Wildlife Crime

A Guide to
Wildlife Law Enforcement in the United Kingdom

574.94~

Compiled and Edited by

Michael Bradley Taylor QPM

London : The Stationery Office

Department of the Environment, Transport and the Regions
Eland House
Bressenden Place
London SW1E 5DU
Telephone 0171 890 3000
Internet service http://www.DETR.gov.uk/

Second Impression 1998

ISBN 0 11 753317 3

Printed in Great Britain on material containing
75% post-consumer waste and 25% ECF pulp.
June 1998

foreword

Sir Paul Condon QPM
Commissioner of Police of the Metropolis

METROPOLITAN POLICE SERVICE

New Scotland Yard
Broadway
London SW1H 0BG

The Police Service has a commitment to maintaining the quality of life for those it serves, and this includes protecting the environment in which we live.

In the UK wildlife crime takes three main forms: the illegal trade in endangered species, badger baiting, and the illegal trade in wild birds, principally birds of prey, but the legislation and various controls are more far reaching and the overall problem is beyond the capabilities of any one agency.

Wildlife crime is a very lucrative business and Interpol estimate that the worldwide trade is worth US$5 billion each year. There are indications that the illegal exploitation of wildlife, including the international smuggling of endangered species, is on the increase.

Successful policing relies on partnership, and this is especially true of the fight against wildlife crime. Recent successful prosecutions, particularly against traders in illegal oriental medicines containing derivatives of endangered species, have achieved national publicity and would not have been possible without close inter-agency co-operation.

That is why this Guide has been written. It pulls together in one place information about all the controls affecting wildlife and sets it out in a user-friendly and accessible way. I believe that police officers dealing with wildlife cases will find this a helpful guide to the legislation and its provisions. I hope that it will also be of interest to others concerned with matters relating to the protection of wildlife.

I am pleased to join with the wide range of bodies who have welcomed the publication of this Guide and who are fully behind the efforts to crack down on the illegal exploitation of wildlife. In partnership we can make an impact on this type of crime, and it is my hope that the Guide will be a valuable tool in that fight.

P L Condon

acknowledgements

Compilation of the Guide has only been possible with the tremendous help so kindly given by the following contributors, to whom I gratefully acknowledge my heartfelt thanks:

Mark Barrett	Wiltshire Police
Paul Beecroft	Thames Valley Police
Paul Butt	ADAS
Phil Cannings	Bedfordshire Police
David Cove	Metropolitan Police
Tony Crittenden	RSPCA
Graham Elliott	RSPB
Andy Fisher	Metropolitan Police
Neil Forbes BVet Med MRCVS	Avian Specialist Veterinary Surgeon
John Francis	Metropolitan Police
Lynn Garvey	DETR
Andy Jones	Montgomeryshire Wildlife Trust
Steve Kourik	Hertfordshire Police
Mark Mason	Royal Ulster Constabulary
George Oxendale	HM Customs and Excise
Bob Philpott BA (Hons)	Wiltshire Police
Charlie Parkes	Derbyshire Police
Nick Ridley	RSPCA
Paul Sayers	ADAS
John Sellar FRGS	Grampian Police
David Shepperd PhD BSc	English Nature
Guy Shorrock	RSPB
Peter Slimon GM Dip Ecol	Metropolitan Police
John Thornley	Derbyshire Police
Michael Wellman	Cheshire Police
Graham Wellstead	National Council for Aviculture

Additional administrative help and support was kindly given by Jane Withey (DETR) and Janet Woodward (secretarial services).

I am also deeply indebted to Rob Hepworth, Head of Global Wildlife Division, DETR and his colleagues whose continuing support and helpful advice has ensured the production of the Guide.

M Bradley Taylor
October 1996

contents

4 poaching, cruelty, trapping and poisoning

5 native plants

6 habitat protection

7 wildlife law in Scotland

8 wildlife law in Northern Ireland

9 the trade in non-native and endangered species

10 miscellaneous legislation

Appendices

a the Schedules to the Wildlife & Countryside Act 1981

b checklist of legal status of selected British birds

c guide to general licences

d species list with scientific names

e useful addresses

f further reading

g abbreviations

introduction

1.1 INTRODUCTION

This publication is intended as a practical guide for anyone in wildlife law enforcement. It is not a legal document, but it does contain many of the legal provisions that apply to the protection of wildlife. It also gives useful and pragmatic advice on the prevention of offences and the detection and prosecution of offenders. It is directed principally at practitioners within the law enforcement, government and conservation agencies.

The majority of people who live in the countryside respect the country and the diversity of wild and domesticated bird and animal life, and wish to see it flourish. There is, though, a very small percentage of the population who are prepared to disregard the law and who, in some cases, are prepared to deny the ability of some species to continue to exist in order to trade in these species for considerable sums of money. Of course the rarer the species the greater the incentive to trade illegally, and the greater the financial reward.

For the newcomer to wildlife law enforcement, the relevant legislation can initially appear to be a daunting mass of statutes of disparate ages and intentions. These range from early 19th century game laws, aimed at preventing people from poaching the squire's rabbits, to recent European Community regulations intended to curtail the activities of organised international criminals in the multi-million pound trade in endangered species.

This working guide to the principal legislation should serve you well, but no one can be expected to know the answer to every query on wildlife law. What you really need to know is:

*   where to look for the answer;

*   where and/or whom to ask for specialist advice, if you cannot find it.

This Guide has been compiled with these objectives in mind.

David Parsons of the Metropolitan Police

1.2 USING THE GUIDE

The Guide is divided into chapters on birds, other animals, plants, and non-native species. There are chapters on the variations in enforcement which apply in Scotland and Northern Ireland, and details of some additional legislation. Finally, there is also a short chapter on habitat protection.

If you are using the Guide to deal with a particular wildlife topic, you should find this listed in the contents pages. If you have a query about an individual species, go straight to the index for the relevant page references.

Some offences are mentioned in more than one part of the Guide. This has been deliberately done to allow the reader to research one subject without constantly having to refer to different parts of the book. Some cross-referencing has, however, been unavoidable.

NOTE: If you are considering investigating an alleged offence, it is strongly recommended that you refer to the legislation itself, obtaining your own specific legal advice where necessary.

Furthermore, aspects of the legislation, including the species covered by it, are altered from time to time, and it is well worth checking that you have up-to-date information, especially if legal proceedings are likely.

If, despite searching the Guide, you are unable to resolve a particular wildlife problem, then turn to Appendix E. This contains a comprehensive list of organisations and individuals with particular responsibilities, skills and expertise. You will find these a ready source of professional advice and guidance, and your call will be welcomed.

NOTE: Few post-holders have been named as there are frequent changes. What remains constant is the willingness amongst agencies to provide mutual assistance and support.

In Appendix F you will find details of recommended reading material, providing further information on general and specialist aspects of wildlife law enforcement.

A number of abbreviations are used throughout the Guide. You will find these listed in Appendix G.

Doubtless you have and will develop your own contacts within wildlife law enforcement, both locally and nationally. The final page of the Guide provides space for you to add your own 'useful contacts' details.

1.3 THE WILDLIFE AND COUNTRYSIDE ACT

The Wildlife and Countryside Act 1981 (WCA) is the principal legislation in Britain for the protection and conservation of our wildlife and its habitat. It is supplemented by the Conservation (Natural Habitats, &c.) Regulations 1994 ('the Regulations'), implementing Council Directive 92/43/EEC on the conservation of natural habitats and of wild fauna and flora ('the Habitats Directive').

NOTE: The WCA applies to England, Wales and Scotland. It does **not** apply to Northern Ireland, although the legislation there has a similar format (see Chapter 8).

Where other statutes apply only to England and Wales or only to Scotland, this is clearly shown.

Under the WCA it will be helpful to remember these general maxims:
- some species of wildlife and most wild birds are protected at all times;
- some wild birds and some other species are protected some of the time; and
- some species are protected only against certain methods of killing or taking.

Details of protected species are listed in Schedules to the WCA which show the degree of protection in each case (see 1.7 and Appendix A). All species are formally identified by their scientific name, which should always be used in cases of doubt. The most frequently used of these are listed at Appendix D.

The Regulations contain provisions relating to the protection of European sites and to the protection of European species of animals and plants. Details of protected species are listed in the Schedules to the Regulations (see Appendix A). All species are formally identified by their scientific name, which should be used in cases of doubt. You should note that nothing in the Regulations shall be construed as excluding the application of the provisions of the WCA relating to the protection of animals and plants.

There are several differences between the Regulations and the WCA in relation to European protected species. In particular, where under the WCA it would be an offence to intentionally kill, injure or take a protected animal (section 9(1)), the Regulations render it an offence where the action was carried out deliberately (Regulation 39(1)(a)). Whereas the WCA makes it an offence to disturb any such animal whilst it is occupying a structure or place which it uses for shelter or protection (section 9(4)(b)), the Regulations more simply make it an offence to deliberately disturb a protected animal (Regulation 39(1)(b)). Additionally, the WCA offence of intentionally damaging, destroying or obstructing any such place (section 9(4)(a)), is reflected in the Regulations more simply by the offence of damaging or destroying a breeding site or resting place of any protected animal (Regulation 39(1)(d)). Other equally important differences exist, and in any proceedings for an offence involving an European protected species you are advised to contact the DETR for advice.

The WCA and the Regulations make provision for licences to be issued to allow activities to take place which would otherwise be prohibited. When you are investigating any offences always check whether a licence has been issued authorising the particular activity which you are looking into. The WCA and the Regulations also allow for certain birds and certain wild animals to be killed or injured in 'emergency' situations.

In addition, under the Wild Mammals (Protection) Act 1996 all wild mammals are protected against certain cruel acts carried out with the intention of causing unnecessary cruelty (see 4.2.1).

1.4 POLICE POWERS

If a constable suspects with reasonable cause that any person is committing or has committed any offence under sections 1 – 18 of the WCA, then the constable may, under the provisions of section 19 of that Act, without warrant:

- stop and search that person if the constable suspects with reasonable cause that evidence of the commission of the offence is to be found on that person;
- search or examine any thing which that person may then be using or have in his possession if the constable suspects with reasonable cause that evidence of the commission of the offence is to be found on that thing;
- seize and detain for the purpose of proceedings any thing which may be evidence of the commission of the offence or may be liable to be forfeited;
- arrest a suspect who fails to give his name and address to the constable's satisfaction;
- for the purpose of exercising these powers, enter any land other than a dwelling.

NOTE: This specific power of arrest under the WCA applies only in Scotland. In England and Wales, powers under section 25 of the Police and Criminal Evidence Act 1984 should be used if appropriate. In Scotland, powers under section 13 of the Criminal Procedure (Scotland) Act 1995 should be used.

1.5 SEARCH WARRANTS

Under section 19(3) of the WCA a justice of the peace may issue a warrant to a constable to enter and search any premises (this includes dwellings) if there are reasonable grounds for suspecting that:

- an offence under sections 1, 3, 5, 7 or 8 has been committed, where a special penalty is provided for; or
- an offence under sections 6, 9, 11(1) or (2), 13 or 14 has been committed; and
- that evidence of the offence may be found on the premises.

The warrant may authorise another person or persons to accompany the constable.

In Scotland, 'justice of the peace', includes a sheriff.

This provision allowing the issue of search warrants is very important and should never be overlooked. Gaining sufficient evidence to prosecute offenders can be very difficult, so the ability to search premises including dwellings is a tremendous advantage. Always seek to take an appropriate expert with you when you search, and have that person's name or his status included on the warrant (for example, the warrant could state that a member of staff of the RSPB is to accompany you).

1.6 PENALTIES

Anyone found guilty of an offence punishable by a special penalty is liable to a fine of up to £5,000 (level 5). For offences other than the setting of snares, uprooting protected plants or making a false declaration, where a fine of up to £2,500 (level 4) can be imposed, the maximum fine is £1,000 (level 3).

Fines may be imposed in respect of each bird, nest, egg, animal, plant or thing. If more than one such item is involved, then the total fine is determined as if the person had been convicted of a separate offence in respect of each bird, nest, egg, animal, plant or thing.

The courts **must** order the confiscation of any bird, nest, egg, animal, plant or thing involved in the offence, and **may** order the confiscation of any vehicle, animal, weapon, climbing gear or other thing which was used to commit the offence.

1.7 SCHEDULES TO THE WCA 1981

These list the species which are protected in varying degrees and are shown in full at Appendix A. Schedule 2 of the Conservation (Natural Habitats, &c.) Regulations 1994 is also reproduced in Appendix A.

In summary, the Schedules to the WCA list species as shown on the following page.

Schedule 1 Rare birds which require special protection	Birds which are protected by special penalties. Part I – At all times Part II – During the close season
Schedule 2 Game birds and some wildfowl Pest species	Birds which may be killed or taken. Part I – Outside the close season Part II – By authorised persons at all times **NOTE:** Part II repealed and species included on General Licences issued by MAFF/DETR. These licences impose certain conditions.
Schedule 3 For aviculture Woodpigeons Game birds and some wildfowl	Birds which may be sold. Part I – Alive at all times if ringed and bred in captivity Part II – Dead at all times Part III – Dead from 1 September to 28 February
Schedule 4 Aviculture and falconry	Birds which must be registered (with the DETR) and ringed if kept in captivity.
Schedule 5 Rarer species	Protected animals (includes some mammals, reptiles and invertebrates).
Schedule 6	Animals which may not be killed or taken by certain methods.
Schedule 8	Protected plants.
Schedule 9 Protects native wildlife	Animals and plants which may not be released into or caused to grow in the wild.

native birds

2.1 PROTECTION

All **wild** birds, their nests and their eggs are protected by law. The level of this protection depends on whether the bird is rare or endangered (these are shown on **Schedule 1** of the WCA) but even very common birds such as robins and blackbirds are protected. Some birds can be shot for sport but only at certain times of the year. Other birds may be killed because they are pests (for example, magpies or crows) but this can only be done under certain conditions by authorised persons – see definition below.

2.2 DEFINITIONS UNDER THE WILDLIFE AND COUNTRYSIDE ACT

Section 27 of the WCA gives the following definitions:
- wild bird: *any bird of a kind which is ordinarily resident in or is a visitor to Great Britain in a wild state.* Except for offences involving the use of illegal weapons and articles, the WCA does not cover the following game birds: pheasant, partridge, black grouse, red grouse and ptarmigan. These species are covered by the Game Acts, but details of their close seasons can be found in the checklist of legal status in Appendix B. In respect of section 1 offences, 'wild bird' does not include any bird which is shown to have been bred in captivity.
- authorised person: *the owner or occupier of any land on which the action takes place or any person authorised by the owner or occupier.* It can also be someone authorised in writing by a local authority, English Nature (EN), Scottish Natural Heritage (SNH), the Countryside Council for Wales (CCW), a district fishery board (Scotland) or local fisheries committee, a water authority or any other statutory water undertakers. Authorisation does not confer a right of entry on to any land.
- occupier (see above): includes any person *having the right of hunting, shooting or fishing, on any land other than the foreshore.*

2.3 OTHER DEFINITIONS
- Close season: inclusive dates of a period when a bird is fully protected; outside that period it may be killed or taken.

- Licence: issued by one of a number of authorities, including the DETR, EN, SNH, the CCW, WOAD, MAFF and SOAEFD, to permit an otherwise illegal act. The licence will specify precisely what action is permitted under it.

- General licence: licences which permit authorised persons (in some cases anyone) to carry out an otherwise illegal act, provided certain conditions are complied with and certain requirements are met. Such licences need not be applied for. These are listed in Appendix C.

2.4 PRINCIPAL OFFENCES

Wildlife and Countryside Act 1981

Section 1(1)(a)
Killing, injuring or taking wild birds
It is an offence for any person to
intentionally kill, injure or take
any wild bird

NOTE: Need to prove intentionally.

This section gives protection to any wild bird.

EXCEPTIONS: It is permissible for a person to take a diseased or injured wild bird (as long as it was not intentionally injured by them) in order to tend it provided that it is released as soon as it has recovered. If the bird is one of those on Schedule 4 then the finder must either hand it over to a licensed person, (see 2.9.8) or register it with the DETR in order that he may keep the bird until it has recovered. It is also lawful to kill a wild bird that is so sick or injured that there is no hope of it recovering, provided that the killing is carried out humanely.

It is permissible for an authorised person to kill (or injure whilst attempting to kill) any bird formerly listed on Schedule 2 (Part II), now under general licences. These are birds considered to be pest species. They often need to be controlled to protect crops, game and livestock, or to prevent damage to trees.

It is not an offence to kill or take a wild bird if it can be shown that it was the incidental result of an otherwise lawful operation, for example a road accident.

It is not an offence to kill or take a wild bird if it is done in accordance with a notice issued by MAFF under section 98 of the Agriculture Act 1947; or under an order made under sections 21 or 22 of the Animal Health Act 1981; or, except for birds listed on Schedule 1 to the WCA, an order made under any other part of the Animal Health Act 1981.

It is not an offence to kill (or injure whilst attempting to kill) any bird in Schedule 2 (Part 1) provided that this is done outside the close season. These exceptions allow certain species of birds to be hunted for sport.

The close season is the time of year when birds may not be shot for sport. This rule enables the species to raise its young and allows it to maintain a viable population. The close season varies for different species of birds.

It is a defence under section 4(3) as amended to kill or take any wild bird, except one on Schedule 1, in emergency situations for preserving public health and safety and air safety; preventing the spread of disease; and damage to agriculture. However, this defence is only available in relation to the prevention of damage to agriculture where there is no other satisfactory solution. Neither is the defence available if it was known beforehand that the action would be necessary and a licence had not been applied for as soon as reasonably practicable or where a licence application had not been determined.

> ### Wildlife and Countryside Act 1981
>
> #### Section 1(1)(b)
> #### *Taking, damaging or destroying birds' nests*
>
> It is an offence for any person to **intentionally take, damage or destroy** the nest of any wild bird while that nest is in use or being built

EXAMPLE: If a person intentionally knocks down a house martin's nest that is being built by the birds under the eaves of his house, he would be committing the offence described above, unless he has obtained a licence under section 16 of the WCA.

EXCEPTIONS: It is not an offence to take, damage or destroy the nest of any bird formerly listed on Schedule 2 (Part II) of the WCA. This is now permitted by general licences.

2.5 THE TAKING AND COLLECTING OF WILD BIRDS' EGGS

Bird-nesting and egg-collecting emerged as an almost exclusively British pastime during the Victorian era. Almost all professional collectors, as opposed to 'schoolboy' collectors, kept meticulous notes of eggs which they collected.

Such egg collections have played an important part in the development of ornithology and natural history.

However, the need for collecting eggs has now diminished to the point where such activity is illegal and needs licensing if undertaken. Modern technology and recording techniques are able to fill the need for monitoring and understanding the breeding biology of British birdlife.

While young offenders will still come to police notice through bird-nesting, a more serious threat is still posed by a small number of fanatical egg collectors who have,

Part of an egg collection siezed by the police

in recent years, been responsible for carefully planned thefts of whole clutches of rare eggs. The osprey and red kite have particularly suffered.

NOTE: The RSPB's Species Protection Department has excellent intelligence information on persistent egg collectors. Do not hesitate to contact the Investigations Section to search their database if you have information on possible suspects.

2.5.1   Legislation and offences

Wild birds and their eggs are fully protected by the WCA. The taking of wild birds' eggs has been illegal since at least 1954. Since the WCA came into force on 28 September 1982 it has been illegal merely to possess or control the eggs of wild birds.

Those who choose to be in possession of items such as wild birds' eggs are obliged to show, on a balance of probabilities, that their possession is lawful. The prosecution merely has to prove possession.

Section 18(2) of the WCA allows for the defendant to be summonsed for being in possession of items capable of being used to commit an offence, namely the taking and keeping of wild birds' eggs.

Section 21(5) of the WCA allows a court to fine separately for each item involved in an offence as if separate summonses had been issued for each item.

Wildlife and Countryside Act 1981

Section 1(1)(c)
Taking or destroying birds' eggs

It is an offence for any person to
intentionally take or destroy
an egg of any wild bird

EXCEPTIONS: It is lawful for any person to remove eggs from nest-boxes from August to January. This means, for example, that if you have nest-boxes in your garden you can clean them out and remove any eggs that are remaining, because these will certainly be dead during the months specified.

An authorised person may take or destroy the eggs of any of the 'pest' species, formerly included in Schedule 2 to Part II of the WCA, under general licence.

Wildlife and Countryside Act 1981

Section 1(2)(a) and (b)
Possession of eggs and wild birds

It is an offence for any person to
have in his possession or control
any live or dead wild bird or any part thereof; or
an egg of a wild bird or any part of such an egg

EXCEPTIONS: A person shall not be guilty of an offence if he shows that the bird or egg had not been killed or taken, or had been killed or taken otherwise than in contravention of the relevant provisions or had been sold (to him or another) otherwise than in contravention of the relevant provisions (that is the provisions of Part I of the WCA).

This means that you do not commit an offence if you came by the bird or egg innocently. For example, if you find a dead bird at the side of the road or your cat brings home a dead bird you are entitled to keep the bird for, say, having it mounted by a taxidermist (see 2.7).

Birds listed in Schedule 1 to the WCA are protected by special penalties, by virtue of the fact that they are rare, declining or vulnerable species. Special penalties apply under section 1(4) for any person who is convicted of an offence under sub-section 1(1) or (2) in respect of:
* a bird included in Schedule 1 or any part of, or anything derived from, such a bird;
* the nest of such a bird; or
* an egg of such a bird, or any part of such an egg.

Wildlife and Countryside Act 1981

Section 1(5)(a)
Disturbing wild birds

It is an offence for any person to
intentionally disturb any wild bird
included in **Schedule 1** while it is building a
nest or is in, on or near a nest containing eggs
or young; or to disturb dependent young of such
a bird

This does not include any bird bred in captivity.

EXAMPLE: The offence, which you will note only applies to birds on Schedule 1 (the specially protected birds), may be committed for example by over-enthusiastic photographers who disturb nesting birds whilst trying to photograph them. Some people do have a licence (normally issued by EN, the CCW or SNH) to photograph or film these birds, which they must have with them to produce if required. Bird-watchers can commit this offence if they intentionally disturb a bird at or near its nest.

The offence can also be committed by egg thieves who take the eggs from the nest. Hence, egg thieves can commit several offences if they take the eggs of a bird on Schedule 1, namely:
- disturbing a bird (section 1(5)(a));
- taking the eggs (section 1(1)(c)); and
- possessing eggs (section 1(2)(b)).

Section 18(1) of the WCA makes it an offence for any person to 'attempt to commit an offence under the foregoing provisions of this Part'. That person 'shall be punishable in like manner as for the said offence'.

Section 18(2) of the WCA makes it an offence if 'any person who for the purposes of committing an offence under the foregoing provisions of this Part, has in his possession anything capable of being used for committing the offence'. That person 'shall be punishable in like manner as for the said offence'.

'Wild bird' means any bird of a kind which is ordinarily resident in or is a visitor to Great Britain in a wild state but does not include poultry or, except in sections 5 and 16, any game bird (section 27(1) of the WCA).

'Game birds' are protected by the Game Act 1831 in England and Wales. Section 2 of the Game Act defines 'game' as including pheasants, partridges, grouse, heath or moor game, and black game, for the purposes of that Act (see 2.2 for the definition of 'game' in the WCA).

Section 24 of the Game Act 1831 makes it an offence for any person to wilfully take out of the nest or destroy in the nest, or knowingly have in his house, shop, possession or control any eggs of any bird of game, or of any swan, wild duck, teal or wigeon from land for which that person did not have the right of killing game.

2.5.2 Police action

If you have to deal with a 'professional' egg thief, you may well find good evidence on the suspect or in his vehicle. Particularly look for:
- climbing equipment;
- egg-blowing equipment (usually a variety of drills, syringes and needles);
- egg/nest identification guides;
- maps with nest sites marked;
- camera equipment (consider having the film developed);
- mirrors attached to poles;
- drag ropes (for ground-nesting species);
- tins, boxes, cases or even adapted Thermos flasks containing cotton wool or similar material; and
- field notebooks and diaries.

Remember that egg thieves will sometimes raid the nest, then hide the eggs nearby for collection at a later date. Do not overlook the use of a good tracking police dog.

While good evidence can be forthcoming at or near the scene, experience has proven it more likely that this will be found at the home of the suspect.

In any case of suspected 'professional' egg-stealing always:
- check whether the person has obtained a licence under section 16 of the WCA;
- obtain a search warrant under section 19(3) of the WCA (you will usually need evidence that Schedule 1 species are involved);
- obtain the assistance of an expert (perhaps from the RSPB Investigation Section);
- ensure that experts are named on the warrant and that it covers all the items being searched for, such as equipment and documentary evidence; and
- thoroughly search the suspect's address.

2.5.3 Executing the warrant

You are looking for and should seize:
- eggs and the containers they are in;
- any records, data cards or paperwork which show where the eggs were taken and when;
- any items which could be used to take the eggs, for instance climbing equipment, marked maps, or containers in which eggs can be placed;
- any handwritten documents by the occupant where the sites of rare birds, nests or other comments are noted;
- any photographs, slides or negatives of birds, nests, eggs, etc;
- any correspondence between egg collectors which may indicate knowledge of rare bird sites and involvement in these offences; and
- any item used for the blowing of eggs, for example miniature drills, air blowers, pipettes, plastic tubing, syringes etc.

NOTE: You may find bird reference books, with annotations, which are of interest and relevance, especially any book published by Oriel Stringer, or books relating to the study of eggs and egg collecting.

In your investigations you should:
- remember forensic examination. For example, an examination of inks used on cards and eggs can often reveal discrepancies;
- remember you will need an expert to help you identify and catalogue any eggs or other exhibits that you may find in a search;
- be thorough – egg-collecting cases usually involve the accumulation of a lot of different pieces of evidence. A well-documented search record is essential; and
- pay particular attention to the data (usually on cards) which are likely to show when, where and how the eggs were taken, species and clutch size. Any of the following are unusual and merit careful investigation:
  - no data recorded;
  - dates or details added or altered;
  - coded data (can be used to falsify dates);
  - cards apparently aged (consider forensic examination or checking with manufacturers).

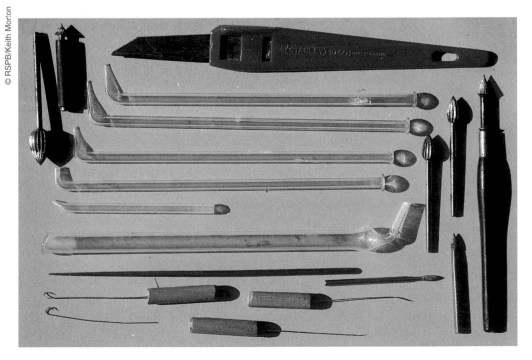

An egg-blowing kit

2.5.4 Points to note in major investigations

If evidence of disturbance to Schedule 1 birds is found during the investigation, remember that the six-month time limitation applies from the date of the offence (if no bird or egg is killed or taken). It may be necessary to lay information if the limitation is about to expire.

If the investigation reveals more than one offender, it can be difficult for one officer to deal with this in its entirety. Consideration should be given to designating a team of officers to complete enquiries to prevent a lengthy enquiry in which only one offender can be dealt with at a time.

Ask the prosecuting authorities to consider nominating a prosecuting solicitor at an early stage. If one solicitor is aware of the case as it progresses the prosecution becomes easier. Such cases can be complicated and unusual, and it will be difficult for a prosecutor to satisfactorily take on a prosecution at its later stages.

Jurisdiction may be an issue in a major case. It is worth gaining written agreement from the defence as to place of trial.

It is impractical to separate a linked enquiry between a number of police forces. If more than one police force is involved, one force should take responsibility for the whole enquiry. Experience has shown a willingness by forces to assist each other in this type of investigation, but this should be resolved at an early stage, and at a senior level.

2.5.5 Storage and retention of exhibits

Eggs (particularly when blown) are extremely fragile. When seizing these, care should be taken in relation to transfer and retention. Where possible transfer the eggs in their original container and request that the alleged offender assists in the package of such items.

Eggs must be stored safely and away from light. If found to be lawfully held they should be returned straightaway to the owner.

2.5.6 Police (Property) Act

Police officers must ensure that any items seized are returned to the rightful owner.

Where eggs are seized and there is dispute over ownership, or if the owner is unknown, the police may apply to a magistrates' court for an Order under section 1 of the Police (Property) Act 1897 to determine ownership. Similarly, it is open to any person claiming property seized by the police to apply under the same procedure for its possession.

If eggs have been seized that are known to have been taken from the wild between 1954 and 1982, a problem can arise. These eggs will have been taken illegally but it is not possible to prosecute for possession.

Under this Act there is a strong legal case for asking magistrates to consider their disposal. As the eggs were originally taken illegally the court should decide whether the current 'owner' can keep them or if they are to be given to a museum or similar institution for the benefit of society.

Such application will often be resisted by the 'owner', but there have been cases where the magistrates have decided that the eggs should be placed in museums.

This Act does not extend to Scotland.

2.5.7 Specimen summonses

In the event of a successful conviction it should be noted that section 21(6)(a) of the WCA makes mandatory an order of forfeiture of any bird, nest, egg, other animal, plant or other thing in respect of which the offence was committed.

In addition, section 21(6)(b) of the WCA allows the court to order the forfeiture of any vehicle, animal, weapon or other thing which was used to commit the offence.

Schedule 1 birds

That you on _____date_____ at _____place_____ in the County of _____county_____ did have in your possession or control wild birds' eggs, namely three little ringed plover eggs, being a species included in Schedule 1 to the Wildlife and Countryside Act 1981.

Contrary to section 1(2)(b) of the Wildlife and Countryside Act 1981.

Non-schedule 1 birds

That you on _____date_____ at _____place_____ in the County of _____county_____ did have in your possession or control wild birds' eggs, namely five blackbird eggs, four song thrush eggs, five robin eggs, ten blue tit eggs and six goldfinch eggs.
Contrary to section 1(2)(b) of the Wildlife and Countryside Act 1981.

(Species can either be named in the summons or listed on a separate sheet).

Possession of equipment

That you on _____date_____ at _____place_____ in the County of _____county_____ did for the purposes of committing an offence under section 1 of the Wildlife and Countryside Act 1981, namely the taking and possession of wild birds' eggs, have in your possession items capable of being used for committing the offences, namely a wooden box laid with sawdust, a glass-fronted display cabinet laid with cotton wool, egg-blowing equipment and maps marked with nest sites.

Contrary to section 18(2) of the Wildlife and Countryside Act 1981.

Game birds

That you on _____date_____ at _____place_____ in the County of _____county_____ did knowingly have in your possession, one egg of red grouse, three eggs of pheasant, two eggs of grey partridge and one egg of red-legged partridge, being eggs taken out of the nest by a person on land where that person did not have the right of killing game.

Contrary to section 24 of the Game Act 1831.

2.6 PROHIBITED ARTICLES

Certain methods of killing or taking wild birds are prohibited under section 5(1)(a–e) of the WCA. This includes, with certain exceptions, authorised persons (see 2.2).

The following articles **may not** be used for killing, taking or injuring any wild bird.

Sub-section	Method
a	springe (noose used for catching small game)+
a	trap+
a	gin+
a	snare+
a	hook and line+
a	any electrical device+
a	any poison or stupefying substance+
b	any net*
b	baited board
b	bird lime or similar substance (to which birds become stuck)
c	bow or crossbows
c	any explosive other than ammunition for a fire-arm
c	any automatic or semi-automatic* weapon
c	any shot-gun with a barrel diameter (muzzle end) more than 1 3/4 inches
c	any device for illuminating a target*
c	any sighting device for night shooting*
c	any artificial lighting or mirror or other* dazzling device*
c	any gas or smoke
c	any chemical wetting agent
d	decoy
d	sound recording or live bird or animal which is tethered or secured by means of brace or which is blind, maimed or injured
e	any mechanically-propelled vehicle in immediate pursuit of a wild bird

NOTE: These methods are a combined list of all the various means prohibited under section 5(1)(a), (b), (c), (d) and (e):

(a) refers to methods that are illegal for use in causing bodily injury to birds;

(b) these methods are prohibited for use in taking or killing; they also include all those under sub-section (a);

(c) these means must not be used to kill or take birds;

(d) outlaws the use as a decoy of any sound recording or any live bird or other animal that is in any way tethered or maimed;

(e) using mechanically-propelled vehicles to pursue birds to kill or catch them is unlawful.

Sub-section (f), introduced by the Wildlife and Countryside (Amendment) Act 1991, makes it an offence to knowingly cause or permit the setting or use of any of the devices mentioned above.

It is not an offence to use, or cause or permit to be used, the items marked with a + for the lawful killing or taking of wild animals if the item was set in the interests of agriculture, public health, forestry, fisheries or nature conservation and all reasonable precautions were taken to prevent injuries to wild birds. This exception does not apply where the item is set to kill or take those animals listed in Schedule 6 of the WCA.

All methods marked with an asterisk may be used by authorised person to kill birds formerly on Schedule 2 (Part II) provided this is done in accordance with the terms of the general licence (ie the pest species) provided this is done to preserve public health, air safety or preventing serious damage to agriculture.

EXCEPTIONS: It is not unlawful for an authorised person (see 2.2) to use a cage trap or net for taking birds formerly on Schedule 2 (Part II) (pest species). An authorised person is also allowed to use a cage-trap or net to catch game birds for the purpose of breeding. Even when the use of cage traps is allowed, any live bird held in the cage must have sufficient room to stretch its wings fully in all directions (however, see Larsen traps – 4.3.23).

Certain people (for example British Trust for Ornithology ringers) are licensed to catch birds for study or ringing by use of some of the normally prohibited methods, usually by netting. They will have and should produce the licence (normally issued by EN, the CCW or SNH) on demand to a police officer.

Also remember that licences can be obtained to allow any of the traps listed above to be used by certain people in certain circumstances; always ask to see any licence that has been issued.

See additional information in 4.3.1 to 4.3.23.

NOTE: If ever you anticipate taking action against someone for taking or killing birds, always remember the offence of using unlawful methods. It is possible that the means used by people for illegal taking or killing will fall into one of the prohibited methods.

2.7 SELLING OF DEAD BIRDS

Until 1 January 1995 the sale of dead birds was restricted under both the WCA, section 6(2) and Regulations arising from the Act. At that stage registered sellers of dead birds (including taxidermists) were required to keep specific records of their transactions.

However, on 1 January 1995 two general licences came into effect:

• WLF 100092 – permits the sale of feathers and parts of wild birds included in Schedule 3 Part III of the WCA; and

• WLF 100096 – permits the sale of certain dead birds (any dead wild bird other than those included in Part I of Schedule 2, Parts II and III of Schedule 3, or barnacle geese and the Greenland race of white-fronted geese).

The effect of these licences is to allow those acts that would otherwise be illegal under section 6(2) of the WCA. These include sale, offering or exposing for sale, possession or transporting for sale, as well as the publishing of or causing to be published any advertisement indicating the buying or selling of such items.

General licences have an expiry date and may be withdrawn or amended. It is worth checking with the DETR that you have the up-to-date position (see Appendix C).

However, failure to comply with the conditions of the licence may involve offences under section 6(2) of the WCA.

For information about the sale of live birds see 2.8, 2.9.6, 2.9.13 and 2.9.15.

2.7.1 Offences

Wildlife and Countryside Act 1981
Section 6(2)(a) ***Sale of dead wild birds*** It is an offence for any person who is not registered in accordance with regulations made by the Secretary of State to **sell or offer for sale or expose for sale** any **dead** wild bird Also It is an offence for any person to **have in his possession or transport** for the purpose of sale any dead wild bird
Section 6(2)(b) ***Advertising to buy or sell dead birds*** It is an offence for any person who is not registered in accordance with regulations made by the Secretary of State to **publish or cause to be published** any advertisement likely to be understood as conveying that he **buys/sells or intends to buy/sell** any dead wild bird

EXCEPTIONS: It would not be an offence if the dead bird was a woodpigeon. Nor would it be an offence in the case of any bird on **Schedule 3 (Part III)** between 1 September and 28 February (ie certain game birds).

In order that the seller can make use of the general licences, certain conditions will apply.

2.7.2 Licensing: terms and conditions

The licences apply only to the sale of small numbers of dead birds, or any part or product of such dead birds that were:

- bred in captivity. A bird is not treated as being bred in captivity unless its parents were lawfully in captivity when the egg from which it hatched was laid. Documentary evidence of captive breeding must accompany any sale; or

- removed from the natural state within Great Britain under legal provisions in force in Great Britain. Documentary evidence that the bird was legally removed from the natural state must accompany any sale.

2.7.3 Records

Any person who sells a dead bird, or part or product of such a dead bird, under this licence must keep a record for a minimum of two years from such sale. This record must contain details of:

- the person from whom the seller acquired the bird or part or product of such a bird;

- the person to whom the bird or part or product of such a bird was sold; and

- the species of the bird sold, the cause of death (if known) and the age of the bird.

The seller must certify the record is accurate, produce the record for inspection if required to do so, and submit to the DETR at the end of every year a report showing how each bird was acquired, also listing species and numbers.

2.7.4 Investigations

The 'seller' of a dead bird can include the posessor or taxidermist. In investigating such a seller you should:

- establish at an early stage the history of the items in the seller's possession and whether the birds have been taken under licence;

- find out which are possessed and which are commissioned work – birds passed to a taxidermist for preparation and mounting. Payment made to the taxidermist for his services does not constitute a sale of the specimen;

- ask the seller to produce records and check that the receipts of birds are in chronological order;

- check the seller's records against those submitted to the DETR;

- check the names of suppliers of birds, looking closely at regular suppliers, suppliers of large numbers and regular non-local suppliers. Check that the names listed are genuine and not listed from the telephone directory;

- check each specimen against the record, making notes of each relevant entry;

- examine birds in the seller's freezer for signs of injury, looking for signs of wear on the scales of the legs which may indicate that a ring has been removed. Check that injuries are compatible with the cause of death listed in the seller's records. Evidence of shooting can be still found on a bird which has been mounted. Shot lodged in a bone can be revealed by x-ray examination; and

- check the seller's own private collection of birds, since sellers often keep particularly rare birds for themselves.

When choosing which birds to submit for veterinary examination it is worth bearing in mind the following:

- birds of prey are persecuted and are always worth examining;

Stuffed and mounted birds siezed by the police

- other persecuted species such as cormorants, herons, lapwing, goosanders and mergansers are always worth examining;

- it may not be worth x-raying 'pest' species as most will have been shot, unless injury by illegal methods, such as pole-trapping or poisoning, is suspected;

- mounted birds can be x-rayed but the plates require careful interpretation;

- birds of prey with pole trap injuries can be submitted to The Institute of Terrestrial Ecology (ITE) for a 'second opinion';

- birds of prey with full crops but no trauma injuries may be worth examining for poison, but bear in mind that the body will be unsuitable for mounting afterwards. If poisoning is suspected it may be worth contacting ADAS.

Although the regulations apply only to British wild birds, many other species of protected birds and animals are prepared and mounted by taxidermists. Trade in animals protected by the WCA and in CITES species is prohibited except under licence issued by the DETR. Sellers may not be aware of these additional restrictions.

Photograph anything which is of any relevance, however minor, and video the search if possible.

2.8 SELLING OF LIVE WILD BIRDS

Section 6(1) of the WCA makes it an offence to sell, transport for sale or advertise for sale any live wild bird (including those which have been bred in captivity). The only exception to this relates to birds listed on Schedule 3 Part I of the Act, which can be sold if they are bred in captivity and are ringed in accordance with Statutory Instrument 1982/1220.

Licences to sell wild birds (apart from those covered by EC Regulations – see 2.9.6, 2.9.13 and 2.9.15) can be issued under section 16(4) of the WCA.

There are ten species of bird which need an individual licence to allow them to be sold. They are the Brent goose, goldeneye, long-tailed duck, Bewick's swan, mute swan, velvet scoter, common scoter, goosander, red-breasted merganser and ruddy duck.

There are two general licences:

- **WLF 100093** allows the sale of 34 species of waterfowl and their eggs, subject to the following conditions.

   1. The bird must have been bred in captivity and documentary evidence of captive breeding must accompany any sale.

   2. The owner of the bird must, if requested by a DETR official or police officer, make the bird available for a blood sample to be taken, for the purposes of confirming ancestry.

   3. Any egg must have been laid in captivity, by parents lawfully in captivity.

- **WLF 100095** allows the sale of all other wild birds except those covered by EC Regulations, those listed on Schedule 3 Part I and the ten species listed above. This licence does not allow sale of the eggs of these species and is subject to the following conditions.

   1. The bird must have been bred in captivity and documentary evidence of captive breeding must accompany any sale.

   2. The bird must be ringed with an individually numbered close ring.

   3. The owner of the bird must, if requested by a DETR official or police officer, make the bird available for a blood sample to be taken, for the purposes of confirming ancestry.

2.9 FALCONRY

Falconry has been practised in England since Saxon times. The invention of the gun and the enclosure of common land led to its rapid decline, although enthusiasts have kept the sport alive in Britain.

In recent years there has been a dramatic increase in the number of birds of prey in captivity and in the number of people who keep them, frequently more for free-flying or exhibition than for true falconry (the pursuit of quarry).

The principal reason is the success of captive breeding, which has ensured that sought-after foreign species no longer have to be imported. Lanner and saker falcons, red-tailed buzzards and Harris hawks are among the most popular non-native birds that are bred in captivity in this country for falconry. As they have become more readily available, so they have become less expensive. This also applies to native species like the peregrine falcon.

It is the common objective of Government and responsible falconers to achieve sustainable captive breeding to avoid the unnecessary use of wild birds.

2.9.1   Escaped birds

Police officers are often called by members of the public to escaped birds of prey, particularly falcons, which travel much greater distances than hawks and buzzards and so are more readily lost when being flown.

Wherever possible enlist the help of either a knowledgeable member of RSPCA staff or an experienced local falconer to catch the bird. They will have the proper glove, lure and food to ensure a speedy and trouble-free recovery. However tame or tired a bird may seem, its talons can and will inflict serious and painful injury on an unprotected hand – or anywhere else for that matter.

2.9.2   Identification

It is important to develop some skill in identifying the different birds, particularly birds of prey, that you are likely to come across.

A quick and effective way to increase your knowledge is to visit a falconry centre. Alternatively, almost all the county shows and game fairs held during the summer months will have some form of falconry display.

The birds of prey in common use for falconry are as follows:

Falcons

Lanner	non-native	not on Schedule
Merlin	native	Schedules 1 and 4
Peregrine	native	Schedules 1 and 4
Saker	non-native	not on Schedule
Kestrel	native	not on Schedule

Known collectively as long-wings, these birds are trained to 'wait on' at a considerable height above the falconer and then dive in a spectacular stoop to take their quarry in flight or come to a lure swung by the falconer.

Buzzards

Common buzzard	native	not on Schedule
Ferruginous hawk	non-native	not on Schedule
Harris hawk	non-native	not on Schedule
Red-tailed buzzard	non-native	not on Schedule

Collectively known as broad-wings, these birds are flown at feathered or ground game (usually rabbits) from the falconer's fist or by following the falconer across country. They are trained to return to the fist, although a lure may also be used.

True hawks

Goshawk	native	Schedules 1 and 4
Sparrowhawk	native	not on Schedule

The short-wings or true hawks are flown from the fist at similar quarry to the broad-winged hawks.

2.9.3 Hybrids

A hybrid bird is the result of the cross-breeding of different species. Hybrids are now quite common in captivity. There are a number of examples such as peregrine x gyrfalcon, peregrine x saker, lanner x saker. Hybrids are required to be ringed and registered if one of the parent birds or any lineal ancestor is included in Schedule 4. The lanner x saker cross, for example, would not be required to be registered as neither parent is on Schedule 4.

Identification of hybrids can be very difficult. Always consult an expert.

2.9.4 Owls

There are five species of owl which regularly breed in this country and can frequently be found in captivity:

Barn owl	Schedule 1
Little owl	not on Schedule
Long-eared owl	not on Schedule
Short-eared owl	not on Schedule
Tawny owl	not on Schedule

A sixth species has bred irregularly in Shetland:

Snowy owl	Schedule 1

Non-native species which are frequently kept for display purposes are:

Eagle owl	non-native
Bengal eagle owl	non-native

2.9.5 Barn owl release schemes

Barn owls in the wild have declined considerably for a number of reasons, especially the loss of suitable feeding habitat resulting from the intensification of agriculture. Barn owls in captivity can be prolific breeders, with two or sometimes three clutches a year being recorded. This has led to a huge number of surplus barn owls being offered for sale.

Owing to the reduced numbers in the wild, many captive-bred barn owls have been released into the wild by various individuals and organisations. Some of these release schemes were done with great care, but unfortunately some were not. This resulted in many released birds starving to death or ending up in rescue centres, having been found in pitiful conditions where they have not been able to fend for themselves. The release of a bird which is unable to look after itself either because it is unfit or because it was released into unsuitable habitat constitutes an offence under section 1 of the Abandonment of Animals Act 1960 (see also 4.3.30 and 9.1). The barn owl has now been included in Part I of Schedule 9 to the WCA, and section 14(1)(b) of the Act applies.

Wildlife and Countryside Act 1981

Subject to the provisions of this Part, if any person
releases or allows to escape into the wild
any animal which is included in Part I of Schedule 9 he shall be guilty of an offence

---

Barn owls, however, can still be released as long as a licence under section 16 has been issued authorising a person to do so. This licence is obtainable from the DETR.

The barn owl is also a species of bird that is included in Schedule 1 and is, therefore, protected by a special penalty.

2.9.6 Other legislation affecting owls

Certain owls, including the barn owl, short-eared owl, long-eared owl, little owl, snowy owl and tawny owl are also protected by the EC Wildlife Trade Regulation (338 and 939 of 1997).

Many owl species are listed on Annex A of the Regulation, and can only be traded if permits have been issued by the importing and exporting countries.

Trade in Annex A species within the European Community is also strictly controlled. Under Article 8 of EC Regulation 338/97, the purchase, offer to purchase, acquisition for commercial purposes, display to the public for commercial purposes, use for commercial gain and sale, keeping for sale, offering for sale or transporting for sale of Annex A specimens is prohibited unless a certificate has been issued in accordance with Article 10 of that Regulation. These certificates are issued by the DETR. Such specimens will also have to be marked with a close ring, or in certain circumstances a microchip. See 2.9.15 for more details of these provisions.

Sales of certain owl species have taken place in accordance with general exemptions issued under Article 6 of EC Regulation 3626/82. These exemptions are under review and may be revoked, so in any cases where people are relying on them to sell restricted specimens, you should check with the DETR.

See 2.8, 2.9.13, and 2.9.15 for information about the sale of other live birds.

2.9.7 Registration

Registration documents are issued to people who keep Schedule 4 birds; that is to say, those birds that are subject to ringing and registration under section 7 of the WCA.

This document (Form DETR14089) gives a number of details. These include the date of expiry (renewed every three years), and the name and address of the keeper, together with his/her ID number, which is issued by the DETR. It also includes a number of details about the bird, including:
- species;
- gender;
- ring number;
- date the keeper acquired the bird;
- date the bird was hatched if it was born in captivity and parents' ring numbers;
- the origin of the bird.

The origin will normally be given as 'captive bred', 'wild-disabled' or 'imported'. There are times, however, when it may read 'unknown'. This normally occurs when the history of the bird is doubtful, such as a bird that has just been 'found' with falconry equipment attached but is not ringed, or a bird that has been seized at some stage by the police and again the true origin is not known.

There are also transfer details if the bird is passed on or sold. Conditions relating to the sale of the bird are also included.

The document clearly states that registration does not legalise any illegal taking or possession, and the fact the bird has been registered does not automatically mean that it was legally obtained or is being held legally (or was captive bred).

2.9.8 Rehabilitation: licensed persons

A person who is licensed may keep certain wild birds for the purposes of rehabilitation. The details can be found under licence WLF 100099. The licence is a general one, and therefore a check will have to be made with the DETR to ascertain if a person is covered by it or not.

This licence allows persons to have in their possession a wild Schedule 4 bird without the need to ring and register it, as long as it is possessed solely for the purpose of tending it and releasing it when no longer disabled.

However, the licensed person must, within four days commencing from the day on which he takes into his possession/control a disabled wild-bred Schedule 4 bird, notify that fact in writing to the Secretary of State (ie the DETR).

The licence lasts for a total of 15 days commencing from the date the bird came into care. After that the bird must be registered in accordance with the regulations. On applying for registration, a certificate by a qualified veterinary surgeon may be required, to show that it is not possible to return the bird to the wild within 15 days because of its injuries or illness.

In a case where a person is not covered by the licence and cannot meet its conditions, that person is required to inform the DETR immediately.

2.9.9   DETR rings

There are four types of ring found on birds of prey, the close metal ring, the plastic cable-tie, the metal Swiss ring and the split metal ring. All rings issued by the DETR are easily recognisable.

- Close rings are made of brown anodised aluminium and are stamped with four or five numbers followed by the letters DOE (printed sideways on) and then a letter giving the ring size.

- The cable-tie ring can come in a number of colours and the part forming the ring round the bird's leg is usually covered by a clear plastic sleeving (although after time dirt can get into the sleeve making the number difficult to read). The ring number always begins with the letters 'UK' and is immediately followed by five numbers (eg UK24565).

- Swiss rings are made from silver-coloured metal which is closed into a circle ring shape using special pliers. Once closed, a rivet pin is inserted through the joint and the area of metal around the pin is crimped. This crimping holds the rivet pin in place and prevents the ring from being opened without damaging it, to an extent where it cannot be re-used. The ring number always begins with a letter indicating the ring size, followed by a five-digit number and ending with GB (printed sideways).

- Split rings are made from silver-coloured aluminium which is closed into a circle ring shape using special ringing pliers. The ring number always begins with a letter to indicate the size followed by a series of four or five numbers ending with DOE (printed sideways on).

Cable-tie rings can, however, be open to abuse. They can be taken off a bird and put on to another. A cable-tie ring and registration document can be worth considerable sums to criminals. It is always worth examining the registration document for the age and sex of the bird and comparing it with the age of the bird it is fitted to. A number of people have committed an offence in this way, but it takes an expert to prove the offence.

Close rings and cable ties issued by the DETR

Because of these problems, the DETR no longer uses cable-ties: Swiss rings are used in their place. There is currently no plan to replace cable-ties fitted to birds with Swiss rings. Therefore, a number of birds will be fitted with and registered with cable-ties.

It is possible to keep a bird legally without it wearing a ring, provided it is held under an unringed (UR) licence. The bird will be registered under the UR licence number, which will be shown on the registration document. The keeper should be able to produce the licence with the registration document.

2.9.10 Breeders' rings

These rings are obtainable from several sources and are advertised in a number of specialist magazines. They come in a variety of colours and the breeder can choose what he wants stamped on the ring. In the main, breeders use numbers followed by their initials, the ring size and the year. Therefore, such a ring should read something like 001 MBT 96W.

British Bird Council close rings are stamped with a four-digit number, followed by a B over a C, a code letter to indicate the size of the ring, and the year. International Ornithological Association rings are silver in colour and are stamped with a ring number, followed by a size code, IOA, and the year.

2.9.11 Offences relating to the taking and keeping of wild birds of prey

The taking of birds of prey or their eggs from the wild, either to launder them into the legitimate market for profit or simply to save the person the cost of legal acquisition, is a matter of concern.

There are a number of offences committed at different stages, which start off very simply when eggs, chicks or adult birds are taken from the wild.

Additionally, there is evidence of a ready market for peregrine falcon and goshawk eggs and chicks. In one case, a man was sentenced to four months' imprisonment after admitting a number of COTES offences of selling young wild peregrines as aviary-bred.

Wildlife and Countryside Act 1981

Section 1(1)(a)

It is an offence if any person intentionally
kills, injures or takes
any wild bird

Section 1(1)(c)

It is an offence if any person intentionally
takes or destroys
an egg of any wild bird

Both these offences are relatively simple to prove and provide protection for wild birds and their eggs, although it must be noted than an element of the offence is intention, so it is necessary to show intent and to show that the offence was not committed accidentally.

Both these offences and many others under the WCA refer to wild birds. See 2.2 for the definition of 'wild bird' in the Act. Any bird of a kind which breeds and winters in Great Britain, together with all those species which are present either as birds passing through en route elsewhere or as a summer or winter visitor, falls within this definition. All the common species of birds of prey are protected by this legislation.

The WCA then goes on to specifically exclude from the provisions of section 1 any bird which was bred in captivity, but only if the parents of the bird bred were themselves lawfully in captivity when the egg was laid.

To prove offences under the WCA it is essential that the identity of the species concerned is established beyond doubt, and that the status of the bird in the wild in Great Britain is again proven. To do this a statement from an expert ornithologist will be required.

Two other considerations apply to offences of the taking of birds and their eggs from the wild. One is a six-month statutory limitation on proceedings which runs for six months from the date on which sufficient evidence to justify proceedings came to the prosecutor's attention, subject to an absolute limit of two years from the date of the offence (section 20(2)).

The second is that jurisdiction to try offences under the WCA is considered to be where the offender is found, so that if, for example, a bird of prey is stolen in the Midlands, and the offender is found at his home address in London, then he can be prosecuted before a London court (section 21(7)).

Having taken birds or eggs from the wild, continuing possession of those birds or eggs constitutes a further offence under the WCA.

Wildlife and Countryside Act 1981

Section 1(2)(a)

If any person has in his
possession or control
any live or dead wild bird, or any part of, or
anything derived from such a bird
he shall be guilty of an offence

The onus of proof lies with the person who has the bird in his possession to show that the bird is held legally. The prosecution only has to show that the person was in possession or control of the bird.

An additional offence of possession of an unregistered bird may be considered if the species of bird involved is one which is included on Schedule 4 of the WCA, which includes all native diurnal birds of prey except kestrel, sparrowhawk and common buzzard.

The 'regulations' referred to in section 7(1) of the WCA are the Wildlife and Countryside (Registration and Ringing of Certain Captive Birds) Regulations 1982 (S.I. 1982/1221); the Wildlife and Countryside (Registration and Ringing of Certain Birds) (Amendment) Regulations 1991 (S.I. 1991/1478); the Wildlife and Countryside Act 1981 (Variation of Schedule 4) Order 1994 (S.I. 1994/1151); and the Wildlife and Countryside (Registration and Ringing of Certain Captive Birds (Amendment)) Regulations 1994 (S.I. 1994/1152).

Of these regulations, Regulation 3 states that:

- the Secretary of State shall for the purposes of section 7(1) of the WCA maintain a register of birds to which these regulations apply;
- an application for registration shall be made by the keeper, or prospective keeper, of the bird to which the application relates on a form obtained from the Secretary of State; and
- the Secretary of State shall not register any bird which is required by Regulation 5 of these regulations to be ringed, unless he is satisfied that the bird has been ringed as required.

NOTE: The registration provisions apply to the keeper of the bird and the address at which it is normally kept. This is not necessarily the same as the owner of the bird and the owner's address.

Regulation 5 states that:

- every bird included in the Schedule to these regulations (being certain of the birds to which these regulations apply) shall be ringed with a ring obtained from the Secretary of State;
- any person who rings a bird under this regulation shall complete a declaration of ringing on a form obtained from the Secretary of State and return it to him.

This means that all birds on Schedule 4 of the WCA must be close-ringed with a ring of the correct size for that species (or in certain limited circumstances, fitted with a cable-tie or split ring) issued by the DETR, and the keeper or intended keeper must register his possession with the DETR. If any person has in his possession any Schedule 4 bird not registered or ringed accordingly he commits an offence under section 7(1). Exceptionally, a bird may be registered when it is unable to wear a ring (sec 2.9.9).

In the case of a non-Schedule 4 bird, there is no requirement for the bird to be close-ringed in order to possess it. However, keepers are encouraged to fit close rings, because this may be helpful if the keeper is subsequently required to prove the birds are legally held. If the keeper wishes to sell the bird other legislation comes into play.

The requirements of Regulation 5(2) are particularly relevant when investigating offences of taking wild birds of Schedule 4 species, because part of the registration process includes a declaration of claimed parentage which is extremely useful if DNA profiling is subsequently used to investigate a bird's parentage.

2.9.12 Further registration offences

It is an offence to make a false statement to obtain a registration document.

Wildlife and Countryside Act 1981

Section 17

A person who, for the purposes of obtaining, whether for himself or another, a registration in accordance with regulations made under section 7(1)

(a) Makes a statement or representation or furnishes a document or information **which he knows to be false in a material particular shall be guilty of an offence**

(b) Recklessly makes a statement or representation or furnishes a document or information **which is false in a material particular shall be guilty of an offence**

This section also applies these offences to applications for licences under section 16 of the WCA.

2.9.13 Offences relating to the sale of illegally-taken wild birds

Whether further offences are then committed depends on what the keeper subsequently does with the birds.

A keeper commits an offence if he sells a bird illegally taken from the wild. In order to appear to comply with the terms of the general licences which govern the sale of birds held in captivity, he needs to be able to pass the bird off as bred in captivity by attempting to fit a close ring illegally.

A close ring is a continuous metal ring with an individual number which is of such a size that it fits over the leg of a chick that is still growing but which cannot be fitted or removed when the bird is fully grown.

The existence of a close ring is a good indication that a bird has been bred in captivity, but it is not conclusive evidence, since any small chick or egg taken from the wild is going to be capable of being close-ringed.

In the case of a bird included on Schedule 4 of the WCA, the close rings must be obtained from the DETR and the ringing and possession of the bird registered.

If a keeper has two adult birds of breeding age and condition and then claims to have produced young or eggs, it is hard to prove whether they did in fact breed or not. Now with the advent of DNA profiling this can be easily verified.

If the keeper does decide to sell the bird(s) then he commits further offences.

Wildlife and Countryside Act 1981

Section 6(1)(a)

If any person **sells, offers or exposes for sale or has in his possession or transports for the purpose of sale** any live wild bird other than a bird included in Part 1 Schedule 3 or an egg of a wild bird or any part of such an egg **he shall be guilty of an offence**

This section creates several offences which include all forms of trade or offering to trade. Section 27 of the Act defines a 'sale' as including hire, barter and exchange, and cognate expressions shall be construed accordingly.

Any offer to exchange or trade for other birds or goods in kind will still be treated as a sales offence under the Act if it involves a live wild bird.

One further offence can be considered where a keeper is intending to launder birds. If he buys close rings for illegal birds or retains close rings from another bird that has died, intending to use the rings on a replacement bird, then the keeper is guilty of the offence of possessing an article capable of being used to commit an offence under the Act. Rings issued by the DETR remain the property of the DETR, and should be returned when a bird dies or when the rings have not been used for the purpose for which they were issued.

Wildlife and Countryside Act 1981

Section 18(2)

Any person who for the purposes of committing an offence under the foregoing provisions of this Part
has in his possession
anything capable of being used for committing the offence
shall be guilty of an offence
and shall be punishable in like manner as for the said offence.

This section applies to all offences of taking, possessing, sale and registration of wild birds and their eggs.

For further information about the sale of live birds see 2.8, 2.9.6 and 2.9.15.

2.9.14 Offences following conviction

Following a conviction in court for any of the offences mentioned with a special penalty then section 7(3)(a) will take effect.

Wildlife and Countryside Act 1981

Section 7(3)(a)

If any person
keeps or has in his possession or under his control
any bird included in Schedule 4, within five years of him having been convicted of an offence under this part for which a special penalty is provided
he shall be guilty of an offence

NOTE: Following a conviction in respect of a Schedule 4 bird that is the subject of a special penalty, section 7(3)(a) will take effect and will last for a term of five years. This section will not take effect, however, if a conditional discharge was given for the original offence.

Following a conviction in respect of a Schedule 4 bird that is not the subject of a special penalty then section 7(3)(b) will take effect and will last for a term of three years. The three-year ban also applies to anyone convicted of any cruelty offence involving any birds or mammals protected under Part I of the 1981 Act.

2.9.15 The law – non-Schedule 4 birds

The ringing and registration provisions of the WCA apply only to birds listed on Schedule 4 of the Act. Other species may be held in captivity – it is not an offence to keep a non-Schedule 4 bird that is not ringed – but a keeper must be able to prove that it is legally in his possession. The other provisions of the WCA, relating to the taking of birds from the wild (section 1), and their sale etc (section 6) continue to apply.

In addition to the WCA, an EC Regulation prohibits internal trade in certain species unless a certificate has been issued.

These controls arise from the Convention on International Trade in Endangered Species of Wild Fauna and Flora (CITES) (see Chapter 9). The aim of this Convention is to control and regulate trade in certain endangered species.

Since 1 June 1997 CITES has been implemented throughout Europe by EC Regulation 338/97. All European birds of prey are included in Annex A of the EC Regulation. This means that international trade and internal sale of wild-taken specimens are generally banned. The legislation which provides offences for this in the UK is the Control of Trade in Endangered Species (Enforcement) Regulations 1997. These are known as COTES.

Article 8.1 of EC Regulation 338/97 states:
The purchase, offer to purchase, acquisition for commercial purposes, display to the public for commercial purposes, use for commercial gain and sale, keeping for sale, offering for sale or transporting for sale of specimens of the species listed in Annex A shall be prohibited.

Regulation 8(1) of the Control of Trade in Endangered Species (Enforcement) Regulations 1997 makes it an offence to purchase, offer to purchase, acquire for commercial purposes, display to the public for commercial purposes, use for commercial gain, sell, keep for sale, offer for sale or transport for sale any specimen of a species listed in Annex A. The COTES Regulations provide for a custodial sentence to be imposed in the event of a successful prosecution, and it is always worth considering whether these provisions can be used when dealing with cases involving the sale of birds illegally taken from the wild. In one case an 18-month sentence was given for the sale of illegally-taken peregrine falcons.

Regulation 8(2) makes it an offence to sell any Annex B specimen if it has been illegally imported.

EXEMPTIONS TO ARTICLE 8 OF REGULATION 338/97: Within the Regulation there is provision for exemptions to permit the purchase, sale, display etc of certain captive-bred Annex A species. Some species are covered by a general exemption (see Article 32 of EC Regulation 939/97).

AVES ANSERIFORMES Anatidae	Anas laysanensis
	Anas querquedula
	Aythya nyroca
	Branta ruficollis
	Branta sandvicensis
	Oxyura leucocephala
GALLIFORMES Phasianidae	Crossoptilon crossoptilon
	Crossoptilon mantchuricum
	Lophophorus impcianus
	Lophura edwardsi
	Lophura swinhoii
	Syrmaticus elliott
	Syrmaticus humiae
COLUMBIFORMES Columbidae	Columba livia
PSITTACIFORMES Psittacidae	Cyanoramphus novaezelandiae
	Psephotus dissimilis

PASSERIFORMES Fringillidae	Carduelis cucullata

For other species the CITES Management Authority (the DETR in Great Britain and the DANI in Northern Ireland) need to issue a certificate. These certificates may be issued for only one of the purposes set out in Article 8.3 of EC Regulation 338/97.

Specimens for which certificates are issued must be marked. For captive-bred birds, this must be a close ring (ie a ring in a continuous circle which cannot be removed from the bird when its leg is fully grown), or if this is not possible due to the physical or behavioural characteristics of the bird, a microchip transponder.

The information contained on the close ring or microchip code will be recorded on the certificate.

If a certificate has been issued for a sale, or it is covered by a general exemption, a separate certificate is not required for the purchase, offer to purchase or acquisition for commercial purposes of a specimen.

However, certificates are holder-specific and valid for just one transaction. The new owner must apply for a further certificate if he or she wishes to sell the bird.

The only exception to this is certificates for breeders. These are only available for captive-bred specimens and are valid for all subsequent sales provided the certificate travels with the specimen.

Any breeders' certificates which are lost will not be replaced, and a new certificate will be required for each subsequent sale of that specimen.

Sales of certain species have taken place in accordance with general exemptions issued under Article 6 of EC Regulation 3626/82. These exemptions are under review and may be revoked, so in any cases where people are relying on them to sell restricted specimens, you should check with the DETR.

For further information on the sale of live birds see 2.8, 2.9.6 and 2.9.13.

2.9.16 Other offences

Do not overlook criminal offences of deception or attempted deception, under section 15 of the Theft Act 1968. If a keeper takes a bird from the wild and then sells or attempts to sell it, pretending it is a legitimate captive-bred bird, then he deceives the buyer into believing that it is captive-bred and obtains money by deception. If these circumstances apply then this provides a valuable power of arrest which allows the keeper to be detained and interviewed.

In Scotland this would constitute the common law crime of fraud.

2.9.17 Power to investigate offences and gather evidence

In many of the cases that come to the notice of investigators all the evidence for the offence will be with the keeper, so the investigator needs to be able to gather this evidence and to search for and seize exhibits.

Under section 19(1)(d) of the WCA, powers of seizure and detention are given for the purposes of proceedings under Part I of the Act. The subsection makes it clear that the power extends to anything which 'may be liable to forfeiture under section 21'. This will bring in 'any bird, nest, egg ...' (section 21(6)). The power of seizure is also extended by section 21(2)–(3).

Under section 19(3) of the 1981 Act, where there are reasonable grounds to believe a Schedule 1 species is involved, a justice of the peace and in Scotland a sheriff may issue a warrant to a constable to enter and search any premises for evidence of offences under sections 1, 3, 5, 7 or 8 (these sections include taking from the wild, possession and non-registration).

Section 19(3) allows the presence during the execution of the warrant of such other people as are necessary for the purpose of gathering evidence; this allows the attendance of a vet, falconer, RSPB or RSPCA officer and DETR wildlife inspector.

When applying for a warrant, the magistrate should be informed of all those who will be in attendance when the warrant is executed. This will not only prevent any dispute about who may or may not be allowed to enter and search premises under the warrant, but it will also enable the magistrate to have a clearer picture of what action is proposed and will assist in the consideration of the application. Section 16 of the Police and Criminal Evidence Act 1984 (PACE) requires that entry and search under a warrant must be within one month from the date of issue. (PACE does not apply in Scotland.)

Where there are reasonable grounds to suspect that a sales offence under the Control of Trade in Endangered Species (Enforcement) Regulations 1997 is involved and reasonable grounds for believing that the bird or birds bought have been illegally imported, a justice of the peace can again issue a warrant to a constable.

There are a number of important points to note and a couple of significant differences between the two types of warrant.

A WCA warrant can be issued only where the evidence suggests that one of the species involved is on Schedule 1 to the Act; the offence took place in an area of special protection; one of the species is on Schedule 4, etc.

A COTES warrant covers sales, or possession for sale, of any species listed on EC Regulation 338/97.

COTES provides powers of seizure:

> (a) necessary for the protection of the constable or any person accompanying him; or
>
> (b) otherwise essential to effect seizure of the specimen; or
>
> (c) necessary for the conservation of evidence; or
>
> (d) in the interests of the welfare of the specimen.

A constable can exercise these powers when he is lawfully on any premises.

These warrants serve specific purposes; and the circumstances of each case should be considered individually to determine under which legislation an application should be made to the court.

In cases in which a person has been arrested for suspected involvement in offences of deception under section 15 of the Theft Act 1968, a police officer may, in accordance with section 18 of PACE, enter and search any premises occupied or controlled by that person.

In Scotland this would be the common law crime of fraud and a common law warrant could be issued by a sheriff.

General powers of seizure are also provided by the Police and Criminal Evidence Act 1984. Under section 19(2), where a police officer is lawfully on premises he may seize anything which is on the premises if he has reasonable grounds for believing:

- that it has been obtained in consequence of the commission of an offence; and
- that it is necessary to seize it in order to prevent it being concealed, lost, damaged, altered or destroyed.

This allows a police officer to seize anything if it is potential evidence of an offence, including the bird itself.

The police in Scotland have the powers under section 60 of the Civil Government (Scotland) Act 1982 to seize anything which appears to have been stolen or to be evidence of the commission of the crime of theft.

2.9.18 DNA profiling and birds of prey

It has been possible to obtain birds from the wild and then launder these into the legitimate falconry world by taking young birds or eggs illegally and then claiming to have bred them from legitimately-held captive stock.

Since the development of DNA profiling for certain birds of prey, it has now become a relatively straightforward matter to prove conclusively the heredity and provenance of individual birds.

Sibling relationships (brothers and sisters) and maternity/paternity can be proven by the taking of a blood sample from the claimed parents and young, and analysis of the DNA profiles produced.

It is possible to obtain evidence as to whether an individual adult is related to an individual chick, whether two adults, or any of a combination of adults, are related to a chick, and also whether two chicks are related and were produced by the same parents.

Adult-to-young relationships are easy to prove, especially in combination with declarations of ringing and parentage for Schedule 4 species, but sibling relationships are also valuable as these can still be used where the adults are claimed to have escaped or died.

Chicks or eggs can be taken from more than one nest or site, and if these are claimed to be a single clutch it is possible to negate this claim.

Regulations 9.3 and 9.5 of COTES give the police and DETR wildlife inspectors powers to require the taking (by a qualified veterinary surgeon) of samples of blood or tissue for DNA analysis. Certain conditions must be met.

The WCA does not, however, provide a specific power to obtain a sample of blood or other tissue for DNA analysis. It may therefore be unlawful, in certain circumstances, to take a blood sample from a bird without the consent of a keeper. However, keepers will know that where a person is being charged with an offence under section 1(2) of the WCA of being in possession of a wild bird, the onus is on that person to prove that the bird had been acquired lawfully. DNA can therefore provide keepers with a useful method of showing that a bird is lawfully in their possession.

More detailed information about DNA and its use in the investigation of wildlife offences can be found in *Wildlife Crime: Using DNA Forensic Evidence* published by the DETR in 1997.

2.9.19 Planning and executing a warrant

It is worth selecting a veterinary surgeon who has experience of birds of prey and asking him to examine and comment on the condition of each bird that he sees.

With the exception of very tame pet birds, all birds dislike being handled, and the stress of handling can precipitate fits or collapse, especially in the smaller or highly strung species such as sparrowhawks and goshawks. All injury to birds, including their feathers and beaks which may become damaged if they fly into the aviary fence, must be avoided at all costs. In most situations keepers will be content to catch their own birds, as they will view this as the best way of minimising the risk of injury during the procedure. It should be borne in mind that some keepers may not wish their birds to be examined, and having caught them in the aviary may 'accidentally' let them go once they are outside the safety of the aviary netting. Situations will arise when the owner is either not present or does not wish to co-operate. In view of this, the visiting officers must either comprise or be accompanied by someone suitably experienced to ensure that any birds can be safely caught and handled.

EQUIPMENT:

- net – (for example suitably – sized fisherman's landing net). Remember the birds may be loose in a large aviary. It is important to catch the birds quickly rather than to chase them around an aviary for several minutes;

- gloves – two pairs, one thick (for example commercial 'welders' gloves), one thin for small birds (for example driving gloves);

- clean towel – to help wrap a bird in, or restrain it;

- carrying boxes – safe and secure and suitable for the species and numbers likely to be involved.

ASSISTANCE: If a veterinary surgeon is to be present it must be borne in mind what other tasks the vet may be required to carry out, and whether he can do these as well as catch or restrain birds. It may be necessary to have an additional experienced handler present. People who will accompany an authorised person or police officer should be included in the application to the court for a warrant (see 2.9.17).

BLOOD SAMPLING: If blood samples are required for DNA analysis, a veterinary surgeon with appropriate expertise will need to be engaged.

IDENTIFICATION: If blood samples are taken from a bird which is not identified in a permanent manner (for example a closed metal ring on the leg), it may be advisable for a vet, with the keeper's consent, to implant the bird at the scene of the investigation with an electronic 'identichip' (microchip). Most vets have or have access to suitable equipment; they should be requested to bring such equipment with them, and know how and where to safely implant birds of various sizes. There may, however, be an extra charge for this service, and it is well worth checking with the vet before the warrant is executed. If microchipping is not appropriate then cable-ties can be used (depending on the species). The DETR can assist.

SEIZURE OF BIRDS: Where circumstances dictate that birds may need to be seized, plans should be made in advance to find suitable sites where they may be looked after by experienced and reliable bird-keepers. Suitable carry boxes, which must have non-slip floors (for example, a piece of carpet material), and transport must be arranged in advance. Seized birds should always be transported individually in boxes, unless they are small, non-aggressive and were already living together (for example, wild-taken siskins or other finches).

It is essential that at least one experienced falconer attends to assist with handling and holding of the birds of prey, as the keeper may refuse to co-operate with the catching procedure.

Video or photographic evidence can be extremely valuable and should be considered, for there is no better way to illustrate the conditions under which birds were being kept. This could also provide proof of whether breeding was in fact possible in those conditions. Video film or photographs should be marked with the date.

From the point of view of the birds' welfare, the best time to execute a warrant is early morning or daytime, avoiding the late afternoon or evening after the birds have settled.

If the case involves taking samples from chicks or young birds, then it is important to wait until the chicks are large enough for a sample to be safely taken; in the case of species like goshawk or peregrine this is when the bird is about 18 days old. Obviously, with large broods a median point will have to be calculated, because the birds will be of different ages.

With the chicks of the registrable species, it is also worth waiting until the birds have been ringed and the keeper has applied to register the birds, as this process involves him declaring the parentage of each chick (potentially a further offence under section 17 of the WCA). This can be useful evidence if the keeper subsequently declines to be interviewed.

Birds may be carried hooded and perched on a bow perch or block if necessary. It is very important to see that the birds do not overheat and to remember that birds of prey are very susceptible to exhaust fumes. They should not be left near to the rear of or in a stationary vehicle with its engine running.

If it is anticipated that birds may be seized, then prior arrangements should have been made for their long-term care and maintenance, bearing in mind that a case can take many months to be resolved through the courts.

2.9.20 Theft of birds

Always be prepared to give advice to bird-keepers on security. If in doubt, consult your local crime prevention officer.

Bird theft is rapidly increasing, principally because of rarity and/or value. Rare parrots and good hunting female goshawks command four-figure prices, and even less sought-after birds of prey change hands at £100 and upwards.

The majority of thefts occur from aviaries, but falcons are known to have been stolen by thieves prepared to lure a flying bird down from a distance, and escaped birds are often the subject of stealing by finding.

2.9.21 Security

Security against bird theft is a difficult problem. Physical entry into an aviary is usually relatively easy, owing to the materials used to construct them. Many aviaries are situated some distance from the keeper's house, which does not help security. There are, however, a number of things that an owner/keeper can do to help protect his birds and cause a problem to any would-be thief. The main objective of any thief is to be in and out as quickly as possible, making the minimum noise, and above all, not to be detected and certainly not to get caught.

The most obvious deterrent is an alarm. Alarms can be very 'hi-tech' and can be used quite easily to protect aviaries. Audible bells do not have to be fitted near the aviary itself, so panic to birds during any activation can be avoided. Systems can be installed to suit keepers' wishes, for example with bells inside the house or garden. The drawback is the cost, as some systems can be very expensive.

There are, however, cheaper ways that provide some deterrent effect. Movement-detector lights are useful as no thief wants to be in the spotlight. These must be sited high enough so that the thief cannot quickly knock them out. Heavy-duty padlocks on doors are also a hindrance, especially those designed so that they cannot be bolt-cropped. Any wire can easily be cut but this takes longer. Gravel paths are useful, as the sound of walking on gravel is quite loud and most house dogs will hear it. One simple but very effective alarm system that can be very cheaply installed consists only of fishing line and a bell. The line is strategically placed about a foot from the ground across the front of the aviary and leads into the house, where a bell is attached to the end. Trellis-work placed on the tops of walls and on solid fences also make entry difficult for intruders.

There is one other security method that keepers can be advised about, and that is to curtail 'loose talk'. Keepers must be careful what they say and in whose presence they say it. Captive birds have almost always been stolen by other keepers or agents working on their behalf. The only people that are interested in these birds are other keepers. In virtually all detected cases of theft the victim has either known the defendant or has a friend close by that knows him. Where birds are being displayed or exhibited, security is very difficult indeed, but consider the use of an address which is not where birds are actually located.

2.9.22 Other special measures: microchips

Keepers are also well advised to have their birds fitted with a microchip or microtag. This is an injectable passive transponder about the size of a grain of rice which provides an electronic means of identification. The chip is protected by special glass and is inserted into an animal or bird where it becomes encapsulated by tissue/muscle. Once a chip is inserted it is virtually impossible to remove except by a veterinary operation. The transponder does not need a battery. It is activated by a reader and transmits its own unique code/number, which in turn is then displayed on the reader.

There are two types of microchips: Destron and Trovan. Each type operates in a slightly different way, so Destron readers cannot read Trovan chips and vice versa.

The Destron chip is most commonly used by vets for implanting birds of prey and most other domestic pets. The Trovan chip is mainly used by zoos and other such establishments. Details of suppliers are included in Appendix E.

There are two types of readers.

- Static readers are generally found at veterinary surgeries, RSPCA hospitals, etc. They are now widely used by vets and you should not have too much difficulty obtaining access to one.

- Portable readers are also normally held by vets, RSPCA inspectors, RSPB investigations officers, the DETR and some police officers.

In using the portable readers, you need to be as close to the bird or animal as possible. Ideally, when you scan the reader should virtually be touching the bird. Some chips are easier to find than others, so cover every inch of the bird/animal and sweep the area more than once.

Details of suppliers can be found in Appendix E.

2.9.23 Registration schemes

Keepers can also be advised to join a private registration scheme. A number of private schemes exist to enable keepers to continue to register the birds that have been removed from Schedule 4 of the 1981 Act, or any other birds. Registration documents are made available, similar to those of the DETR, and rings can also be issued. The schemes also run a lost/found register for birds of prey.

Details are shown in Appendix E.

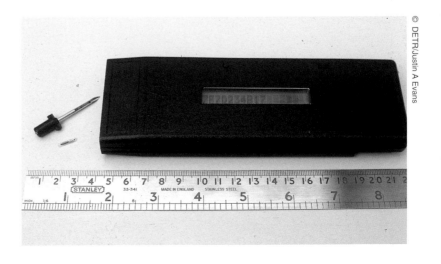

© DETR/Justin A Evans

A microchip, implanting needle and reader

Peregrine being scanned for a microchip

2.10 INJURED BIRDS AND BIRD DESTRUCTION

Section 4(2)

A person shall not be guilty of an offence under section 1 of the WCA if:

- he takes a wild bird which has been disabled so that he can tend it and release it when recovered. Remember, if it is a bird on Schedule 4 he must register it with the DETR or hand it over to a person operating under general licence WLF 1000999;

- he kills a wild bird for humane reasons (ie he destroys a seriously injured bird);

- he carries out a lawful act which results in the death or injury of a wild bird if this could not reasonably have been avoided.

Section 4(3)(a) Preserving public health and safety

A person may kill or injure a wild bird, except those on Schedule 1, if necessary for preserving public health or for reasons of air safety.

Section 4(3)(b) and (c) Prevention of disease and protection of crops and livestock.

A person may kill or injure a wild bird, except those on Schedule 1, if necessary to:

- prevent the spread of disease (subsection (b));
- prevent serious damage to livestock, foodstuffs for livestock, crops, vegetables, fruit, growing timber, fisheries or inland waterways (subsection (c)).

Under subsection (c) a person controlling birds must show that there was no other satisfactory solution, and if it had been apparent beforehand that the action would be necessary, a licence should have been obtained. Anyone using this defence must also notify MAFF as soon as reasonably practicable.

2.11 PROTECTION OF CAPTIVE BIRDS

Wildlife and Countryside Act 1981

Section 8(1)

It is an offence for any person to
keep or confine any bird whatsoever
in any cage or other receptacle which is not
sufficient in height or length or breadth to permit
the bird to stretch its wings freely
(this person is liable to a special penalty)

NOTE: This applies to all birds, both wild and domestic. Always remember this offence when considering prosecution for illegal use of a cage trap. Almost invariably, the part where the captive bird is held will be too small to allow the bird to stretch its wings in each direction.

EXCEPTIONS: This section does not apply to:

- poultry;
- any bird that is in the course of conveyance;
- while that bird is being shown at any public exhibition or competition, as long as the total time spent confined does not exceed 72 hours;
- while that bird is undergoing examination or treatment by a vet; and
- anything done in accordance with a licence issued under section 16 of the WCA.

2.12 AVICULTURE (BIRD-KEEPING)

Keeping caged birds is a popular hobby. In theory, captive birds are not wildlife. However, many species of British native birds, all protected by one or more statutes, and many foreign species of exotic birds subject to CITES or the laws in their country of origin, are kept by bird-keepers throughout the United Kingdom.

The great majority of bird-keepers are law-abiding and careful to keep their birds well cared for in proper surroundings. However, the following offences do occur within the cage-bird trade:

- trapping from the wild (see Chapter 4);
- ringing illegally-taken birds to pass them off as captive-bred;
- theft of birds from aviaries or, to a lesser extent, from shows or exhibitions; and
- importation of endangered species in contravention of CITES (see Chapter 9).

Where a breach of the law is suspected, it is often difficult for an investigating officer to decide what species the bird belongs to and how to show that the law has been broken. Many bird-keepers produce hybrid species which are frequently difficult to identify, and there is no user-friendly guide to give the investigator an instant answer.

Frequently the problem is simply whether a bird is held legally in captivity. As an aid to proof either way, birds are often required to be close-ringed. Species required to be fitted with close rings are listed in Schedule 3 to the WCA, together with their size code letter, usually stamped on the ring.

Close rings can only be fitted to birds at an early infant stage. With small British finches, rings would need to be applied to the baby bird at between five and seven days of age. With larger birds, the rings may be fitted up to two weeks of age, after which the ankle joint becomes too large for the correct-sized ring to pass on or off. The rings are designed to fit in such a way as to be able to freely rotate without undue slack. Therefore an oversized ring, capable of being fitted to an adult bird, becomes obvious once a small degree of experience has been obtained.

In addition to the use of oversized rings, it is the practice of some keepers attempting to 'legalise' a bird to use rings which have been stretched sufficiently to be fitted to the bird. Such rings will show distention, either in the figuring, or the vertical plane, in that the ring is wider at one end than the other.

Parrot species do not have to be ringed and it needs considerable expertise to identify species, particularly with Amazon parrots, where there is little variation in plumage and both rare and common species are essentially green birds. Imported specimens will, if ringed, only carry a sexing ring fitted by a veterinary surgeon as proof of surgical or DNA sexing. These rings are no guide to the legal status of the bird; they show only that the bird has been sexed, and because they are not closed they can easily be removed and refitted to other birds.

When viewing captive birds suspected of being taken from the wild illegally, do not regard the birds' nervous behaviour or feather condition as proof of wildness. Many keepers hold their birds in conditions which keep them isolated from humans, especially strangers, in order to produce better breeding results. Feather condition has, in the past, been used to show that birds have been recently trapped; colour and condition indicating that the birds were 'field moulted'. This is no longer considered to be a reliable indication as 'colour feeding' of some native species (which lose their natural pink or red coloration on a captive diet), replaces the lost ingredients and produces birds of excellent natural colouring.

Some indication of the scale of theft comes from the register of bird theft maintained by the National Council for Aviculture (NCA). The register has grown from 142 reported thefts in 1994 to a dramatic increase of 1,154 reported thefts in 1995. While some increase may be due to improved reporting, there has been a huge increase in theft of caged birds. Prior to 1992 the theft of large parrots, such as valuable macaws, was almost unheard of. Since then, several hundred of these birds, including some very rare and valuable CITES-listed birds, have been taken.

The NCA gives a free service to every police force. Any investigating officer can make use of the NCA intelligence network, which has been responsible for the successful prosecution of a number of bird thieves, some of whom have received substantial prison sentences. Calls are also welcome from officers seeking advice on any aspect of bird-keeping. Full details of the NCA are in Appendix E.

NOTE: See 2.9.21, 2.9.22 and 2.9.23 on security of aviaries and crime prevention measures.

2.13 INTRODUCING NON-NATIVE SPECIES

Wildlife and Countryside Act 1981

Section 14(1)

It is an offence for any person to
release or allow to escape into the wild
any animal which
(a) is of a kind which is not ordinarily resident in and is not a regular visitor to Great Britain in a wild state;
or
(b) is included in Part I of Schedule 9

EXCEPTIONS: No offence would be committed if the person could show that:
- he can prove that he took all reasonable steps and exercised due diligence to avoid committing the offence; or
- a licence has been issued under section 16 of the WCA and all the conditions have been complied with.

native animals

3.1 PROTECTION

Under the Wildlife and Countryside Act 1981 (WCA) all wild birds are protected. However, the same is not true of other animals. Only selected species which are included in Schedule 5 enjoy protection. These are creatures that are most at risk or endangered.

NOTE: The Conservation (Natural Habitats, &c.) Regulations 1994 augment the provisions of the WCA in many areas. When considering whether an offence has been committed, due regard should also be given to these Regulations.

Wild mammals are protected against certain acts of cruelty (see Chapter 4). Schedule 5 of the WCA lists all species that have protection, but this protection can be at a number of levels, singly or in combination, namely:

- full protection;
- may not be sold;
- may not be killed or injured;
- may not be taken; or
- may not be possessed – dead or alive.

3.2 PRINCIPAL OFFENCES

Wildlife and Countryside Act 1981

Section 9(1)
Killing, injuring or taking

It is an offence for any person to
intentionally kill, injure or take
any wild creature on Schedule 5

EXAMPLES: Anyone who catches a dormouse to keep it as a pet would be guilty of this offence. Likewise, a person who kills an adder would be liable to prosecution.

EXCEPTIONS: It is not an offence if the animal was killed as a consequence of a lawful action which could not have been reasonably avoided. It is for the person to show good reason for any action which would otherwise be unlawful.

Likewise, it would not be an offence if the animal was killed or injured by an authorised person if this was necessary to prevent serious damage to livestock, crops, vegetables, fruit, growing timber, any other form of property or to fisheries. However, an authorised person will not be able to rely on this defence if he knew beforehand that injuring or killing the animal was necessary and that an application for a licence under section 16 of the WCA had not been applied for, or had been applied for but not determined.

It is not an offence for a person to take a disabled animal for the purpose of tending it and releasing it when it is no longer disabled, provided that the animal had not been disabled by that person's unlawful act. Nor would it be an offence for a person to kill an animal that is so seriously disabled that there is no reasonable chance of it recovering. Again, this is provided that it had not been disabled by that person's unlawful action.

Furthermore, it is not an offence if the animal is killed or taken as a requirement of a notice issued under section 98 of the Agriculture Act 1947 by the Agriculture Minister or under an order made under the Animal Health Act 1981.

No offence will be committed if the action has been taken in accordance with a licence issued under section 16 of the WCA.

NOTE: Section 11 of the WCA prohibits certain methods of killing or taking wild animals (see Chapter 4).

Wildlife and Countryside Act 1981

Section 9(2)
Possession of a wild animal

It is an offence for any person to
have in his possession or control
any live or dead Schedule 5 wild animal
or
any part or anything derived from such an animal

EXCEPTIONS: No offence would be committed if the keeper/possessor can prove legal possession because:

- the animal had not been killed or taken, or had been killed or taken otherwise than in contravention of Part I of the WCA or the Conservation of Wild Creatures and Wild Plants Act 1975;
- a licence has been issued under section 16 of the WCA;
- the animal had been disabled otherwise than by that person's unlawful act and was taken to be tended and released when recovered. Likewise, no offence would be committed if the animal was killed if there was no reasonable chance of it recovering; or
- the animal or other thing had been sold otherwise than in contravention of Part 1 of the WCA or the Conservation of Wild Creatures and Wild Plants Act 1975.

An example would be where a person finds a red squirrel that had been hit and killed by a car accidentally. If the finder takes it to a taxidermist to have it stuffed neither he nor the taxidermist would commit an offence. However, if a person shoots a red squirrel he would commit an offence. If he gives the carcass to a friend that other person would also commit an offence.

Wildlife and Countryside Act 1981

Section 9(4)(a)
Protection of animals' nests or roosts, etc

It is an offence for any person to
intentionally damage, destroy
or obstruct access to any structure
or place
which any wild animal on Schedule 5 uses for shelter or protection

---

EXAMPLE: Anyone blocking the entrance to an otter holt (an otter's den) would commit this offence if they did so intentionally.

Wildlife and Countryside Act 1981

Section 9(4)(b)
Disturbing wild animals

It is an offence for any person to
intentionally disturb
any wild animal included on Schedule 5 while it is occupying a structure or place it uses for shelter or protection

---

EXCEPTION: Sections 9(4)(a) and 9(4)(b) of the WCA do not apply to anything done within a dwelling house. This exception does not apply to bats unless they are within the living area of the building (see 3.3 below).

Some animals also receive protection from the 1994 Conservation Regulations (see list of species in Appendix A). Disturbance of European protected species is an offence regardless of whether they are occupying a place or shelter. It is also an offence to damage or destroy a breeding site or resting place regardless of whether this is intentional or not.

3.3 SPECIFIC OFFENCES: BATS

3.3.1 Introduction

Bats are protected by section 9 of the WCA, all British bats being listed on Schedule 5. They are further protected by a restriction of the exceptions normally permitting action against protected species. And they are also protected by the provisions of the Conservation (Natural Habitats, &c.) Regulations 1994.

NOTE: In the investigation of offences relating to bats, as with all wildlife, the most important thing is knowing where to obtain the necessary information and expertise. The employment of someone with expert knowledge of the animal is essential and it is important that all police wildlife liaison officers know their local bat group and their local Country Conservation Agency office (ie English Nature, the Countryside Council for Wales or Scottish Natural Heritage).

Nearly half of all bat colonies are found in houses less than 25 years old

3

People involved in possible offences against bats may well be annoyed, either because they cannot understand the need for police involvement where the subject of the investigation is a small animal that is causing them problems, or because these small animals are holding up work and possibly costing a company time and money. It is therefore important in any investigation to start by calming all parties and also not voicing any opinions that could be construed by anyone concerned as supporting them in any way.

The legislation makes it an offence to kill, injure or take the animal, and to possess or control any live or dead bat, except where that possession is specifically exempted. Most importantly so far as bats are concerned, the legislation affords protection to any structure or places the animal uses for shelter or protection, by making it an offence to damage, destroy or obstruct access to such places, as well as to disturb the animals whilst they are using such a place.

All these offences are subject to a qualification within the wording of the relevant sections, in that the person suspected of committing any of the above offences must 'intentionally' carry out one of the above acts. This makes the proving of these offences very difficult, and particular care must be taken in the investigation.

Further offences are created by the sale and transport, or possession for sale and the advertising for sale, of these animals. These offences also relate to parts of the animal; occasionally offences may be committed which relate to 'parts', particularly in relation to alternative medicine.

Also worth mentioning here are police powers to enter and search. It is normally necessary to enter and search some form of structure when investigating offences relating to bats. Section 19 of the WCA provides police with a broad power of entry, but this power excludes dwelling houses. In circumstances where entry into a house is required, this is usually by asking consent of the householder. However, if you suspect that an offence has been committed, a warrant under section 19(3) (b) of the WCA can be applied for.

Bats may be discovered by householders, usually as a result of the discovery of droppings on the ground below the entrance to the roost or within the loft area of a dwelling. This is often followed by an actual sighting of the bats emerging from the roost.

It is often at this point that householders consider attempting to remove the bats from their house. Police may be called by a neighbour, or the local bat group, aware of the protection afforded these animals, when the householder is seen sealing the roost entrance or doing some other act that is likely to have an effect on the bats. When challenged, householders usually defend their actions on the grounds that:

- the bats may transmit some disease;

- the bats droppings are unsightly, or may carry disease;

- the bats will damage the fabric of the house in some way; or

- they simply do not like bats in the confines of the house.

All the above reasons for a householder attempting to remove any bats are unfounded. Bats in this country do not normally carry any diseases that are communicable to humans, either from the animal itself or its droppings. One or two bats suffering from rabies were believed to have originated outside the UK. Normally bats do not bite unless they are handled, but anyone who is bitten should seek medical advice. Bats do not build nests or engage in any sort of behaviour that will damage the fabric of any building. They simply group together, utilising space that already exists. This information, although it can be communicated to a householder by the investigator, should ideally be left to an expert who can cover the details in more depth.

It must be remembered that householders have a defence in law if the bat or bats are within the actual living area of the house. This defence would relate to offences covered by section 9(4)(b) of the WCA that relate to the disturbance of animals. The defence would only extend to the removal of the bat from the living area, and it must then be released immediately. It would not extend to the intentional killing of the animal to remove it. It may be that in their efforts to catch the animal they accidentally kill it. In such circumstances clearly no offence has been committed.

Also remember that householders with bats using their house to roost are not compelled to keep them; they must simply liaise with the relevant Country Conservation Agency to obtain the correct advice as to how any exclusion should be carried out and to the timing of such an operation.

If police are called to a household where attempts have been made to exclude bats from the house, particularly from the roof area by sealing off the access point, then it is important that the access point is re-opened so that any bats trapped inside can escape, or nursing females can return to the non-flying offspring inside.

It is important that the local bat group is involved at an early stage of any investigation. They have the expertise to be able to direct the investigator in the right direction. They can also indicate early on if the matter is one that requires investigation for possible offences, or if they can deal with the matter simply by way of advice to the householder.

At all times where it is proposed to conduct an investigation that relates to bats, and more particularly bat roosts, the relevant Country Conservation Agency must be consulted. This is because entry into and acts conducted within a roost would be contrary to the relevant legislation. A person who possesses a licence issued by the relevant Country Conservation Agency to enter a bat roost would need to be present to facilitate the gathering of any evidence within a roost.

Contact details for English Nature (EN), the Countryside Council for Wales (CCW) and Scottish Natural Heritage (SNH) are given in Appendix E.

3.3.2 Bats discovered by commercial organisations

Bats discovered by commercial concerns will invariably involve some form of building renovation. The most likely circumstances are those where remedial timber treatment is being carried out. The types of chemical used and the manner and time that they are applied can have catastrophic effects on bats. Indeed, the remedial treatment of timber is cited as one of the major causes of the decline in the bat population in Great Britain.

In these circumstances, investigators will require the assistance of a licensed bat worker, particularly as the local bat group will probably have already visited the roost at an earlier stage, possibly prior to any work starting.

Treating timbers with chemicals to prevent wood rot and to kill beetles, etc, is the greatest threat to bats in houses

3

Prior to construction work within an identified bat roost the developer should liaise with the relevant Country Conservation Agency, to give them the opportunity to 'give advice' about the proposed work to be carried out. The legislation states that advice should be taken when any works affecting bats or their roosts are proposed. Any advice offered must be adhered to. This advice is offered in the form of a letter from the relevant Country Conservation Agency office. This can range from advice about the dates between which work may be conducted or the areas where the work may be prohibited because of the presence of bats, to the chemicals that may be used. The investigator should contact the relevant Country Conservation Agency as soon as possible to find out what advice, if any, has already been given to the developer or occupier.

It may be that the presence of bats was not identified by the developer during any early survey of the location, and the bats have been discovered during the course of the works. In such circumstances it is unlikely that offences will have been committed at the time of discovery. Following discovery, the contractor must immediately stop work in that area so that no further disturbance takes place, and must immediately seek advice from the relevant Country Conservation Agency office. This is normally in the form of a

voluntary bat warden being asked to attend the site. The attendance of the voluntary bat warden is normally fairly prompt, so that any solution to the problem can be set in motion as soon as possible, and also to cause minimal disruption to the planned works. It must be remembered that the bat warden who attends – although responding to a request from, and acting on behalf of, the relevant Country Conservation Agency – cannot offer formal advice to the developer. The bat warden will decide on the most appropriate course of action and communicate that to the relevant Country Conservation Agency office.

The Country Conservation Agency will offer the formal advice necessary under the WCA.

In most circumstances the developers accept the advice given and comply. If a developer ignores the advice given and continues with any work, this may be sufficient to satisfy the 'intentional' requirement of the legislation if the bats are disturbed or their roosts damaged. Clearly any accidental disturbance of a previously unknown roost would not constitute an offence. If no advice was sought at this later stage, this then might become an offence if work was to continue.

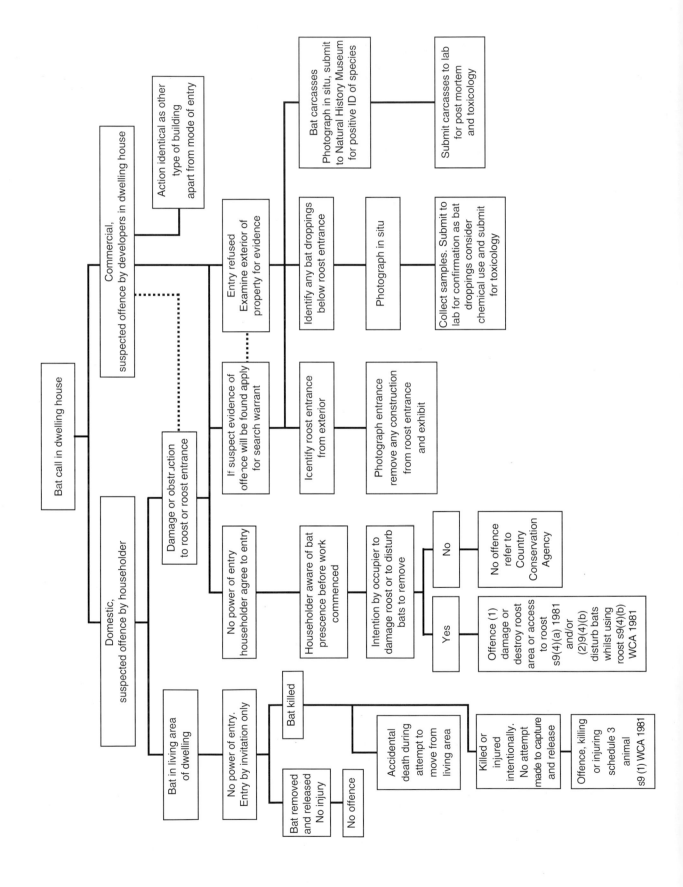

Bat call in dwelling house

Domestic, suspected offence by householder

Commercial, suspected offence by developers in dwelling house

Action identical as other type of building apart from mode of entry

Damage or obstruction to roost or roost entrance

Bat in living area of dwelling

No power of entry. Entry by invitation only

Bat killed

Bat removed and released No injury

No offence

Accidental death during attempt to move from living area

Killed or injured intentionally. No attempt made to capture and release

Offence, killing or injuring schedule 3 animal s9 (1) WCA 1981

No power of entry householder agree to entry

Householder aware of bat prescence before work commenced

Intention by occupier to damage roost or to disturb bats to remove

No

Yes

No offence refer to Country Conservation Agency

Offence (1) damage or destroy roost area or access to roost s9(4)(a) 1981 and/or (2)9(4)(b) disturb bats whilst using roost s9(4)(b) WCA 1981

If suspect evidence of offence will be found apply for search warrant

Identify roost entrance from exterior

Photograph entrance remove any construction from roost entrance and exhibit

Entry refused Examine exterior of property for evidence

Identify any bat droppings below roost entrance

Photograph in situ

Collect samples. Submit to lab for confirmation as bat droppings consider chemical use and submit for toxicology

Bat carcasses Photograph in situ, submit to Natural History Museum for positive ID of species

Submit carcasses to lab for post mortem and toxicology

When dealing with possible offences against bats in instances where remedial timber treatment is involved, it is crucial to be aware that some form of chemical has been employed. These chemicals can be toxic to both bats and humans, and extreme care should be taken when dealing with any of these substances. Do not accept the labelling of chemicals as they are displayed. If in doubt get them tested. Cases have been known of far more harmful chemicals being used at bat sites than those indicated on the containers. Always consider the possible effects on yourself and employ an expert to take the samples if necessary. In any event, always wear protective clothing, particularly covering the hands and eyes.

3.3.3 Investigating offences involving bats

The following is a summary of points to bear in mind.

1. Before entry into an alleged bat roost contact the relevant Country Conservation Agency.

2. Always take a licensed roost visitor or bat handler with you, as their assistance will be invaluable.

3. If no licensed expert is available you will need to obtain a licence to enter a roost from the appropriate Country Conservation Agency.

4. Although section 19 of the WCA provides a power of entry to any place other than a dwelling house to enter and investigate offences (or entry to a dwelling house if a search warrant has been obtained), entry to a bat roost will require the issue of a licence by the relevant Country Conservation Agency (see 1 and 3 above).

5. Do not touch or handle any bat carcasses or chemicals without rubber gloves. Consider the use of suitable protective clothing and respiratory equipment to counter any fumes from chemical use. Also consider other forms of protective clothing, such as hard hats and coveralls.

6. Do not disturb any bats still roosting at the site.

7. If in an underground site do not touch the walls, roof or any roof supports. Always ensure that someone knows that you are entering an underground site. Pre-arrange a time when you will contact them, so if you fail to report in the alarm will be raised.

3.4 SALE OF LIVE AND DEAD WILD ANIMALS

Wildlife and Countryside Act 1981

Section 9(5)(a)
Selling protected wild animals

It is an offence for any person to
sell/offer/expose for sale
or
possess/transport for the purpose of sale
any live or dead wild animal on Schedule 5
or
any part of, or anything derived from, such a wild animal

Section 9(5)(b)
Publishing advertisements

It is an offence for any person to
publish or cause to be published
any advertisement likely to be understood as conveying that he
buys/sells or intends to buy/sell
any live or dead wild animal on Schedule 5 or anything derived from such an animal

PRESUMPTION: In any proceedings for an offence under section 9(1), 9(2), 9(5)(a) or 9(6) of the WCA the animal in question shall be presumed to have been a wild animal unless the contrary is shown. For example, if a defendant uses the defence that the animal was not wild but captive-bred then it is for him to prove this and not for the prosecution to refute the claim.

Some animals are also subject to sales controls under the EC Wildlife Trade Regulation (338/97). Article 8 of the Regulation states that the purchase, offer to purchase, acquisition for commercial purposes, display to the public for commercial purposes, use for commercial gain and sale, keeping for sale, offering for sale or transporting for sale of the specimens listed in Annex A (eg otters) shall be prohibited.

Anyone acting in breach of these prohibitions may be guilty of an offence under Regulation 8(1) of the Control of Trade in Endangered Species (Enforcment)

Regulations 1997, unless the activity is authorised because it is covered by a general exemption, or a certificate issued by the CITES Management Authority (the DETR in Great Britain and the DANI in Northern Ireland) under Article 10 of Regulation 338/97.

Sales of certain species have taken place in accordance with general exemptions issued under Article 6 of EC Regulation 3626/82. These exemptions are under review and may be revoked, so in any cases where people are relying on them to sell restricted specimens, you should check with the DETR.

For advice and guidance on taxidermy see Chapter 2.

3.5 PROHIBITION OF CERTAIN METHODS OF KILLING OR TAKING WILD ANIMALS

Section 11 of the WCA details various offences relating to methods of killing or taking wild animals. The Wildlife and Countryside (Amendment) Act 1991 added offences relating to causing or permitting the prohibited methods of killing or taking wild animals.

These are fully set out in Chapter 4 – Poaching, Cruelty, Trapping and Poisoning.

3.6 THE PROTECTION OF BADGERS ACT 1992

3.6.1 Introduction

Previous legislation which protected badgers has now been consolidated in the Protection of Badgers Act 1992. The level of protection they receive is unique for an animal which is not endangered.

However, although badgers are not endangered nationally, in certain areas they have been persecuted, most notably in South Wales and South Yorkshire. Offences against badgers do occur, most commonly at the badger sett.

© LACS

Television picture of man with dogs and dead badgers

The definition of a sett is 'any structure or place which displays signs indicating current use by a badger'. Many of these setts have existed for decades, and their locations are well known locally. Offenders put terriers into the sett to attack the badger and/or dig it out. The badger is either killed or taken away alive to be used subsequently for baiting, ie being set upon by dogs.

Section 10 of the Badgers Act 1992 does allow licences to be issued to permit otherwise prohibited activities. Such licences may for example allow setts to be interfered with, or badgers to be killed or taken, in certain circumstances. You should contact the local MAFF Regional Service Centre (or WOAD, as appropriate), and the relevant Country Conservation Agency office (ie. EN, the CCW or SNH) to find out whether a licence has been issued.

MAFF Regional Service Centres and WOAD will only release details of whether a licence has been issued or not to the police.

Although setts are usually found to have been dug out well after the event, you may come across or be called to suspects (diggers seldom work alone) at or near a sett. If a licence has not been issued, look for and seize:

- any dead badgers. It sounds obvious, but if the diggers have been caught red-handed you may find that they have already killed a badger and thrown it aside or concealed it while they continue their dig. If they have seen you coming, any dead badger may have been hidden or thrown away as far as possible. Any dead badgers found in the vicinity should be taken away for post mortem examination;

- cameras or video equipment. Diggers sometimes pose at setts with their dogs and dead badgers. It provides the best possible evidence, particularly when diggers have not been caught in the act;
- digging equipment. Preserve any soil on spades or other implements by bagging these individually. Take control samples of soil from the sett. Be careful to avoid possible cross-contamination of exhibits – or affording the possibility of this to be alleged later;
- any implements to hold the badger – thick gloves, tongs, sacks or nets. If you suspect that badgers have been chased above ground to drive them back to a netted sett, look for the mark of the netting stake beside the entrance to the sett;
- clubs or instruments to kill or subdue the badger. Preserve these for examination for badger hair;
- 'ferret-finding' equipment to detect a small transmitting device, attached to the collar of a terrier to help to locate the dog underground if it fails to surface;
- maps marked with sett locations or any other documentary evidence;
- first-aid equipment for injured dogs; and
- injured dogs. If they have been down the sett and fought with a badger they are likely to have serious bites or tears to their jaws, chest and tops of the front legs. (**NOTE:** When dogs meet foxes below ground they are more likely to get small puncture-wound bites to the top of the muzzle and lower legs.)

If faced with strong denials and injured dogs, or if you have good reason to believe dogs have been in contact with badgers, seize the dogs and take them to a veterinary surgeon, who will isolate them and subsequently preserve faeces for examination. If the dogs have been below ground fighting badgers then badger hair may well be present in the faeces.

NOTE: Police officers may not interfere with badger setts even to obtain evidence unless they are licensed by the relevant Country Conservation Agency to do so for the purpose of investigating offences against badgers. Badgers are also protected against being killed or taken by certain means under Schedule 6 to the WCA.

If you are likely to be dealing with these offences, contact the relevant Country Conservation Agency and apply for a licence.

3.6.2 Police powers

In England and Wales, where a police officer has reasonable grounds for suspecting that a person is committing or has committed an offence under the provisions of the Act and that evidence of the commission of the offence is to be found on that person or any vehicle or article he may have with him, the police officer may:

- without warrant stop and search that person and any vehicle or article he may have with him; and
- seize and detain, for the purposes of proceedings under any of those provisions, anything which may be evidence of the commission of the offence or may be liable to be forfeited (badger, badger skin or any weapon or article used in the commission of the offence).

There is no power of arrest other than within the terms of section 25 of the Police and Criminal Evidence Act 1984 (PACE). In Scotland the police officer may arrest without warrant if a suspect fails to give their name to the police officer's satisfaction. Furthermore, because the badger legislation carries imprisonment as a penalty, Scottish officers may use section 13 of the Criminal Procedure (Scotland) Act 1995 in order to detain persons for questioning/further enquiries.

3.6.3 Principal offences under the 1992 Act

Protection of Badgers Act 1992

Section 1(1)
Unlawfully killing, injuring or taking

It is an offence for any person to
wilfully kill, injure or take
any badger or attempt to do so

EXCEPTIONS: A person is not guilty if he can show that his action was necessary to prevent serious damage to land, crops, poultry or other property.

This defence can only be used in the case of an unforeseen emergency. For example, a badger found in a chicken house killing poultry could legitimately be shot if there was no other reasonable way of preventing the damage.

Whenever necessary action against badgers can be foreseen (for example, where badgers are damaging golf greens or causing serious agricultural damage) a licence must be obtained from the relevant Country Conservation Agency, MAFF, or WOAD in Wales or SOAEFD in Scotland.

It is not an offence for a person to take or attempt to take a badger which had been disabled otherwise than by his lawful action and is taken or to be taken solely for the purpose of tending it.

Nor is it an offence to kill or attempt to kill a badger which appears to be so seriously injured, other than by his own unlawful act, or in such a condition that to kill it would be an act of mercy.

ONUS OF PROOF: Section 1(2) of the 1992 Badgers Act places the onus of proof upon the defendant. It states that:

> 'If, in any proceedings for an offence under subsection (1) consisting of attempting to kill, injure or take a badger, there is evidence from which it could reasonably be concluded that at the material time the accused was attempting to kill, injure or take a badger, he shall be presumed to have been attempting to kill, injure or take a badger unless the contrary is shown.'

This means that the onus is upon the defendant to show that there was no attempt to kill, injure or take a badger. This closes a loophole whereby a defendant would maintain that he was trying to kill or catch an unprotected animal such as a fox.

Protection of Badgers Act 1992

Section 1(3)
Possession of dead badgers

It is an offence for any person to possess or control
a dead badger or part of a dead badger or anything derived from a dead badger

---

EXCEPTION: No offence is committed if the person can show that:
- the badger had not been killed, or had been killed otherwise than in contravention of the provisions of the Act; or
- the badger or part of a badger or thing derived from a badger had been sold and, at the time of the purchase, the purchaser had no reason to believe that the badger had been killed in contravention of any of those provisions.

For example, if you find a badger that had died otherwise than in contravention of the Act, (for example, a road casualty), you can take possession of it. It also means that you would not commit an offence if you had a badger-hair shaving brush if it were bought before the Act came into force.

A person found on any land committing an offence under section 1 of the Act may be required by the owner or occupier of the land, or his servant or a police officer, to quit the land and give his name and address. If he refuses to do either he commits an offence.

David Parsons of the Metropolitan Police

Protection of Badgers Act 1992

Section 2(1)(a)
Cruelty

It is an offence for any person to
cruelly ill-treat
any badger

Section 2(1)(b)
Badger tongs

It is an offence for any person to
use
tongs in the course of
killing, taking or attempting to kill or take a
badger

Section 2(1)(c)
Badger digging

It is an offence for any person to
dig for any badger

ONUS OF PROOF: In any proceedings for an offence under this last subsection, if there is evidence from which it can reasonably be concluded that the accused was digging for a badger, he shall be presumed to have been digging for a badger unless the contrary is shown.

Again this removes the 'fox defence' – a defendant would have to prove that he was looking for foxes.

Protection of Badgers Act 1992

Section 2(1)(d)
Killing badgers by prohibited means

It is an offence for any person to
kill or take any badger
by use of any firearm other than a shotgun of
bore greater than 20 bore
or
a rifle using ammunition of muzzle energy not
less than 160 footpounds and bullet greater than
38 grains

Section 3
Interfering with a badger sett

It is an offence for any person to
interfere with a badger sett by
damaging a sett or a part thereof; obstructing
access to any entrance of a sett; destroying a
sett; causing a dog to enter a sett or disturbing a
badger when it is occupying a sett and
intending to do any of these things

EXCEPTIONS: A person is not guilty of committing this offence if he shows that his actions were necessary to prevent serious damage to land, crops, poultry or any other form of property. However, this defence can only be used if the action was required immediately to prevent serious damage. Otherwise the person must apply for a licence to carry out the action from either the relevant Country Conservation Agency or MAFF.

A person would not be guilty of disturbing a badger sett by damaging it or part of it, obstructing access to any entrance or disturbing a badger occupying a sett if his actions were incidental to a lawful operation and could not have been avoided.

3.6.4   Fox hunts and sett-stopping

The purpose of stopping earths or setts is to prevent a fox being hunted from seeking refuge underground. Traditionally, this is done the day before the hunt or early in the morning on the day of the hunt. It is normally undertaken by hunt employees, terriermen or hunt followers. Complaints of badger digging have turned out to be over-exuberant stopping, with sett entrances being dug out or stopped with large stones, drums, concrete or tree trunks. Complaints were, and still are, received from owners of land where hunting and stopping is not permitted.

A person is not guilty of an offence under section 3(a), (c) or (e) of the 1992 Badgers Act by reason of obstructing any entrance to a badger sett for the purpose of hunting foxes with hounds if he:

- is acting with the authority of the owner or occupier of the land and the authority of a recognised hunt;
- takes no action other than obstructing entrances;
- does not dig into the tops or sides of the entrance; or
- complies with the following conditions as to the material and manner of the obstructing by the use of:
  untainted straw or hay, or leaf-litter, or bracken, or loose soil placed in the entrances on the day of the hunt, or after midday of the preceding day; or a bundle of sticks or faggots, or paper sacks either empty or filled with untainted straw, or hay, or leaf-litter, or bracken, or loose soil, placed in the entrances on the day of the hunt and removed the same day.

A 'recognised hunt' means one recognised by the Masters of Fox Hounds Association, the Association of Masters of Harriers and Beagles or the Central Committee of Fell Packs.

The Act permits limited interference or disturbance by hounds marking a fox that has gone to ground in a sett provided they are removed as soon as practicable. Any further operations to extract the fox, such as entering a terrier or digging, are not permitted.

3.6.5   Fox control and badgers

The 1992 Badgers Act has restricted the traditional methods of fox control by farmers, landowners and gamekeepers. General licences granting permission to enter dogs or dig setts are not issued. Applications must be made for a particular sett when the need arises. A sett or setts must be identified on a map or by grid reference.

A licence to lightly stop setts during fox control operations, (for example, a fox drive) can be granted to prevent foxes bolting into a sett. The manner of stopping would be as for fox-hunting.

Licences may be issued to allow dogs to be entered into badger setts for the purposes of fox control. Before taking action, always check whether or not a licence has been issued.

To find out if a licence has been issued, contact the relevant Country Conservation Agency or MAFF. However, please note that MAFF Regional Service Centres will only release details of whether or not a licence has been issued to the police.

3.6.6   Dogs lost in setts

In these cases the first port of call is often the police or RSPCA, who must be satisfied that there is no criminal offence in terms of sett interference or badger digging. In such cases the following actions should be taken.

- MAFF Regional Service Centres should be notified. A licence must be applied for, and advice received, before interference takes place.

- Dogs should be left for 48 hours to free themselves. Reaching in to remove the dog or removing stopping materials are allowed in immediate life-threatening situations.
- Familiar scents should be left at the entrance.
- Encouraging sounds, like rattling a food bowl, should be made.
- Dogs lose weight rapidly and free themselves naturally but, if not, an assessment of the necessity to enter the sett is made.
- The RSPCA can assist with reassuring the dog owner and obtaining the services of a badger worker.
- The RSPCA could also assist in assessing whether or not the owner committed an intentional or reckless act by allowing the dog to enter the sett.

This assessment would include the following questions.
- Is the sett occupied?
- Is there a likelihood of the dog being alive (barking)?
- Will the dog be driven further into the sett?
- Will animals suffocate as a result of sett collapse due to interference?
- Will the dog be driven into confrontation with a badger?

3.6.7 Ferrets

Rabbits, which can be an attraction to the ferreter, sometimes live alongside badgers. Entering a ferret into a sett is not a specific offence. Expert opinion would be needed to show that a badger was disturbed by the act.

Ferrets have a reputation of getting lost underground or killing down (killing a rabbit underground). Having killed down, the ferret may gorge itself on the rabbit and then lay up to sleep it off.

If the ferret has killed and eaten, it may lay up for 12 to 18 hours. Electronic locators on a collar are used in ferret work to pinpoint its position underground. Any attempt to dig it out of a sett would obviously be an offence.

A cage trap for mink, baited with something smelly (for example a rabbit paunch), should be placed near the sett. A ferret-carrying box containing food and hay can also be effective in enticing out the ferret.

3.6.8 Possessing badgers

Protection of Badgers Act 1992

Section 4
Possessing a live badger

It is an offence for any person to
sell or offer for sale or possess or control
a live badger

Section 5
Marking or ringing live badgers

It is an offence for any person
not authorised by licence to mark or attach a
ring/tag/other device
to any badger

NOTE: Researchers can be granted licences to mark badgers for purposes of study.

3.6.9 Orders with respect to the destruction or custody of dogs

Under the 1992 Badgers Act, where a dog has been used in or was present at the commission of an offence under sections 1(1), 2 or 3, a court, on convicting the offender, may, in addition to or in substitution for any other punishment, make an order:
- for the destruction or other disposal of the dog; and/or
- disqualifying the offender, for such period as it thinks fit, from having custody of a dog.

3.7 FOXES

3.7.1 Fox-hunting and hunt disruption

The fox is not protected by the WCA, nor is it an offence to interfere with a fox earth.

It may be hunted with hounds by a recognised hunt or by anyone else who has permission. Public disorder may occur at meets or during hunts occasioned by clashes between hunt saboteurs and hunt supporters.

Although public order offences are not strictly within the scope of this Guide, it is quite likely that wildlife specialists will become involved in matters affecting fox-hunting, and the principal legislation is reproduced here for that reason.

In addition to existing legislation relating to violence or public disorder, sections 68 and 69 of the Criminal Justice and Public Order Act 1994 are aimed at providing protection for those engaging in lawful activities, whoever they might be, from all trespassers (including hunters as well as saboteurs) who intentionally disrupt, or seek to disrupt, a lawful activity on land.

Section 68(1) Aggravated trespass

1. A person commits the offence of aggravated trespass if he trespasses on land in the open air and, in relation to any lawful activity which persons are engaging in or are about to engage in on that or adjoining land in the open air, does there anything which is intended by him to have the effect of:

   - intimidating those persons or any of them so as to deter them or any of them from engaging in that activity;

   - obstructing that activity; or

   - disrupting that activity.

2. Activity on any occasion on the part of a person or persons on land is 'lawful' for the purposes of this section if he or they engage in activity on the land on that occasion without committing an offence or trespassing on the land.

3. A person guilty of an offence under this section is liable on summary conviction to imprisonment for a term not exceeding three months or a fine not exceeding level 4 on the standard scale, or both.

4. A police officer in uniform who reasonably suspects that a person is committing an offence under this section may arrest him without a warrant.

Section 69

1. If the senior police officer present at the scene reasonably believes:

   - that a person is committing, has committed or intends to commit the offence of aggravated trespass on land in the open air; or

   - that two or more persons are trespassing on land in the open air and are present there with the common purpose of intimidating persons so as to deter them from engaging in a lawful activity or of obstructing or disrupting a lawful activity

   he may direct that person or (as the case may be) those persons (or any of them) to leave the land.

2. A direction under subsection (1) above, if not communicated to the persons referred to in subsection (1) by the police officer giving the direction, may be communicated to them by any police officer at the scene.

3. If a person knowing that a direction under subsection (1) above has been given which applies to him:

   - fails to leave the land as soon as practicable; or

   - having left again enters the land as a trespasser within the period of three months beginning with the day on which the direction was given

   he commits an offence and is liable on summary conviction to imprisonment for a term not exceeding three months or a fine not exceeding level 4 on the standard scale, or both.

4. In proceedings for an offence under subsection (3) it is a defence for the accused to show:

   - that he was not trespassing on the land; or

   - that he had a reasonable excuse for failing to leave the land as soon as practicable or, as the case may be, for again entering the land as a trespasser.

5. A police officer in uniform who reasonably suspects that a person is committing an offence under this section may arrest him without a warrant.

3.7.2 Fox control

Foxes can be killed or taken, but the ways in which this can be done are subject to control.

The use of gas is regulated by the Control of Pesticides Regulations 1986 (there are currently no authorised gas mixtures); the use of snares is subject to section 13 of the WCA; and the use of a spring trap is covered by the Pests Act 1954 and the Spring Traps (Approval) Order 1995. It is always worth checking the relevant legislation if the use of a particular fox control method is questioned.

If a fox has been ill-treated or intentionally caused unnecessary suffering, the provisions of the Protection of Animals Act 1911 and the Wild Mammals (Protection) Act 1996 may be relevant.

Information on fox-hunting is given in 3.6.4, 3.6.5 and 3.7.1.

3.8 DEER ACTS

In England and Wales the Deer Act 1991 is the principal legislation dealing with offences against deer and replaces numerous other enactments covering the subject. In Scotland, the law relating to deer is dealt with in separate legislation. See 7.8 for details.

3.8.1 Police powers

Section 12 of the Deer Act 1991 provides that a police officer may enter without warrant any land except a dwelling house where he has reasonable cause to suspect that someone is committing or has committed an offence. He may do so in order to:

- stop and search any person suspected of the offence;
- search or examine any vehicle, animal, weapon or other thing;

- seize and detain anything that is evidence of the offence;
- exercise the general arrest conditions contained in section 25 of PACE.

Any deer or venison seized under this section may be sold and the proceeds detained and forfeited.

For full details of deer poaching and offences see 4.1.14. For the relevant laws in Scotland, see Chapter 7.

3.9 SEALS

There are two species of seal to be found in Britain's coastal waters: the grey seal and the common seal. Both are protected by the Conservation of Seals Act 1970, which provides for close seasons during which it is an offence to take or kill any seal except under licence in certain particular circumstances.

The 1970 Act creates offences relating to the use of poisons or rifle ammunition less than 600 footpounds muzzle energy and bullets less than 45 grains. The close season for grey seals is from 1 September to 31 December inclusive and for common seals from 1 June to 31 August inclusive. These close seasons coincide with the puppy seasons when the seals are at their most vulnerable. The Act provides a general exception which makes it lawful to kill a seal to prevent it from causing damage to a fishing net or tackle or to any fish in the net, providing the seal is in the vicinity of the net or tackle at the time. The effect of the close season can be extended by the Secretary of State where it appears necessary for the proper conservation of seals.

It is also an offence to attempt to commit anything unlawful under the Act and/or to be in possession of poisonous substances, firearms or ammunition prohibited by the Act.

This statute provides powers of arrest, search and seizure for the police. A police officer may stop any person he suspects with reasonable cause of committing an offence under the Act and may:

- without warrant arrest that person if he fails to give his name and address to the police officer's satisfaction;

- without warrant search any vehicle or boat the person may be using at that time; and
- seize any seal, seal skin, firearm, ammunition or poisonous substance.

The Conservation (Natural Habitats, &c.) Regulations 1994, Regulations 41(3) and 41(5), list a range of unlawful methods for taking and killing seals. This legislation also creates the offence of using aircraft or motor vehicles to take or kill seals. Interestingly, the species covered by these Regulations are more than those in the 1970 Act and include bearded, common, grey, harp, hooded and ringed seals.

Police powers under the 1994 Regulations match those of the WCA.

See Appendix E for details of specialist assistance, for example for species identification.

3.10 DOLPHINS, PORPOISES AND WHALES

Whilst not generally subject to criminal activity, these creatures have suffered in some parts of Great Britain, for example from speedboats. In some areas, commercial dolphin and whale 'spotting trips' are now organised by boat owners.

All whales, dolphins and porpoises receive protection from the 1981 Act and the 1994 Conservation Regulations. Importantly, Regulation 39(1)(b) creates the offence of deliberately disturbing any such animal and this can be employed where necessary. The law applies to these animals when they are in 'territorial waters', ie within 12 miles of the coast.

Staff of Veterinary Investigation Service units, especially at the Institute of Zoology in London and the Scottish Agricultural College in Inverness, have extensive experience of autopsies of such creatures and can be of considerable forensic science assistance to the police.

Police may also be called to deal with stranded whales. For details of specialist assistance, see Appendix E.

3.11 INVERTEBRATES

Most children enjoy looking for insects in their gardens or for shrimps and crabs in rock pools. Invertebrates are easy to find, most are harmless to handle, and they can be reared to adulthood in a very short time with the minimum of equipment. For some this becomes a fascination, leading to a deeper understanding of the natural world, and for others will be the first step towards a career in the biological sciences. Legislation, rightly intended to protect our most threatened species, should not inhibit the activities of interested naturalists nor hinder the development of this next generation of scientists.

3.11.1 Taking from the wild

The collecting of insects and other invertebrates has a long history in Britain. Indeed, our knowledge of these animals far exceeds that of other countries largely because of the activities of collectors over the last 200 years. Much current collecting is part of the process of recording the present distribution of species throughout Britain (biological recording) or the detailed investigation of their life-cycles and habitat requirements.

Responsible, targeted collecting is not seen as a serious conservation problem. It is, therefore, with a few exceptions, perfectly legal to collect insects and other invertebrates from the wild, to possess specimens either alive or dead and to trade in them. Similarly, it is legal to possess collecting equipment, even if such equipment could be used to collect protected species.

Nevertheless, there are some species which are so rare that to remove any specimens at all would be a serious threat to their continued survival in the wild in Britain. These species are given full protection either by the WCA or by international agreements such as the Convention on the Conservation of European Wildlife and Natural Habitats (Bern Convention) and the Council of the European Communities Directive on the Conservation of Natural Habitats and of Wild Fauna and Flora (Habitats Directive) implemented, in Britain, by the Conservation (Natural Habitats, &c.) Regulations 1994. The species involved are listed in various schedules, annexes and appendices, but the listings are periodically revised so that the currently enforceable lists may not be those attached to the original documents.

There are approximately 30,000 species of large invertebrate in Britain. Only 46 species are currently protected from being taken from the wild (ie collected) in Britain.

Crabs, shrimps and crayfish (Crustacea)

Atlantic stream crayfish	WCA Schedule 5 (1981)
Three shrimp species	WCA Schedule 5 (1988)

Spiders (Araneae)

Fen raft spider	WCA Schedule 5 (1981)
Ladybird spider	WCA Schedule 5 (1981)

Dragonflies (Odonata)

Norfolk aeshna	WCA Schedule 5 (1981)
Orange-spotted emerald dragonfly	Bern Convention appendix II (1988) EC

This species is thought to be extinct in Britain but under Directive annex IVa (1992) would be likely to receive full protection if found.

Bugs (Hemiptera)

New Forest cicada	WCA Schedule 5 (1988)

Grasshoppers and crickets (Orthoptera)

Wart-biter	WCA Schedule 5 (1981)
Mole cricket	WCA Schedule 5 (1981)
Field cricket	WCA Schedule 5 (1981)

Beetles (Coleoptera)

Long-horned beetle	Bern Convention appendix II (1988); EC Directive annex IVa (1992)

This species is thought to be extinct in Britain but would be likely to receive full protection if found.

Rainbow leaf beetle	WCA Schedule 5 (1981)
Water beetle	WCA Schedule 5 (1992)

This species is thought to be extinct in Britain but would be likely to receive full protection if found.

Lesser silver water beetle	WCA Schedule 5 (1992)
Violet click beetle	WCA Schedule 5 (1988)
Three water beetle species	WCA Schedule 5 (1992)

Butterflies and moths (Lepidoptera)

High brown fritillary butterfly	WCA Schedule 5 (1992)
Large copper butterfly	WCA Schedule 5 (1989)

This species became extinct in Britain in the 1860s. The single 'wild' colony is of Dutch origin but would still receive protection, as should any future introductions. Livestock of long-term captive-bred origin is readily available from dealers.

Large blue butterfly	WCA Schedule 5 (1981); Conservation Regs. Schedule II (1994)

This species became extinct in Britain in 1980. Several colonies of Swedish origin are now present and are fully protected.

Heath fritillary butterfly	WCA Schedule 5 (1981)
Swallowtail butterfly	WCA Schedule 5 (1981)

Reddish buff moth	WCA Schedule 5 (1981)
Viper's bugloss moth	WCA Schedule 5 (1988)
Barberry carpet moth	WCA Schedule 5 (1981)
Curzon's sphinx moth	Bern Convention appendix II (1988); EC Directive annex IVa (1992)

A rare vagrant to Britain and never known to have bred here. Should it become established naturally, it would be likely to receive protection. Livestock is regularly available and would need to be subject to control unless it was of captive-bred origin.

Black-veined moth	WCA Schedule 5 (1981)
Sussex emerald moth	WCA Schedule 5 (1992)
Essex emerald moth	WCA Schedule 5 (1981)
New Forest burnet moth	WCA Schedule 5 (1981)

Sea mats (Bryozoa)

Trembling sea-mat

Snails, slugs and sea-shells (Molluscs)

De Folin's lagoon snail

Sandbowl snail

Glutinous snail

Lagoon snail

Lagoon sea slug

Northern hatchet shell

Worms (Annelida)

Tentacled lagoon worm

Lagoon sandworm

Medicinal leech

Sea anemones and allies (Cnidaria)

Ivell's sea anemone

Pink sea-fan

Starlet sea anemone

Legitimate scientific study does, sometimes, involve taking specimens from the wild. Where these studies involve protected species, a licence can be granted if the study is considered to be in the interests of science, education or conservation. There is a presumption that specimens taken were wild, unless the contrary can be demonstrated.

3.11.2 Killing or injuring

The collecting of insects and other invertebrates, other than of the 46 protected species, for an educational or scientific study, or to form a collection for whatever purpose, is not an illegal act in Britain. Legitimate scientific study does, sometimes, involve the killing of specimens from the wild, for example for genetic or pathology screening. It is important that the law does not hinder these activities, because the naturalists and scientists involved in these studies provide the information necessary to protect the sites and habitats of Britain's wildlife. Where these studies involve protected species, a licence can be granted if the study is considered to be in the interests of science, education or conservation. It is, therefore, legal to possess poisons and other equipment used for killing invertebrates, even if they could be used to kill protected species.

With the exception of Atlantic stream crayfish all of those species which are protected from being taken from the wild are also protected from being killed or injured. The native crayfish is exempt from this part of the WCA in order to allow water quality monitoring and other potentially lethal activities to take place without the need of a licence. Together with these 45 species, the pearl mussel is also protected from killing or injuring, but not from taking. This allows pearl fishing to remain legal so long as the mussels are returned, unharmed, to the water.

3.11.3 Possession

Building and possessing a collection of insects was a popular pastime for generations up until the 1970s. Since then attitudes have changed, and collecting specimens has become difficult to justify, in the popular mind, unless part of a scientific study. Many collections, which include specimens of protected species, exist in private hands. It is most likely that the species now in these collections protected from 'possession' were taken many years ago, long before they became protected by law. Their current possession is no offence against conservation and the confiscation of these specimens serves no purpose in promoting conservation. What is more, if the owner of the collection desires a complete collection, he would have to collect or purchase replacement specimens, thereby committing or encouraging other, possibly illegal, acts which would be much more damaging to wildlife conservation.

Most researchers retain a reference collection of invertebrates which can often contain species beyond their immediate sphere of research. Voucher specimens are retained to help in validating problematical identifications. However, it is not usually necessary to take voucher specimens of easily identifiable species (for example butterflies), and it is also likely that only a few specimens of the most abundant species will be held in a personal reference collection. There may, therefore, appear to be a disproportionately high number of rare, but difficult to identify, species in a collection because these are the specimens that would require validation in the future should any doubts about their identity arise.

It is not an offence to possess specimens of unprotected species either in a collection or as a decorative display. Neither is it an offence to possess mounting (setting) equipment, storage boxes or specimen cabinets for invertebrates even if they could be used to store protected species. Collections were traditionally laid out using printed species labels and there will probably

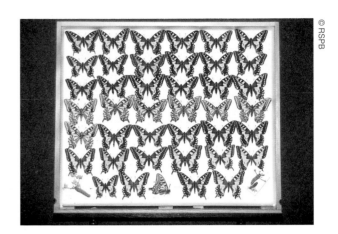

A drawer of swallowtail butterflies from a collection

be spaces labelled to receive protected species. This does not suggest that the owner is actively seeking specimens of those species, that he has any intention of ever filling these gaps or that he has removed the specimens and is hiding them elsewhere.

There is the presumption that the specimens were taken from the wild unless the opposite can be proven. The burden of proof rests with the owner of the specimens. The origin of the specimens should be detailed on a label attached to the pin on which the specimen is mounted. This should give a locality and a date, and there may be other details as well, such as the name of the collector or whether it was reared or caught in a particular way. The details on a label could easily be false, which could be interpreted as an attempt to mislead a purchaser or anyone authorised to inspect the collection, and thus as a criminal attempt at deception.

The Atlantic stream crayfish is an exception to the general rule in that, although it is protected from being taken from the wild, it is not an offence to possess specimens. This is in order to allow fishermen, trying to catch other species of crayfish, to 'possess' Atlantic stream crayfish in their traps prior to their release.

3.11.4 Selling livestock or deadstock

All of the species which are protected from being taken from the wild are also protected from being sold, offered for sale, exposed for sale, possessed for the purpose of sale or transported for the purpose of sale. Any part of, or anything derived from, any of these species is also similarly protected.

In addition to those species, there are a further 21 species of butterfly which are protected in this way, but not from being taken from the wild in the first place. This apparent anomaly is to protect the rarer, but not threatened, butterfly species from excessive collecting by dealers, whilst not deterring scientists, responsible collectors or children from catching butterflies.

The following species of butterfly are protected from trade (section 9(5) of the WCA only) but are still permitted to be taken, killed or possessed:

Purple emperor	Northern brown argus
Pearl-bordered fritillary	Chequered skipper
Large heath	Small blue
Marsh fritillary	Mountain ringlet
Duke of Burgundy fritillary	Silver-spotted skipper
Wood white	Large copper
Adonis blue	Chalkhill blue
Glanville fritillary	Large tortoiseshell
Silver-studded blue	Black hairstreak
White-letter hairstreak	Brown hairstreak
Lulworth skipper	

Dealers visit the largest or most convenient sites and take as many perfect specimens as possible in the time available. These have to be perfect, undamaged specimens, so are likely to be the youngest, fittest individuals and, if female, may be carrying a large complement of fertile eggs. They are all killed immediately, usually in the field, and later mounted for sale to collectors. The large numbers taken are to offset the cost of the collecting trip and to allow for damaging specimens during the mounting (setting) process and during transport to and from trade fairs. The street value of these species is not high, so many need to be taken to make the collecting trip pay. This is especially so when the specimens are sold on to other, larger dealers.

The restrictions on trade refer also to the immature stages. There is no wish to deter anyone from finding and rearing caterpillars but there is a need to put a stop to dealers collecting large numbers of eggs, caterpillars or pupae, selling them and returning to plunder the same site year after year until the population of the desirable species had fallen to such a low level that it is no longer worthwhile to make the trip. The restrictions to trading in immature stages also cover the developmental stages which follow, up to adult. It is therefore illegal to sell a specimen reared from any of its immature stages, for example to sell a pupa reared from a wild-taken egg. It is difficult to prove whether livestock offered for sale has been taken from the wild or bred in captivity. However, the objective of the law is to protect vulnerable populations of British wildlife and should not be abandoned because of difficulties in proving a case. The origin of any protected species should be clearly stated by dealers and dead specimens labelled accordingly. If they are from captive-bred stock this should be clearly stated on the label, otherwise they may be presumed to have been taken from the wild.

3.11.5 Captive-bred versus captive-reared

A captive-bred specimen is one derived from a mating in captivity between parents who were themselves either reared or bred in captivity. A captive-reared specimen is one derived from a mating in the wild or between parents at least one of which was taken from the wild.

Many dealers do not differentiate between these two origins, with the result that illegal specimens are offered for sale as 'captive-bred' when they were taken from the wild at an earlier developmental stage, eg as eggs or larvae.

Wildlife and Countryside Act 1981

It is an offence under Section 9(5) to
sell any wild specimens
of species protected under Schedule 5 of
the Wildlife and Countryside Act.

However, no offence will be committed if a licence has been granted under section 16 of the WCA. There is no advantage to conservation in prohibiting the sale of specimens which were taken before the Act came into force. This date is that on which the species was added to Schedule 5 and is different for different species. Although a licence is required for the sale of these old specimens, it is likely that such a licence would be issued. A licence is unlikely to be issued for the sale of specimens caught after they had become protected in Britain, even if the specimens originated from outside Britain.

3.11.6 Advertising

Dealers advertise in specialist entomological journals, in 'wants and exchange' lists and provide detailed listings of their stock in sales lists which are available as hand-outs or through subscription. The smaller dealers and enthusiasts form special interest groups (for example Entomological Livestock Group, Phasmid Study Group) and have their own newsletters available on subscription.

3.11.7 Habitat

With the exception of three species – the Atlantic stream crayfish, the pearl mussel and the pink sea-fan – all of the species which are protected from being taken from the wild are also protected in their places of shelter. It is an offence to damage, destroy or prevent access to such places or to disturb the creature whilst it is there. The two exceptions are to allow accidental damage or disturbance to their habitats during legitimate fishing. Conversely, the mire pill beetle is protected solely with respect to its habitat. The species occurs in good numbers in its few localities; it has no sale value and the numbers taken by collectors are of no concern to conservation. The threat to this species was solely the destruction of its habitat. In this special case, the most effective means of achieving its protection was to add it to Schedule 5 of the WCA.

The large blue butterfly is further protected from disturbance by the Conservation (Natural Habitats, &c.) Regulations 1994, in that it is an offence to disturb the butterfly at any time, not just while it is occupying a place of shelter or protection.

3.11.8 Prosecutions

The police are the enforcement authorities for Part I of the WCA, and decide whether to investigate information received. The Crown Prosecution Service or Procurator Fiscal will decide whether a case is brought to court. Specialist advice is available from the Country Conservation Agencies (EN, SNH and the CCW), including an expert witness role if needed. The maximum fine available for these offences is £5,000 per specimen. The only successful prosecution brought so far (offering and transporting for the purpose of sale) resulted in a fine of £36 per specimen. This may seem a paltry sum compared to the initial fines imposed by the court in cases involving birds of prey, but it must be viewed in the light of the smaller street value of the specimens involved. In this case the fine amounted to about 12 times the value of the specimen. No case involving the illegal capture, killing or possession of protected invertebrates has yet gone through the courts.

3.11.9 Import/export controls

Regulations implementing the Convention on International Trade in Endangered Species of Wild Fauna and Flora (CITES) restrict the import and export of approximately 790 species of invertebrates (see Chapter 9). Only one, the medicinal leech, is native to Britain. The indefinite number of species involved is because in some cases whole families of species are protected, but the taxonomy is so difficult that it is not known exactly how many species are involved. The CITES list contains a large number (about 730 species) of corals, sponges, sea anemones and sea-shells which are protected because of their large-scale collection for sale as tourists' curios. Whilst many of these can be identified using specialist literature, sculpted or decorated pieces require the attention of an expert to determine their original identity. The butterflies on the CITES list are mostly large tropical species, including all of the large 'bird-wings' of South-East Asia. These have been heavily collected in the past because of their outstanding beauty and the high prices which they consequently command from collectors. Many species are now captive-bred or 'ranched' in their native areas, providing an income for the local people, allowing trade in specimens to continue and relieving the collector pressure on the wild populations. Wild-caught specimens are often more damaged than captive-bred or ranched ones. All of the protected species, although not all of the sub-species, are illustrated in *The Illustrated Encyclopedia of Butterflies* by John Feltwell, published by Blandford, London, in 1993.

All of the red-kneed spiders are also listed in CITES Appendix II (see Chapter 9). These species were taken in such large numbers for the exotic pet trade that their continued existence in the wild became threatened. When import/export controls were implemented, the dealers were forced to rear them in captivity, and in this they have been very successful. These are readily available via specialist dealers from a flourishing series of captive colonies. There is even a society for 'Tarantula' enthusiasts which arranges mates for lonely spiders reared in isolation.

There is also a series of orders restricting the import and release of known plant and tree pests. The Plant Health (Forestry)(Great Britain) Order 1993/1283 and the Plant Health (Great Britain) Order 1993/1320 lists those species which cannot be imported. The list is regularly revised, but generally the importation of non-indigenous or pesticide-resistant strains of plant-feeding species is prohibited without a licence issued either by the Forestry Authority or by MAFF. A licence is required to possess living specimens of some species considered to be serious threats to crop or tree production.

The Dangerous Wild Animals Act 1976 prohibits the keeping of live specimens of dangerous spiders and scorpions. A licence from the local authority is required to keep the following species:

Wandering spiders	Sydney funnel web spiders
Brazilian wolf spiders	Brown recluse spiders
Black widow spiders	Scorpions (some species)

3.12 AMPHIBIANS

By a general licence, the sale (transport for sale, possession for sale etc) of adult specimens of common frogs, common toads, smooth newts and palmate newts is permitted except during their breeding seasons:

Common frog   – 15 January to 15 April (inclusive);

Common toad   – 1 February to 1 May (inclusive);

Smooth newt   – 1 April to 1 August (inclusive);

Palmate newt   – 1 April to 1 August (inclusive).

Specimens may not be sold, bartered or exchanged at any time if they were taken from the wild during the breeding season.

Smooth newts taken at any time from the wild in Devon, Cornwall or Somerset may not be sold. A similar restriction applies to palmate newts taken from the wild in Cambridgeshire, Lincolnshire, Leicestershire, Northamptonshire, Staffordshire, Warwickshire, Norfolk, Suffolk or Essex.

3.13 INTRODUCING NON-NATIVE SPECIES

Wildlife and Countryside Act 1981

Section 14

It is an offence for any person to release or allow to escape into the wild any animal which
(a) is of a kind which is not ordinarily resident in and is not a regular visitor to Great Britain in a wild state;
or
(b) is included in Part I of Schedule 9

EXCEPTIONS: No offence is committed if the person can show that:
- he took all reasonable steps and exercised due diligence to avoid committing the offence; or
- a licence has been issued under section 16 of the Act and all the conditions have been complied with.

poaching, cruelty, trapping and poisoning

4.1 POACHING

4.1.1 Introduction

In law, poaching is not theft. Poaching is the unlawful taking or killing of game, whereas theft is the dishonest taking of property belonging to another. Wild animals at liberty are ownerless; they can be poached but not stolen.

EXAMPLE: Taking wild fish from a river is poaching, but removing dead fish from a fisherman's car boot is theft.

Many people still perceive a poacher as a one-for-the-pot man taking a rabbit to feed his starving family. It is an image which markedly affects the enthusiasm of the police, the 'public interest' influence in Crown Prosecution Service decision-making and punishments awarded in the courts.

The reality is very different. The lone poacher is a rarity. Poachers often work in sizeable groups, counting on the intimidation of numbers to prevent their arrest, and taking game to a considerable value.

Police officers need to be aware of the involvement of poachers in other forms of crime; notably burglary and theft from houses, farms and gardens in the countryside. People are prepared to travel long distances to commit these offences, which adds to the difficulty of subsequent detection.

The right to take and kill game is one of the incidents of land ownership. No one has the right to enter land to take game without the owner's permission. The right to take and kill game can be sold and leased separately.

4.1.2 Cost of poaching

Game rearing is time-consuming and costly. In early spring gamekeepers catch up wild birds (for example pheasants) and keep these in enclosed pens, removing the eggs for artificial incubation and hatching. Young birds are subsequently kept in enclosed pens and, in

common with deer on deer farms or fish in enclosed waters, are subject to the Theft Act or the common law crime of theft in Scotland if they are stolen.

In the late summer or early autumn, pheasant poults are put in large release pens, which are open to the sky. Despite feeding, they start to wander on to adjoining land. They are no longer protected by the Theft Act, but now have their liberty and are thus subject to the laws on poaching.

Both as young poults and in the release pens, pheasants are frequently taken by night in large numbers, effectively ruining the season's work.

The cost of the careful husbandry during the rearing process is reflected in the expense of shooting. It is big business, albeit the profit margin is considerably reduced by the keeper's and beater's wages, the cost of eggs and chicks, heaters, feed, cover crops and vehicles.

One night's activity by poachers seriously affects the next day's shooting. Constant poaching leads to dissatisfied shooters, loss of business and eventually a substantial impact on a small rural community.

The same adverse effects will result from poaching fish from preserved waters or taking deer.

The financial and commercial aspects need to be considered when preparing case files for prosecution and liaising with the prosecuting authority (Crown Prosecution Service or Procurator Fiscal). Cautioning poachers, particularly where there is more than one offender, does not encourage gamekeepers to put themselves at risk in preventing these offences or in assisting the police.

Always remember to seek proper compensation in a successful poaching prosecution. The gamekeeper, as a witness, should be ready to explain and quantify the real expense involved, and emphasise the detrimental effect of the offence.

Any threats or intimidation should also be brought out in the evidence.

4

4.1.3 The police and gamekeepers

The gamekeeper or stalker can be the police officer's eyes and ears in a rural community.

Get to know the gamekeepers in your area. Visiting them at work in the pens will enhance your knowledge and should produce useful local information. It should also serve to prevent any keeper so inclined from raptor-trapping or considering the illegal release of, for example, chukar partridges.

Your visit should be welcomed as providing support for a fellow professional with a difficult job to do, and seen as an opportunity to share and exchange useful information.

4.1.4 Preventive measures

The keeper can be the police officer's eyes and ears at all times of the day and night, but intelligence is worthless if not used. Some watch schemes have set up their own network of recording and reporting sightings to all members and the police. Police officers need to tap this resource and feed information back to the keeper in order to demonstrate that it is being used, maintain enthusiasm and generate more information. There are other sources waiting to be tapped, such as countryside rangers and members of fishing clubs.

There is much information that can be passed on without incurring problems of data protection. The poacherwatch scheme in the Vale of Belvoir is a good example of this.

Publicise the watch scheme's inaugural meeting and announce your intentions to the press. Subsequent meetings may involve fund-raising for a local charity and generate further publicity. Publicity needs careful planning and staging to ensure a sympathetic approach.

The term 'poacherwatch' can be provocative and may deter farmers and residents from joining. Poacherwatch is better allied to farmwatch, countrywatch or riverwatch schemes which cover all aspects of rural crime and green issues, like pollution.

Establish the purpose of the scheme and what each party is prepared to put into it. Do not make promises you are unable to keep about resources.

Gamekeepers can take a proactive approach by:

- establishing lines of communications and rendez-vous points;
- supplying estate maps with areas coded so as not to reveal locations to poachers and thieves equipped with scanners;
- considering physical security, alarm systems and securing gates to make access difficult;
- encouraging farm workers and residents to be on the look-out and to report suspicious vehicles or activity;
- considering use of signs to advertise the scheme. Sponsorship is often available;
- considering using warning signs that release pens are protected by alarms. Signs can also be placed around woods where there are no birds. Keep poachers guessing and show them there is positive activity on the estate;
- using one or two people to carry high-powered lamps. Poachers can be deterred by briefly shining lights along a riverbank or through a wood;
- improving communications by using a mobile phone or radio. When night-watching for poachers, let someone know where you are working and arrange to contact them at set times. If you fail to make contact establish a plan of action for someone to look for you;
- using the grapevine to let poachers know you are equipped with night-vision equipment, radios, mobile phones and alarms – even if you do not have this equipment yet! If you catch poachers at night tell them you saw them on your night-vision equipment. If you do have such equipment let them look through it. The word will soon get about;
- setting up an early warning telephone network;
- considering night-watching with a keeper from an adjoining shoot;
- asking police to visit the owners of vehicles sighted at unusual times and places to verify their reasons for being there. This again sends a positive message to the poacher to keep off the area;

- encouraging the local media to publish poaching cases. If the poacher lives in the next county it may be worth a phone call to his local paper;

Poacherwatch schemes need the support and enthusiasm of all involved. Two meetings a year are usually enough and can develop into useful social occasions, with guest speakers on law, firearms, game-rearing etc.

4.1.5   Game poaching

Game Act 1831

Section 30

It is an offence for any person to
trespass in the daytime
by entering or being upon any land in search or pursuit of game, woodcock, snipe or rabbits

NOTE: Proceedings must commence within three months of the offence being committed.

Game is defined as:

hares	pheasants
partridges	grouse
black game	heath or moor game

Daytime is defined as one hour before sunrise to one hour after sunset.

Greater penalties can be imposed if five or more people are acting together. Additional offences are committed if one or more of the gang is armed with a gun and any of them, by violence, intimidation or menace, prevents or endeavours to prevent any authorised person from exercising his powers under section 31 of the 1831 Act.

An authorised person may ask any person found committing the above offence to give his full name and address and to quit the land forthwith. If the person gives a false name or address, or refuses to quit the land or give his name and address, or returns to the land, he may be arrested. A police officer is not, in this instance, an authorised person.

In Scotland, the law relating to game poaching is dealt with in the Game (Scotland) Act 1832. See Chapter 7 for details.

4.1.6   Authorised person

An authorised person is defined as:
- anyone having a right to kill game on the land;
- occupiers;
- anyone authorised by 1 or 2 above;
- gamekeeper or servant; or
- wardens, rangers and others employed in a similar capacity in Royal Forests and parks.

NOTE:
Trespass – Must be a physical entry by a person who has no legal right to be on the land in question. Shooting from private land into a field and sending a dog to retrieve may not be a personal trespass.

Entering land – A person poaching from the public roadside is a trespasser. Public roads and paths are there to travel from one point to another. Any abuse of that right, particularly by unlawful activities, amounts to a trespass (Harrison *v* Duke of Rutland 1893). Several cases have included poaching on and from roadsides. It would not be an entry where the poacher shoots from his own land into another's land and sends the dog to retrieve.

Search/pursuit – It is sufficient to be looking for game, but it needs strong evidence to rebut probable excuses.

Game – The target species should be named and this should be evident from the nature of the pursuit (for example, slipping a lurcher to pursue a hare).

NOTE: Evidence must show use of the relevant item in a manner which killed or pursued game (which includes game birds and hares but not rabbits or deer).

Killing is the best evidence. Pursuit produces many excuses, for example exercising the dog, taking the gun/nets etc to land where permission exists, or that nets have just been bought and are being taken home.

4.1.7　Night offences

Night Poaching Act 1828

Section 1(a)

It is an offence for any person to
take or destroy
any game or rabbits on any land unlawfully at
night

NOTE:

Game is defined as:

hares   pheasants

partridges   grouse

heath or moor game   black game

bustards

Land includes any:
public road, highway or path
verges at the openings, outlets or gates from any land
into a public road, highway or path

However, the Ground Game Act 1880, as amended by
the WCA, allows certain people to shoot rabbits at
night. These are:

- owner-occupiers with shooting rights;
- landlords who have reserved the shooting rights;
- shooting tenants not in occupation who have
  derived the shooting rights from the owner; and
- occupiers or one other person authorised in
  writing by the person with shooting rights.

Night Poaching Act 1828

Section 1(b)

It is an offence at night to
**unlawfully enter or be on any land
with any gun, net, engine or other
instrument** for the purpose of taking or
destroying game

NOTE: Offenders must be in possession of one of the
items listed. The term 'instrument' is open to debate
bearing in mind the year the Act was passed, ie 1828.
One view is that instrument could mean anything used
for the purpose, and consequently includes lamps and
slip leads (used as a quick-release device for lurchers).

This offence only includes game birds and hares – not
rabbits. If a rabbit is taken then a section 1(a) of the
Night Poaching Act 1828 offence may be committed. If
it is coursed the offence is not committed. Lampers are
aware of this and you need to refer to the game licence
offences detailed in 4.1.8.

Under section 9 where three or more act together and
any one of them is armed with a gun, crossbow or other
offensive weapon a further offence is committed.

Police powers

Where a police officer has reasonable grounds to
suspect that a person is committing an offence under
section 1 of the Night Poaching Act 1828 (see above)
on any land, he may enter any land for the purpose of
exercising his power of arrest. The power of arrest
comes from section 25 of the Police and Criminal
Evidence Act 1984 in England and Wales. In Scotland,
an individual suspected of committing an offence can
be arrested under section 13 of the Criminal Procedure
(Scotland) Act 1995.

4.1.8 Game Licences Act 1860

Game Licences Act 1860
It is an offence for any person to unlawfully use any **dog/gun/net/engine** to **take/kill/pursue** any game or woodcock/snipe/deer/rabbit without a proper licence

NOTE:

Unlawfully – Without permission, right or authority.

Engine – Trap, snare or device.

Rabbit – A licence is not normally required to take rabbits, as anybody with permission to take rabbits is exempt from the need for a licence. Poachers, however, would require a licence and this fills a loophole in night poaching offences.

4.1.9 Poaching Prevention Act 1862

Game includes pheasant, partridge, grouse, black game, hare, rabbit, woodcock and snipe.

A police officer may stop and search a person or vehicles in any highway, street or public place if the officer has reasonable cause to suspect the person or vehicle of coming from land having been unlawfully in pursuit of game.

The relevant points are that the search must take place on the highway, in the street or in a public place. A public place means somewhere that a police officer would be in the ordinary performance of his duties and does not include a public house to which the poacher was followed. The power to stop and search is not applicable to persons going poaching.

The power to search is obviously useful when dealing with a stop-check of a bag or vehicle containing game and an unsatisfactory explanation.

Anyone found with game unlawfully obtained, or any gun, ammunition, nets, traps, snares or other device for taking game, such as a lamp, can commit one of the following offences:

- obtaining game unlawfully by trespass;
- using a dog, gun, net etc for unlawfully killing or taking game; or
- aiding or abetting a poacher to commit either of the above offences.

It is not necessary to prove that game has actually been taken, nor is it necessary to prove by direct evidence either the specific land where poaching has taken place or, in the case where game is found, the unlawful means used to take it. The prosecution must satisfy the court by either direct or circumstantial evidence and not merely speculation that the defendant has been poaching.

It is a good defence to prove that the person had a bona fide belief that he had permission to go on the land.

A police officer may seize game and equipment but not dogs or ferrets under this Act, although these could now be seized, in England and Wales, under section 19 of PACE. General powers under PACE apply.

4.1.10 Fish poaching and other offences

Fishing for salmon, trout, freshwater fish and eels in England and Wales by rod and net is governed by provisions of the Salmon and Freshwater Fisheries Act 1975 and local byelaws made by the Environment Agency under the Water Resources Act 1991, which are enforced by the Agency's water bailiffs. These bailiffs are deemed to be constables for the purposes of the 1975 Act. The rules regulate, amongst other things, when and where fishing may take place and the gear, method and baits that may be used. Non-compliance constitutes an offence, as does fishing without an Environment Agency licence (see 4.1.12). Local Environment Agency offices can advise on the rules and byelaws applicable in their area.

In England and Wales the Theft Act usually applies to fish in enclosed waters and breeding tanks where they can be classed as property and not as wild creatures.

Under section 32 of and Schedule 1 to the Theft Act, however, it is an offence unlawfully to take or destroy or attempt to take or destroy any fish in private waters. Any person may arrest anyone who is committing such an offence unless they are using rod and line in daytime. In all cases conviction for an offence may lead to the forfeiture or seizure of the fishing tackle involved.

Poachers target principally salmonids (game fish), although sometimes 'prize' coarse fish are taken. They employ mainly gill and trammel nets, which may either be used actively or left anchored in a river for a few hours. Poachers may work from small boats, use waders or set nets from the shore; they may even use car tyres to float down the river. Another method used, particularly for taking trout from lakes, is set lines.

Salmon may also be taken by chemical poisoning. Cyanide-base products are readily available to the agriculture industry and will asphyxiate fish over a wide area, which can then be lifted from the water. Be wary of any tins or powder residues at the scene, as they are potentially lethal to humans. Explosives are a rarely used means of poaching salmon.

The methods described are mainly those that may be left unattended. However, active methods (including netting described above) are also important. Poaching is also conducted by 'snatching' fish using large weighted treble hooks dragged over the fish. 'Snaring' is also used, mainly for sea trout, and involves putting a loop round the tail of the fish.

Eels are also targeted by poachers. The normal commercial nets are used, but fishermen enter land covertly and without the authorisation (net licences) of the Environment Agency or riparian owners.

If any offence is suspected, other than the illegal use of rod and line in the daytime, **the Environment Agency Emergency Hotline on 0800 807060, which operates 24 hours a day seven days a week, should be called immediately** to inform local fisheries enforcement officers.

Poachers usually travel by car to and from the river. Such vehicles may be seized by Agency water bailiffs or any police officer. Any suspicious vehicle containing fish and/or nets should be reported at once to the Agency hotline.

Illegally-caught fish are often sold at the door, particularly to pubs, restaurants and hotels. Such sales are illegal and again should be reported to the Environment Agency hotline.

4.1.11 Specimen charges

Contrary to paragraph 2(1) of Schedule 1 to the Theft Act 1968, unlawfully did (take/destroy/attempt to take/attempt to destroy) otherwise than by angling in the daytime at __time__ __number of fish__ called __specify types of fish__ in certain water namely __name__ which was the private property of __name__ and/or (in which __name__ had a private right of fishery).

Contrary to paragraph 2(2) of Schedule 1 to the Theft Act 1968, by angling in the daytime did (take/destroy/attempt to take/attempt to destroy) otherwise than by angling in the daytime at __time__ __number of fish__ called __specify types of fish__ in certain water namely __name__ which was the private property of __name__ and/or (in which __name__ had a private right of fishery).

In Scotland the offence is contrary to common law.

4.1.12 Fishing licences

Anyone who fishes for salmon, trout, freshwater fish or eels in England and Wales must have an Environment Agency rod fishing licence (children under 12 are exempt). There are two types of licence:
- non-migratory trout and coarse fish; and
- salmon and sea trout.

A salmon and sea trout licence is also valid for non-migratory trout and coarse fish. Holders of an appropriate licence can, with the permission of the owners or tenants of fishing rights where necessary, fish with rod and line anywhere in England and Wales. Where local byelaws and rules allow, a licence allows two rods to be used to fish for coarse fish. In some areas local byelaws allow the use of more than two rods for fishing for any species provided that additional licences are held. Local Agency offices can advise on the rules in force in their areas (tel: 0645 333111). Anglers should carry their licences with them at all times when fishing and produce them when requested by an Environment Agency water bailiff or other authorised person, including a police officer. The request can be made of anyone fishing or reasonably expected to be about to fish, or having fished in the preceding half hour. The maximum penalty for non-compliance is £2,500. Those taking salmon, migratory trout and eels by nets also require a licence from the Environment Agency.

These provisions do not apply in Scotland or Northern Ireland.

In Scotland it is an offence to fish for salmon without having the legal right or without written permission from whoever has that right (section 1, Salmon and Freshwater Fisheries (Protection)(Scotland) Act 1951).

4.1.13 Salmon and Freshwater Fisheries Act 1975

Salmon & Freshwater Fisheries Act 1975
It is an offence to **fish for, take, kill or attempt to take or kill fish** during the close season or close time

The close season and close time during which fishing for salmon and trout by rod and net is prohibited vary throughout England and Wales. The annual close season for freshwater fish runs from 15 March to 15 June; there is, however, no close season on certain stillwaters and certain canals. Restrictions also apply to eel fishing. Local Environment Agency offices can advise on the rules applicable in their area (tel: 0645 333111).

In Scotland there is no close season for freshwater fish except for trout which is from 7 October to 14 March. The close time for salmon varies from district to district.

The Salmon and Freshwater Fisheries Act 1975 applies only in England and Wales; for relevant law in Scotland see Chapter 7.

4.1.14 Deer poaching

NOTE: The Deer Act 1991 applies to England and Wales; for the relevant law in Scotland see Chapter 7.

The Deer Act 1991 is the principal legislation dealing with offences against deer, and replaces numerous other enactments covering the subject.

Deer Act 1991
Section 1(1) **Entering land** It is an offence for any person without the consent of the occupier or other lawful authority to **enter any land in search or pursuit** of any deer with intent to **take, kill or injure it** **Section 1(2)** **Taking, killing or injuring deer** It is an offence for any person whilst on land to **take, kill or injure any deer or attempt to do so** or to **search for or pursue any deer** with intent to remove the carcass of any deer

EXCEPTIONS: Under section 1(3) of the Deer Act 1991 the person would not be guilty of either of the above two offences if:

- he believed he would have had the owner's or occupier's consent; or

- he believed he had lawful authority.

This would cover the case where a person accidentally strays on to land where he does not have consent to shoot but where he believes he has such consent. Another example would be where an injured deer runs on to neighbouring land and the person follows it believing the occupier would have consented.

Deer Act 1991

Section 2(1)
Killing or taking deer

It is an offence for any person to **intentionally take or kill** any red, fallow, roe or sika deer during the close season

---

The close season does not apply to deer that are raised as farm stock.

Muntjac and Chinese water deer do not have a close season at present, though it is advised that 1 March to 31 October be treated as a close season for these species.

Deer Act 1991

Section 3
Killing or taking deer at night

It is an offence for any person to intentionally take or kill deer or take a carcass of deer at night

---

NOTE: Night is defined as the period from one hour after sunset to one hour before sunrise.

This section applies to any species of deer.

EXCEPTIONS: Under section 6 of the Deer Act 1991 it is not an offence to kill or take deer outside the close season or at night if this is done in order to prevent an injured or diseased animal suffering.

MAFF may issue notices under section 98 of the Agriculture Act 1947 which require deer to be shot at night and/or during the close season.

Deer may be legally hunted either by stalking and shooting or by the use of hounds.

4.1.15 Firearms that are permitted for killing deer

The weapons that may be used to shoot deer are limited to the following.

Rifles	Rifles of calibre not less than .240 ins of muzzle energy of not less than 1,700ft/lb (2,305 joules).
	Ammunition – Bullet MUST be soft-nosed or hollow-nosed.
Shotguns	Not less than 12 bore. Can only be used by the occupier of the land, who must be able to prove that the deer were causing serious damage.
	Ammunition – Rifled slug not less than 350 grains or AAA shot.

PROHIBITED FIREARMS:
Any air-gun, air-rifle or air-pistol.

CLOSE SEASON			
Species	1 May – 31 July	1 March – 31 October	1 November – 31 March
Red	Male (Stag)	Female (Hind)	
Fallow	Male (Buck)	Female (Doe)	
Roe		Female (Doe)	Male (Buck)

4.1.16 Traps, snares, poison, nets

Deer Act 1991

Section 4(1)(a)
Injuring deer

It is an offence for any person to
set in position
any trap or snare or poisoned/stupefying bait calculated to injure deer coming into contact with it

Section 4(1)(b)
Killing or taking deer

It is an offence for any person to
use
any trap or snare or poisoned/ stupefying bait or net to
kill or take
any deer

Section 4(2)
Use of prohibited weapons or drugs

It is an offence for any person to
use to injure or kill any deer
any arrow, spear or similar missile, rifle less than .240 or muzzle energy less 1,700ft/lb (2,305 joules), rifle bullet other than soft or hollow-nosed, air weapon, shotgun or shotgun ammunition, missile containing poison/stupefying drug or muscle relaxant

EXCEPTIONS: A shotgun may be used to kill a deer if it is not less than 12 bore, has a barrel less than 24 inches and the ammunition used is AAA or larger. Because of the short barrel length the holder/user must have a firearms certificate.

It is also lawful to kill a deer with a shotgun of any calibre for humane reasons. This excuse does not apply if the deer was injured by that person's unlawful act.

Deer Act 1991

Section 4(4)
Use of motor vehicles

It is an offence for any person to
discharge a firearm or project any missile
at any deer from a powered vehicle

NOTE: Powered vehicle means any powered vehicle whatsoever. This includes motor boats and aircraft.

It is not an offence to use a powered vehicle if this is done on enclosed land with the written authority of the occupier.

4.1.17 Attempts to commit offences

Section 5(1) makes it an offence for any person to attempt to commit any offence under sections 2, 3 or 4 of the Deer Act 1991.

4.1.18 Damage caused by deer

Section 7(3) permits an authorised person to kill or take deer that are causing damage on cultivated land, pasture or enclosed woodland. This may be done even during the close season.

This may only be done if the authorised person can show that:
- he had reason to believe that deer of the same species were causing or had caused damage to crops, vegetables, fruit, growing timber or other property on the land;
- it was likely that further serious damage would be caused; and
- the action was necessary to prevent this further serious damage.

4

4.1.19 Authorised person

An authorised person is:

- the occupier of the land;
- a resident member of his household (authorised in writing by the occupier);
- an employee of the occupier authorised in writing; or
- a person having the right to take or kill deer or a person authorised in writing by the occupier. This includes the shooting tenant, his gamekeeper and invited guests.

4.1.20 Police powers

Section 12 of the Deer Act 1991 provides that a police officer may enter without warrant any land except a dwelling house where he has reasonable cause to suspect that someone is committing or has committed an offence. He may do so in order to:

- stop and search any person suspected of the offence;
- search or examine any vehicle, animal, weapon or other thing;
- seize and detain any thing which is evidence of the offence;
- exercise the general arrest conditions contained in section 25 of PACE (in England and Wales).

Any deer or venison seized under this section may be sold and the proceeds detained and forfeited.

4.1.21 Coursing

Hare-coursing was a mainly seasonal pursuit dependent upon large areas of stubble after the harvest. The use of dogs to hunt or course hares is not in itself illegal. Coursing becomes illegal when the person coursing does not have the permission of the landowner. There is no specific offence of hare-coursing, but hares are defined as 'game', and anyone who enters land to hunt or take game without the landowner's permission commits an offence of poaching (see 4.1.5–7 and 4.1.9).

Large tracts of set-aside land provide an ideal habitat for the hare and may also provide an arena for illegal coursing throughout the year. This particular activity attracts large groups who use four-wheel-drive vehicles to drive the hares towards the dogs. Landowners and their families may also be subjected to intimidation.

In order to deal with this problem, a concerted intelligence-led operation with adequate resources is likely to be required.

Another form of illegal coursing occurs when a group of three or four people risk being charged with the offence. In this situation the gamekeeper has no power of arrest and the poachers may move on to another piece of land nearby and continue with their sport.

A police officer's powers are limited to the general powers under PACE, and if identification is satisfactory then the only action is to report for summons. Paragraphs 1 and 4 of Schedule 9 of the Criminal Justice and Public Order Act 1994 increase the penalties for certain poaching offences under the Game Act 1831 and amend the Game Laws (Amendment) Act 1960 to provide for the forfeiture of vehicles in certain circumstances.

4.1.22 Game dealers

The game dealer can be a source of valuable information. All game and venison should be sold to a licensed game dealer who may then supply shops, restaurants, butchers and the public.

Local environmental health departments should keep a record of registered dealers for the purpose of public health inspections.

A dealer is required to keep records of deer purchased, including the seller, vehicle registrations, and type of any firearm used. Police officers may inspect the record, invoices and other documents.

Game can also be sold or given to consumers direct.

4.2 CRUELTY TO WILD ANIMALS

4.2.1 Legislation

The Wild Mammals (Protection) Act 1996 is the principle legislation protecting wild animals from cruelty, although the provision of the Protection of Animals Act 1911 (1912 in Scotland), primarily applicable to domestic animals, also applies to wild animals if they are in captivity.

The Wild Mammals (Protection) Act does not apply to Northern Ireland, which has had similar legislation since 1972 (see Chapter 8).

The Act creates one offence.

Wild Mammals (Protection) Act 1996

Section 1

Any person who
mutilates, kicks, beats, nails or otherwise impales, stabs, burns, stones, crushes, drowns, drags or asphyxiates
any wild mammal with intent to inflict unnecessary suffering
shall be guilty of an offence

EXCEPTIONS: A person is not guilty of an offence under the Act in the following circumstances:

- the attempted killing of any such wild mammal as an act of mercy if he shows that the mammal had been so disabled, other than by his unlawful act, that there was no reasonable chance of its recovering;
- the killing in a reasonably swift and humane manner of any such mammal if he shows it had been injured or taken in the course of either lawful shooting, hunting, coursing or pest control activity;
- doing anything which is authorised or under any enactment;
- any act made unlawful under section 1 if the act was done by means of any snare, trap, dog or bird lawfully used for the purpose of killing or taking any wild mammal; or

- the lawful use of any poisonous or noxious substance.

These exceptions place an onus on a person to 'show' good reason for any particular action which would otherwise be deemed unlawful.

EXAMPLES: The exceptions mean that it is not an offence under this Act:

- to try and despatch a wild mammal that has been seriously injured in a road accident; or
- to humanely kill a rat caught in a legal trap or a fox injured by hounds.

4.3 TRAPPING

Snares, spring traps and live-catch traps are all methods commonly used to control 'pest species', but a number of offences can occur involving both wild and domestic animals. There are a number of animals and birds that can be controlled (killed or taken) by certain authorised methods.

NOTE: For ease of reference, offences are separately listed in this chapter under snares, spring traps or live-catch traps. Some of these relate to more than one type of trap and hence there is some duplication in the lists of offences.

4.3.1 Snares

Snares have been in use for nearly as long as man has hunted animals, and there are many different types in use throughout the world. They are extremely light and cheap to buy and can be very effective. They are designed to kill either by strangulation or by dislocation of the neck. However, by clever use of a stop knot, some can be used to hold an animal alive until the trapper arrives to dispatch it. Snares are now a very popular and widely-used method of controlling foxes and rabbits. However, when they are not used properly they can be indiscriminate and can catch non-target species.

Badger killed by a snare

4.3.2 Free-running snares

Also known as the boot-lace snare, or in traditional terms 'a wire'. The free-running snare takes its name from the method used to allow the snare to run freely; normally a boot eyelet is used, hence the name boot-lace. This type of snare allows the noose to slacken off so that it relaxes slightly when the animal ceases to struggle. The use of these snares can be permitted.

There has recently been a new design of fox snare introduced called the 'rocking eye snare'. It is a registered design which will close quickly under its own weight and this reduces the risk of a fox backing out of the noose. The design differs from traditional snares in that the running eye is a little heavier than normal, preventing the snare from springing back open when it starts to draw.

4.3.3 Self-locking snares

This type of snare should no longer be on sale, but there are certain types of free-running snare (normally fox snares) that can be converted. The noose on this type continues to tighten as the animal struggles, inflicting terrible injuries should the snare become caught around the middle of any animal. The use of these snares is illegal.

4.3.4 Investigation

Check the snare to establish whether or not it runs freely or locks up when closed. Remember that free running snares can be converted. There are a number of points to prove.

- Is the person an 'authorised person' (see 4.3.10 and 2.2)?
- Who set the snare?
- Has it been inspected at least once daily?

The legislation that applies to snares is the WCA sections 5(1)(a), (b) and (f), 11(1)(b) and (d), 11(2)(a) and (b), 11 (3)(a) and (b) and 18(2); the Deer Act 1991 sections 4(1)(a) and (b) and 5(1) and (2); the Protection of Animals Act 1911, section 1(1)(a); and the Criminal Damage Act 1971, section 1 (not Scotland).

Wildlife and Countryside Act 1981

Section 11(1)(a)

Any person commits an offence if they
set in position any self-locking snare
which is of such a nature and so placed as to be
calculated to cause bodily injury
to any wild animal coming into contact with it

NOTE: The legislation does make reference to wild animals, therefore it could be a defence if the accused claimed that they set a self-locking snare to catch a domestic animal such as a cat. However, an offence could then be committed under the Protection of Animals Act 1911 (1912 in Scotland). Although self-locking snares are banned for use against any wild animal, other types of snares are banned only for Schedule 6 animals.

Wildlife and Countryside Act 1981

Section 11(1)(b)

Any person commits an offence if they use for the

purpose of killing or taking any wild animal any self-locking snare

whether or not of such a nature or so placed as aforesaid

Section 11(1)(d)

Any person commits an offence if they knowingly

cause or permit to be done

an act which is mentioned in the foregoing provisions of this section

Section 18(2)

Any person who for the purpose of committing an offence

has in his possession

anything being capable of being used for committing an offence

shall be guilty of an offence

Wildlife and Countryside Act 1981

Section 11(2)(a)

Any person will commit an offence if he

sets in position any article

of such a nature and so placed as to be calculated

to cause bodily injury to any wild animal

included in Schedule 6 (these include badger, hedgehog etc) which comes into contact with it, that is to say any trap or snare etc

Section 11(2)(b)

Any person will commit an offence if he uses for the purpose of

killing or taking

any such wild animal (Schedule 6) any such article, eg trap, snare

4

A set snare

Wildlife and Countryside Act 1981

Section 18(2)

Any person who for the purpose of committing an offence
has in his possession
anything being capable of being used for committing an offence
shall be guilty of an offence

4.3.6   Dead or decomposed bodies in the snare

Wildlife and Countryside Act 1981

Section 11(3)(a)

Any person will commit an offence if he
sets in position or knowingly causes or permits
to be set in position any snare which is of such a nature and so placed as to be
calculated to cause bodily injury
to any wild animal coming into contact with it

Section 11(3)(b)

Any person whilst the snare
remains in position
fails, without reasonable excuse, to inspect it, or cause it to be inspected at least once every day
shall be guilty of an offence

4.3.7   Birds caught in snares

Wildlife and Countryside Act 1981

Section 5(1)(a)

Any person who
sets in position
any article which is of such a nature and so placed as to be
calculated to cause bodily injury
to any wild bird coming into contact therewith, that is to say any spring, trap, gin, snare, hook and line etc, shall be guilty of an offence

Section 5(1)(b)

Any person who
uses for the purpose of
killing or taking any wild bird
any such article as aforesaid
ie spring, trap, gin, snare etc,
shall be guilty of an offence

Section 5(1)(f)

Any person who knowingly
causes or permits to be done
an act which is mentioned in the foregoing provisions, shall be guilty of an offence

Section 18(2)

Any person who for the purpose of committing an offence
has in his possession
anything being capable of being used for committing an offence
shall be guilty of an offence.

4.3.8 Deer caught in snares

Deer Act 1991

Section 4(1)(a)

Any person who
sets in position any article
which is a trap, snare or poisoned
or stupefying bait and is of such a nature and
so placed as to be
calculated to cause bodily injury to any deer
coming into contact with it,
shall be guilty of an offence.

Section 4(1)(b)

Any person who
uses for the purpose of
taking or killing any deer
any trap, snare or poisoned or stupefying bait,
shall be guilty of an offence

Section 5(1)

Any person who
attempts to commit
an offence under sections 2 to 4,
shall be guilty of an offence

Section 5(2)

Any person who for the purpose of committing
an offence under any of the sections 2 to 4
has in his possession
any article the use of which is prohibited by
section 4(1)b, ie trap, snare, shall be guilty of
an offence

4.3.9 Domestic animals caught in snares

Protection of Animals Act 1911

Section 1(1)(a)

Any person shall commit an offence by
unreasonably doing or omitting to do any act, or
causing or procuring the commission of any act
causing unnecessary suffering
or being the owner permit any unnecessary
suffering to be so caused

In Scotland, the equivalent provision is section 1(1)(a) of the Protection of Animals (Scotland) Act 1912.

Criminal Damage Act 1971 (not Scotland)

Section 1

Any person shall commit an offence if they
deliberately or recklessly
kill or injure domestic and captive animals
which belong to or are in the custody, control or
charge of another

4.3.10 Persons allowed to use snares

The WCA refers to 'authorised persons' being entitled to kill or take certain animals or birds. It should be established in any investigation whether the person who set the snare was allowed to do so. The definition of 'authorised person' is given in section 27(1)) as follows:

- the owner or occupier; or
- any person authorised by the owner or occupier of the land on which the action authorised is taken; or
- any person authorised in writing by the local authority for the area within which the action authorised is taken.

A set pole trap

4.3.11 Spring traps

All spring traps in this country have to be approved by MAFF. They are then put on the Spring Traps (Approval) Order 1995. This legislation approves the trap, conditions for its use and the species of animal that it can be used to control. There are a number of different types of traps that you will come across. Some are legal if used correctly, some are not. They are all based on a similar design: a set of jaws is held in an open position by a plate; when the animal or bird treads on the plate it releases a strong steel spring which closes the jaws, thus killing or trapping the prey.

4.3.12 Illegal traps

The gin trap

This trap has been banned in Britain since 1958. It was basically designed as a 'leg-hold' trap, the idea being not to kill the prey but to hold it until the gamekeeper or trapper came to dispatch the animal. Gin traps were usually placed in the entrances to burrows or in artificial tunnels. The main difference between the gin trap and any other is that the jaws of the trap are toothed or serrated and this is what gave the trap its ability to hold its prey, mainly by the leg. When investigating gin trap complaints always check the underside of any trap for signs of soil or fresh rust, also check the spring mechanism for oil and scuff marks. These signs may indicate the recent use of the trap. Be aware that legal spring traps which have been modified by having teeth cut into the jaws, or even having fencing staples welded on to them, are illegal. These modifications alter the trap into a form of gin.

The pole trap

This type of trap was used to catch birds of prey and owls. The trap was round in shape and of the same basic design as the gin. The jaws (which did not have teeth) were slightly curved, which, if the bird was caught correctly, did not damage the leg. However, this did not always happen and on occasions the leg would be severed and the bird would fly off only to suffer and die.

Live crow in a spring trap

The jaws were held open by the trigger plate, and when the bird landed on this the spring would shut the jaws. Because of the light weight of the birds these traps were very sensitive. The trap would be placed on 'perching' or 'plucking' posts, where the birds of prey perch while waiting for their next meal or to pluck their prey.

EC Regulation 3254/91 banned the use of 'leg-hold traps', devices defined as 'designed to restrain or capture an animal by means of jaws which close tightly upon one or more of the animals limbs, thereby preventing the withdrawal of the limb or limbs from the trap', throughout the European Union from 1 January 1995.

4.3.13 Legal spring traps

The Pests Act 1954 and the Spring Traps (Approval) Order 1995

Under this legislation, 'approved traps' refers to traps of types and makes specified by MAFF as approved by the Minister subject to the conditions as to the animals for which, or the circumstances in which, the spring traps may be used. The approved traps and their uses are listed below.

Type of trap	Circumstances of use
Imbra Mk 1 & 2	To take rabbits, or grey squirrels, stoats, weasels, rats, mice or other small ground vermin in natural or artificial tunnels
Fenn vermin trap Mk 1, 2, 3&4	To take grey squirrels, stoats, weasels, rats, mice or other small ground vermin in natural or artificial tunnels.
Fenn vermin trap MK 6 dual purpose	To take rabbits, grey squirrels, mink, stoats, weasels, rats, mice or other small vermin in natural or artificial tunnels.
Fenn rabbit trap Mk 1	To take rabbits in natural or artificial tunnels.
Juby trap	As for the Imbra.

Type of trap	Circumstances of use
Fuller trap	To take grey squirrels in artificial tunnels.
Sawyer and Lloyd traps	To take grey squirrels, stoats, weasels, rats, mice or other small ground vermin in natural or artificial tunnels.
BMI Magnum 55	For taking and killing rats, mice and other small ground vermin in natural or artificial tunnels.
BMI Magnum 110	As for the BM Magnum 55 plus grey squirrels, stoats and weasels.
BMI Magnum 116	As for the BM Magnum 110 plus mink and rabbits.
Aldrich spring-activated snare	To kill or take large non-indigenous mammalian carnivores.
Kania trap 2000	To kill or take grey squirrels, mink, stoats, weasels, rats, mice and other small ground vermin in artificial tunnels.

Scotland makes its own orders, eg the Spring Traps (Scotland)(Approval) Order 1996.

4.3.14 Using an unapproved trap

Pests Act 1954

Section 8(1)(a)

Any person shall commit an offence if for the purpose of
killing or taking animals,
he uses, or knowingly permits the use of, any spring trap other than an approved trap or
uses or knowingly permits
the use of an approved trap for animals or in circumstances for which it is not approved.

Section (8)(c)

Any person shall commit an offence if he has any spring trap
in his possession
for a purpose which is unlawful under this section

4.3.15 Setting an approved rabbit trap in the open

Pests Act 1954

Section 9(1)

Any person shall be guilty of an offence under this subsection if, for the purpose of
killing or taking hares or rabbits,
he uses, or knowingly permits the use of, a spring trap elsewhere other than in a rabbit hole.

NOTE: A point to remember is that although this section refers to traps for taking hares, at this time there is not an approved trap as specified in the Spring Traps (Approval) Order 1975 for trapping this animal. Therefore if someone admitted to using a spring trap to catch hares they would be committing an offence. It is also worth noting that a rabbit trap can be set elsewhere than in a rabbit hole if it is in accordance with the conditions of use set out in the Spring Traps (Approval) Order 1995.

4.3.16 Using an approved trap to catch birds

Wildlife and Countryside Act 1981

Section 5(1)(a)

Any person who sets any article which is of such a nature and so placed as to be
calculated to cause bodily injury
to any wild bird coming into contact therewith, that is to say any spring trap, gin, snare, hook and line etc, shall be guilty of an offence and liable to a special penalty

NOTE: Fenn traps (or other approved animal traps) cannot be used to kill or take birds.

Wildlife and Countryside Act 1981

Section 5(1)(b)

Any person who uses for the purpose of
killing or taking any wild bird
any such article as aforesaid, ie spring trap, gin, snare etc

Section 5(1)(f)

knowingly
causes or permits to be done
an act which is mentioned in the foregoing provisions shall be guilty of an offence and be liable to a special penalty

No offence will be committed if a licence has been issued under section 16 of the WCA.

Pests Act 1954

Section 8(1)(a)

A person shall commit an offence if for the purpose of
killing or taking animals,
he uses, or knowingly permits the use of, any spring trap other than an approved trap or
uses or knowingly permits
the use of an approved trap for animals or in circumstances for which it is not approved

Sparrowhawk caught in a spring trap

No offence will be committed if a licence has been issued under section 16 of the WCA.

Wildlife and Countryside Act 1981

Section 18(2)

Any person who for the purpose of committing an offence
has in his possession
anything being capable of being used for committing an offence shall be guilty of an offence

4.3.18 Dead or decomposed bodies in the trap

Protection of Animals Act 1911

Section 10

Any person who
sets or causes or procures
to be set any spring trap for the purpose of catching any hare or rabbit,
shall inspect or cause some competent person to inspect the trap at reasonable intervals of time and at least once every day between sunrise and sunset

In Scotland, the equivalent provision is section 9 of the Protection of Animals (Scotland) Act 1912.

4.3.17 Using traps to catch protected animals

Wildlife and Countryside Act 1981

Section 11(2)(a)

Any person will commit an offence if
he sets in position any article
of such a nature and so placed as to be
calculated to cause bodily injury
to any wild animal included in Schedule 6 (these include badger, hedgehog, etc) which comes into contact with it, that is to say any trap or snare etc

or
Section 11(2)(b)

Any person who uses for the purpose of
killing or taking any such wild animal
(Schedule 6) any such article
ie trap, snare, etc

4.3.19 Domestic animals caught in spring traps

Protection of Animals Act 1911

Section 1(1)(a)

Any person shall commit an offence by
unreasonably doing or omitting to do
any act, or causing or procuring the
commission of any act which causes
unnecessary suffering
or being the owner permitting any
unnecessary suffering to be so caused

In Scotland, the equivalent provision is section 1(1)(a) of the Protection of Animals (Scotland) Act 1912.

Criminal Damage Act 1971

Section 1

Any person shall commit an offence if they
deliberately or recklessly kill or injure
domestic and captive animals which belong to
or are in the custody, control or charge of
another

NOTE: This legislation does not extend to Scotland.

4.3.20 Deer caught in traps

Deer Act 1991

Section 4(1)(a)

Any person who
sets in position
any article which is a trap, snare, poisoned
or stupefying bait and is of such a nature and
so placed as to be calculated to
cause bodily injury to any deer coming into
contact with it shall be guilty of an offence

Section 4(1)(b)

Any person who uses for the purpose of
taking or killing
any deer, any trap, snare or poisoned or
stupefying bait shall commit an offence

Section 5(1)

Any person who
attempts
to commit an offence under sections 2 to 4 shall
commit an offence

Section 5(2)

Any person for the purpose of committing an
offence under any of the sections 2 to 4 has in
his possession
any article the use of which is prohibited by
section 4(1)b, ie trap, snare, etc
commits an offence

4.3.21 Persons allowed to use spring traps

The legislation makes reference to 'authorised persons' being entitled to kill or take certain animals or birds. It should be established in any investigation whether the person who set the trap was allowed to do so. The definition of 'authorised person' is given in 2.2.

4.3.22 Summary of spring traps and snares

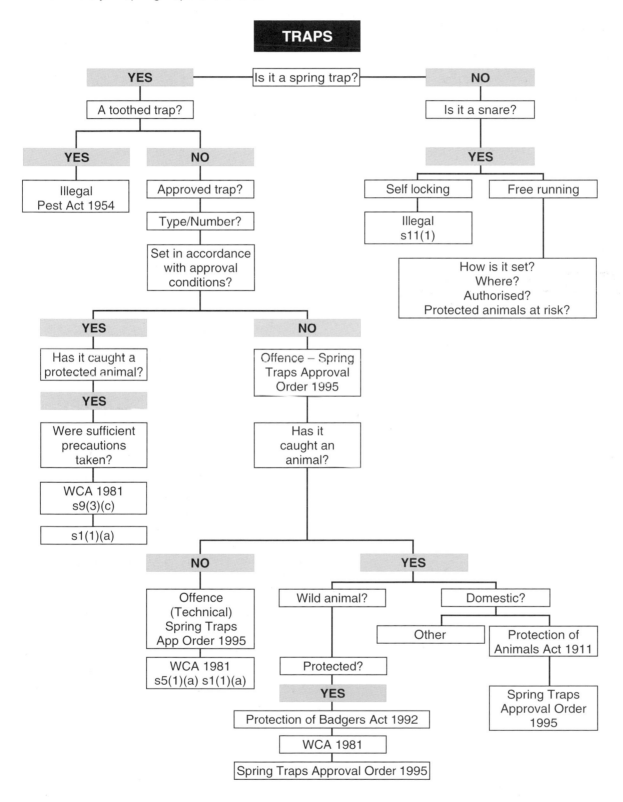

4.3.23 Legal bird traps

There are many types of live-catch traps on the market, which can be used for both mammals and birds.

Larsen trap

These traps are now among the most common live-catch bird traps. They are used for catching members of the Corvid family and are particularly effective in catching magpies. The trap was designed by a Danish gamekeeper in the 1950s and is now available in many different forms. The important factor with this trap is that it employs the use of a live decoy bird, which under normal circumstances may not be legal. However, the issue of a general licence from the DETR allows the operators of the trap to use the decoy bird providing certain conditions are met, ie food, water and shelter should be available, and room to stretch its wings. Most of the traps have three compartments, one larger than the others, in which the decoy bird is usually kept. The other two compartments have spring-loaded doors which are held open by split perches. When the decoy attracts the other birds they alight on the perch, which gives way under their weight and they fall into the trap. The traps often have bait in the form of eggs or eggshells placed on top of or inside the compartments, although in the case of magpies it is the presence of an intruder (ie the decoy bird) which readily attracts them.

A Larsen trap baited with live carrion crow

© RSPB

NOTE: Under the terms of the current general licence only magpies, crows, jays, jackdaws and rooks can be used as decoys. It is illegal to use a Larsen trap to catch goshawks or sparrowhawks.

Ladder traps

These traps were originally devised by MAFF and although still in use are not as popular as the Larsen. The trap is normally about 12 feet square and about six feet high. The roof of the trap is the shape of a flat-bottom 'V', the flat part being formed by the ladder. This has rungs approximately nine inches apart, which allow birds (mainly crows) to enter the trap but prevents them from getting back out. The more that enter the trap, the more effective it becomes. These traps are normally baited with grain, dry bread or sometimes carrion, which is placed on the floor.

Cone or lobster-pot traps

These were also designed by MAFF and work on the same principle as a traditional lobster pot. The traps are normally about six feet square with a cone in the roof section which will allow the birds to enter the trap but not allow them to escape. Baiting is the same as the previous traps.

4.3.24 Other bird traps

Although the use of the following methods is generally prohibited, licences may be issued to allow their use. Always check whether a licence has been issued.

Search warrants can be obtained where there is evidence that someone has been illegally trapping wild birds, even though one cannot be obtained for simple possession of the bird (unless included in Schedule 1).

Smaller wild birds, particularly finches, are trapped in several ways.

Cage traps

The trap is usually constructed as a double- or treble-compartment structure, which enables the trapper to place a tame bird in one compartment to act as a decoy

A cage trap used for finches

bird. As the bird enters the compartment next to the decoy bird, to feed on seed scattered by the trapper, the lid is closed by means of a drop perch design or spring, trapping the bird inside. These traps can be used only if a licence has been issued.

Mist nets

These nets, made of a very fine mesh, are used by illegal trappers; licence-holders carrying out pest control operations; and people lawfully engaged in trapping wild birds to allow an identification ring to be fitted to enable migration routes and habitats to be accurately recorded (see 4.3.25). The mesh is so fine that birds do not see it. These traps can only be used if a licence has been issued.

Bird lime

This is an old method of catching birds. Bird lime is a substance so sticky that once a bird gets it on its wings or feet it is unable to move until released by the trapper, who then cleans off the offending substance and cages the bird ready for the next stage of his operation. Bird lime is usually spread on a bird's favourite perch or feeding place. It is also possible to catch roosting birds with a small amount of the substance on a cane, which is lightly brushed across the bird's wing tips, sticking the bird's wings together and preventing flight and escape. Bird lime continues to be available through southern

Ireland, although the modern availability of adhesive substances means various products can now be used effectively.

Ringing captured birds

Once a bird has been captured it is then necessary to fit the bird with a ring to enable the bird to be sold. As was stated earlier (see 2.9.9–10), the ring is made to be fitted at a very early age, which means the ring has to be stretched to make it fit an adult bird. The old method was to obtain a ring for a species of bird captured then push a nail of a slightly larger size through the ring, stretching it slightly so, with the aid of a smear of Vaseline, the trapper could slide the ring on the bird's leg. The practice of bird-trapping has become a very hi-tech matter; rings are now bored out on a machine to such a fine degree that a micrometer is required to enable the authorities to ascertain if the ring has been tampered with. Even so, illegal ringing often involves the use of vinegar on the bird's leg, which is supposed to make it supple enough to enable the ring to be fitted. One sure sign that illegal ringing has occurred is that the bird's leg is bruised and scales are missing.

Although there is a market for all types of British birds, the main targets are the finch species. These include the bullfinch, goldfinch, linnet, redpoll and siskin. With the exception of the bullfinch, these birds gather in flocks during the winter, enabling the trapper to trap when the birds are hungry and take risks.

Under the terms of a MAFF licence, wild bullfinches can legally be trapped by certain people in some parts of the country and at particular times of the year. These birds can be passed to aviculturists.

4.3.25 Licensed trapping of birds for research

One situation which might be encountered, and which could initially provoke suspicion that the law is being broken, is the trapping and ringing of birds for research purposes.

The WCA, as amended by the Environmental Protection Act 1990, makes provision for the licensing of the trapping of birds for research purposes.

In Great Britain the licence is deposited with the British Trust for Ornithology, which is empowered to issue permits allowing the trapping of birds.

Permits issued by the British Trust for Ornithology can either be 'general', allowing the catching of all species, or specific to a particular species or group of species.

The licences automatically allow the use of traps, but will also specify any additional methods by which the researcher is allowed to catch birds; for instance, mist nets or cannon nets, or by the use of tape recordings to lure species for trapping.

All bird ringers undergo a strict training process before the issue of a licence, and all must abide by the rules of the National Bird Ringing Scheme.

Ringing is conducted for many reasons, and there are numerous specific research programmes involving licensed bird ringers.

Ringing as a research tool is used to monitor the movements and migration patterns of birds, to monitor the fate of individuals within a population, and to monitor mortality rates amongst many other uses.

Licensed ringers will always ring with the landowner's permission and will be able to show proof of identity and licence if requested. When ringing is taking place in a public location there will often be signs displayed on the nets or other traps explaining the purpose of the trap or nets and giving a contact name and address.

A standard bird-ringing permit does not permit the ringing of chicks of species included on Schedule 1 of the WCA, nor the disturbance of such birds at the nest. If these species are involved then the ringer should in addition possess a Schedule 1 licence which he should be able to produce.

Trapping birds without a permit issued by the British Trust for Ornithology will constitute an offence under section 1 of the WCA, and possession of traps or nets without such a licence will be an offence under section 18.

In the event of any doubt about the legality or otherwise of the activities of a ringer, contact the licensing office at: The British Trust for Ornithology, The National Centre for Ornithology, The Nunnery, Thetford. IP24 2PU., tel: 01842 750050, who will be happy to advise.

4.3.26 Mammal traps

Live-catch traps are often seen as the humane solution to problems of urban foxes and other nuisance animals. There are many types of trap on the market but all work on a similar basis. The traps are baited, the animal will enter the trap to get at the bait, and it will either tread on a trigger plate or, by pulling at the bait, release a pin which in turn triggers a spring-loaded door. One advantage of cage trapping is that it allows non-target species such as pets to be released unharmed.

4.3.27 Traps used to catch birds

Wildlife and Countryside Act 1981

Section 5(1)(a)

Any person who sets any article which is of such a nature and so placed as to be calculated to
cause bodily injury to any wild bird
coming into contact therewith, that is to say any spring, trap, gin, snare, hook and line etc

or
Section 5(1)(b)

uses for the purpose of
killing or taking
any wild bird any such article as aforesaid ie spring, trap, gin, snare etc

or
Section 5(1)(f)

knowingly
causes or permits to be done
an act which is mentioned in the foregoing provisions,
shall be guilty of an offence

No offence will be committed if it has been done in accordance with a licence issued under section 16 of the WCA.

4.3.28 Traps used to catch 'pest' birds

Wildlife and Countryside Act 1981

Section 5(5)(a) – allows an authorised person to use a cage trap (ie Larsen, cone, ladder or net) for the purpose of taking a bird formerly included in Part II of Schedule 2 (now revoked and replaced by general licences issued under section 16).

Section 16 – allows the DETR, MAFF, SOAEFD and EN to issue licences, both general and specific. Authorised persons can kill or take 13 pest bird species under the terms and conditions of the general licences. These licences are renewed every two years.

4.3.29 Selling trapped birds

Wildlife and Countryside Act 1981
Section 6(1)(a)
Any person shall commit an offence if he **sells, or offers for sale** or has in his **possession or transports** for the purpose of sale, any live wild bird **other than** a bird included in Part 1 of Schedule 3

NOTE: Although it would be an offence for a gamekeeper to sell a magpie it would not be if he gave the bird away, but 'sale' includes hire, barter and exchange.

4.3.30 Birds or animals in the trap in poor condition with no food or water, or dead

Protection of Animals Act 1911 (in Scotland – 1912)
Section 1(1)(a)
Any person shall commit an offence by **unreasonably doing or omitting to do any act,** or causing or procuring the commission of any act, **or causing the unnecessary suffering or,** being the owner, **permitting any unnecessary suffering** to be so caused to any animal

Abandonment of Animals Act 1960
Section 1
Any person (the owner or person having charge or control of) who **abandons an animal** (whether permanently or not) in circumstances **likely to cause the animal unnecessary suffering** or cause or procure or, being the owner, permit it to be so abandoned without reasonable excuse shall commit an offence

4.3.31 Cage trap containing pheasants

Wildlife and Countryside Act 1981
Section 5(5)(c)
Any person who allows the use of a cage trap or net for the **purpose of** taking any game bird if it is shown that the taking of the bird is solely for the **purpose of breeding**

4.3.32 Traps being used to catch mammals

Live-catch traps can be used to catch any animal which is not protected, ie rabbits, squirrels, foxes and feral cats. However, if badgers, hedgehogs or otters are being trapped the following may apply.

Wildlife and Countryside Act 1981

Section 9(1)

An offence is committed if any person **intentionally kills, injures or takes any wild animal included in Schedule 5** (these include the common otter, dormouse and red squirrel)

Section 11(2)(a)

Any person will commit an offence if **he sets in position any article** of such a nature and so placed as to be **calculated to cause bodily injury to any wild animal included in Schedule 6** (these include badger, hedgehog etc) which comes into contact, that is to say any trap or snare etc

or
Section 11(2)(b)

uses for the purpose of killing or taking any such wild animal (Schedule 6) any such article ie trap, snare etc

---

NOTE: MAFF is currently using cage traps to catch badgers for TB testing in parts of the British Isles. Licences can be issued by the Ministry for the trapping of protected animals. No offence will be committed if it is done in accordance with a licence issued under section 16 of the WCA.

4.3.33 Baits used in the traps

Criminal Damage Act 1971

Non-poisonous baits can be used in traps but if, through being placed too near adjoining fields, it attracts animals which would have not otherwise have been likely to have entered the land, and those animals are injured or destroyed, the person setting the trap could be liable to pay compensation and possibly be prosecuted.

Protection of Animals Act 1911

Section 8(a)

Any person shall commit an offence if they **knowingly put or place, or cause or procure** any person to put in place or knowingly be a party to the putting or placing, in or upon any land or building **any poison or any fluid or edible matter** (not being sown seed or grain) which has been rendered poisonous.

NOTE: There are exceptions to this section: no offence will be committed if the poison was placed by the accused for the purpose of controlling insects, rats, mice or other small ground vermin in the interest of public health etc, and he took all reasonable precautions to prevent injury to dogs, cats, fowls or other domestic animals and wild birds.

In Scotland, the equivalent protection is section 7(b) of the Protection of Animals (Scotland) Act 1912.

Game Act 1831

Under this Act it is an offence to put poison bait on a highway or the ground with the intent to destroy or injure game.

4.3.34 Humane destruction of trapped animals or birds

Protection of Animals Act 1911

Section 1(1)(a)

Any person shall commit an offence by unreasonably doing or omitting to do any act, or causing or procuring the commission of any act which

causes unnecessary suffering

or being the owner permit any unnecessary suffering to be so caused

In Scotland, the equivalent provision is section 1(1)(a) of the Protection of Animals (Scotland) Act 1912.

4.3.35 Trapped animals released in other locations

Wildlife and Countryside Act 1981

Section 14(1)

If any person
releases or allows to escape
into the wild any animal which is of a kind which is not ordinarily resident in and is not a regular visitor to Great Britain in a wild state
or
is included in Part 1 of Schedule 9 (this includes grey squirrel, mink and coypu)
he shall be guilty of an offence

4.4 POISONING

4.4.1 Pesticides

Legislation in the United Kingdom places severe restrictions on the use of pesticides and it is illegal, with certain exceptions, to poison or attempt to poison any mammal or bird. All pesticides have to be approved and users must comply with the specific conditions of approval which relate to the use of a particular pesticide. The relevant legislation is dealt with in more detail later in this chapter.

In the UK the Agriculture Departments operate a scheme to investigate cases of possible pesticide poisoning of animals. This is known as the Wildlife Incident Investigation Scheme (WIIS). In England and Wales this is operated by MAFF and WOAD. Similar arrangements exist in Scotland (SOAEFD) and Northern Ireland.

Incidents which are shown to be due to pesticides are classified as follows.

- Approved use of a product, according to its specified conditions of use.
- Misuse of a product, by careless, accidental or wilful failure to adhere to the correct practice.
- Abuse of a pesticide, in the form of deliberate, illegal attempts to poison animals.

In addition, some reported animal deaths are found to be the result of causes unrelated to pesticide use, such as disease, starvation and trauma or other poisonings.

In cases where animals have been poisoned following the approved use of a pesticide the case history may be reported to the Environmental Panel of the Advisory Committee on Pesticides (ACP) and the information used as a basis for changes to the approval of products. Where there is evidence of misuse or deliberate abuse of a pesticide then the results of those individual investigations may result in enforcement actions.

Each year, an annual report is produced which contains details of all incidents which have been investigated, including the species and pesticides involved and any action which has been taken as a result.

4.4.2 Legislation

For definitive information on legislation it is essential that specific Acts or Regulations are consulted. The following summary is for guidance purposes only.

4

The Food and Environment Protection Act 1985 Control of Pesticides Regulations 1986

Part III of the Food and Environment Protection Act 1985 (FEPA) contains statutory powers to control the use of pesticides. Section 16 of the Act describes the main intentions of the controls as being to:

- protect the health of humans, creatures and plants;
- safeguard the environment;
- secure safe, effective and humane methods of controlling pests; and
- make information about pesticides available to the public.

These aims are achieved by regulations made under the Act. The Control of Pesticides Regulations 1986 (COPR) define those type of pesticides which are subject to control and prescribe that specific approval must be given before any pesticide may be advertised, sold, supplied, stored or used. Additional consents made under the Regulations set out more general conditions relating to these categories.

To gain approval for a pesticide, manufacturers and others must support an application with the necessary data on safety, efficacy and, where relevant, humaneness. Statutory conditions of use will vary depending on the pesticide and product, but in all cases it is important that the user reads the label carefully before purchase and use. Certain instructions must be complied with, including the type of use, operator protection and training requirements and environmental protection measures (which include avoiding or minimising risks to non-target animals). Most pesticide labels now include a 'statutory box' which contains mandatory instructions, and this helps to concentrate the user's attention on these requirements.

It is an offence to use a pesticide for a purpose for which it has not been approved. It is also an offence when using a pesticide to fail to take reasonable precautions to protect the health of human beings and creatures. It is also an offence to store pesticides which are not approved or to store them other than in the original container.

Protection of Animals Act 1911

This Act provides general protection for all domestic or captive animals, in particular making it an offence to cause unnecessary suffering.

Section 8 – prohibits the laying of poisons except for insects, other invertebrates, rats, mice and other small ground vermin (which includes moles).

Where poisoned baits are used for the control of these species, the Act requires that all reasonable precautions are taken to prevent injury to cats, dogs, fowls, other domestic animals and wild birds.

Wildlife and Countryside Act 1981

Part I of this Act deals with the protection of wild birds, animals and plants.

Section 5(1) – prohibits the use of poisonous, poisoned or stupefying substances to kill or take any wild bird. It also prohibits the placing of such substances so as to be calculated to cause bodily injury to any wild bird coming into contact with them.

Licences may be issued to pest control companies allowing the use of stupefying substances to take pest birds.

Section 11(2) – similarly prohibits the use of poisonous, poisoned or stupefying substances against animals included in Schedule 6 of the Act.

These animals include:

badger	pine marten
bats (all species)	polecat
common otter	red squirrel
dormouse (all species)	shrews (all species)
hedgehog	wild cat

An amendment to the Act makes it an offence to cause or permit another person to commit an offence under sections 5 and 11.

Section 16(1) – makes provision for licences to be granted to use prohibited methods in certain circumstances. These include for example the use of stupefying baits against feral pigeons and house sparrows. MAFF, the DETR or other Government Departments are the authorities responsible for the issue of such licences.

Regulation 41 of the 1994 Conservation Regulations also prohibits certain methods of taking or killing specified wild animals.

4.4.3   Other legislation

There are a number of other Acts and Regulations which affect the use of pesticides and have implications for the poisoning of animals. These include the following.

Prevention of Damage by Rabbits Act 1939

Section 4 – allows the use of poisonous gas in rabbit holes (otherwise prohibited under the Protection of Animals Act).

Agriculture Act 1947
Agriculture (Scotland) Act 1948 (Sections 39 and 49)

Section 98.3 – permits the use of poisonous gas in holes, burrows or earths for the purpose of killing rabbits, hares, rodents, deer, foxes and moles (deer and hares are included as a result of a carry-over from another section).

However, currently under COPR there are only products approved for use against rabbits, rats, mice and moles. Use against other species such as foxes and badgers is illegal.

Animals (Cruel Poisons) Act 1962

This Act enables the Secretary of State to prohibit or restrict the use of poisons which may cause unnecessary suffering. Regulations made in 1963 banned the use of phosphorous and red squill against all mammals and restricts the use of strychnine solely to the destruction of moles.

Agriculture (Miscellaneous Provisions) Act 1972

This makes provision for the use of poison (warfarin) against grey squirrels. An order made under the Act restricts outdoor use of this to special hoppers.

Poisons Rules 1982

These Rules are made under the Poisons Act 1972 and they regulate the sale and use of certain chemicals including the following.

- The compounds sodium cyanide and aluminium phosphide, used as fumigants against vertebrates.
- Zinc phosphide employed as a rodenticide.
- Alpha chloralose, which under certain circumstances may be used against rodents and, under licence, against specified bird species.
- Permits are required for the purchase of strychnine to kill moles. These are issued by Agriculture Departments. The use of strychnine is controlled under the Control of Pesticides Regulations 1986.

4.4.4   Agriculture Department powers and enforcement action

Under the Food and Environment Protection Act 1985 Ministers may authorise enforcement officers (in Scotland the authorised enforcement officers are SOAEFD agriculture staff in area and head offices). MAFF and WOAD have provided these powers to their statutory wildlife advisers. This is to assist them in their role of carrying out investigations into cases of suspected poisoning of animals. As a matter of policy only specialist investigation officers will conduct interviews required to be carried out in accordance with the provisions of the Police and Criminal Evidence Act 1984.

Enforcement powers are detailed in Part III, section 19 (as amended), and Schedule 2 of the Act.

The main relevant provisions are summarised as follows.

An authorised person may enter any land, vehicle, vessel, aircraft, hovercraft or marine structure if he has reasonable grounds to believe:

- that any pesticide is being or has been applied to or stored on it; or
- that it is necessary for him to enter for any of the general purposes of this Part of this Act.

For any of these purposes an authorised person may require any person to give him information relating to pesticides.

Under Schedule 2 an officer may take with him:

- any other person; and
- any equipment or materials to assist in the investigation.

The officer may:

- open any containers;
- carry out searches and tests;
- take samples;
- require the production of documents and records;
- photograph certain things.

An officer shall be provided with a certificate of authority which he is required to produce, on request. Also if requested, he must state:

- his name;
- the function he proposes to perform;
- his grounds for proposing to perform it.

In most circumstances an officer must perform his functions under this Act at a reasonable hour. Powers of entry permit access to buildings, stores or other structures but do not allow entry into dwellings.

An officer may use reasonable force, if necessary, in the performance of his functions and shall not be liable for anything done within these functions if the court is satisfied that the act was done in good faith and that there were reasonable grounds for doing it.

Offences include:

- intentionally obstructing an officer;
- failure to comply with a requirement made by an officer;
- making a false or reckless statement; and
- intentionally failing to disclose any material particular.

4.4.5 Enforcement action

When, following the field enquiry, a case has been referred for enforcement action investigation officers will collect further evidence, take statements and interview suspects. The Agriculture Departments have their own legal departments which will undertake prosecutions, although the police and other agencies such as the RSPCA may also take cases involving pesticide-related offences.

The courts have the power to impose heavy fines and costs in relation to such offences.

4.4.6 The role of the police and other agencies

The wildlife adviser investigating a suspected offence may request the assistance of the police to accompany him during a visit to a suspect. The primary purpose of the police presence in such circumstances is to prevent a breach of the peace. Where powers under the Food and Environment Protection Act 1985 are being employed, the police are not sanctioned to exercise any enforcement powers under the Act and the visit is not intended to be used to secure evidence on non-pesticide offences such as illegal traps or poaching.

In Scotland it is increasingly common for SOAEFD investigations staff and police wildlife liaison officers to carry out joint enquiries. A warrant under the WCA will often be obtained to provide police powers of search, and that warrant will cater for the presence of SOAEFD staff. In such cases as these officials provide specialist advice but police will probably prepare subsequent reports for the Procurator Fiscal, including any charges under the Food and Environment Protection Act.

Advisers may take any other person with them to assist with their enquiries. In all cases it is essential that the respective roles of those involved are clarified and established prior to visits being made so that the successful outcome of an investigation is not prejudiced by a failure to comply with legal requirements.

There may be cases which are fully investigated by the police, rather than by Agriculture Departments, where any charges would be brought by the Crown Prosecution Service.

4.4.7 The Wildlife Incident Investigation Scheme (WIIS)

The scheme involves a number of operational groups working within the Agriculture Departments. The Pesticide Safety Directorate (PSD) of MAFF has overall responsibility for the running of the scheme and is also responsible for the evaluation and processing of applications for pesticide approvals. Post-approval monitoring of pesticide use is an important aspect, and the WIIS is part of this.

When an incident which meets the necessary criteria has been accepted for investigation, a wildlife adviser will make a visit to the site involved in order to gather information and secure evidence such as carcasses or suspected baits. This field enquiry will assist in identifying the source or cause of the problem and may be used in enforcement action.

Carcasses are initially forwarded to the appropriate Veterinary Investigation Centre (VIC) (or the Scottish Agricultural Science Agency, SASA, in Scotland) for post-mortem examination. This may identify the cause of death as something other than pesticides, for example, disease, trauma or starvation. If no alternative cause is found then tissue samples and other material are usually submitted for pesticide analysis.

These samples are forwarded to the Wildlife Incident Unit (WIU) at the Central Science Laboratory (CSL) where they are screened for residues of pesticides. The field information is often an important consideration in the decision on which compounds to test for. Suspected poisonous baits and samples or materials which have been seized are also sent direct to the WIU.

The subsequent results may then be used in enforcement action, or they can influence changes to the approval status of an individual pesticide.

4.4.8 Incident reports

The initial report of an incident may originate from a wide range of sources. These include members of the public who discover casualties or suspected baits whilst out walking, pet owners who have suffered an unexpected, suspicious loss of a dog or cat, or gamekeepers and farmers.

Those working in rural environments such as park rangers or countryside wardens may come across suspected pesticide incidents, and conservation or wildlife agencies, including police wildlife liaison officers, RSPCA inspectors and the RSPB can also be the first point of contact.

Agriculture Departments may receive reports either as a result of direct contact being made with advisers or via the freephone number (0800 321 600), which has been widely publicised as a means of reporting incidents where illegal poisoning is suspected.

4.4.9 Action to take

When a report is received either by Agriculture Departments direct or via another agency the following action should be taken.

- Establish the precise nature and location of the incident and contact details for the person reporting it.
- Any carcasses or suspected baits should be identified and their position marked on a map to ensure that they can be found subsequently.
- Where possible, these should be left in position but covered if it is considered that they may pose a risk to other animals or might be removed to eliminate the evidence.

- Individuals should be discouraged from handling or disturbing carcasses or baits, as there may be a risk of pesticide poisoning through contamination and such action might compromise their value as evidence.

4.4.10 Field enquiries

On visiting the scene advisers will seek to obtain as much information as possible that is relevant to the case. The following action should be taken.

- Individuals who discovered the incident, land-owners and others who may be able to assist with the enquiry should be contacted and information sought from them.
- A search of the area should be made and where appropriate, a photographic record obtained or sketch map of the site produced. Notes should be made to assist in producing an incident report.
- In some cases it may be appropriate to make an inspection of outbuildings, stores, vehicles or other sites not within the immediate incident area. These searches are made where there is the suspicion that pesticides or other materials implicated in the incident might be being kept.
- Any carcasses, samples or suspected baits should be collected and individually packaged and labelled. These are then forwarded as appropriate, ensuring continuity of evidence.

Poisoned sparrowhawk at pigeon bait

On the completion of field enquiries and pesticide analysis, reports are sent to the Pesticide Safety Directorate where further action is considered. This could involve prosecution or the issuing of warning or advisory letters. The person who reported the incident is usually informed of the results of the post-mortem examination and any pesticide analysis.

The flow chart on the next page describes the investigation procedure.

4.4.11 Publicity and awareness

Since 1991 Agriculture Departments have been actively promoting a Campaign Against Illegal Poisoning. This involves a number of interested parties, including the DETR, nature conservation organisations, the RSPB, the RSPCA and veterinary surgeons. Shooting and farming interests are represented, as are the police.

The campaign seeks to highlight the dangers and unacceptability of illegal poisoning, and encourages the public and others to report the discovery of suspected incidents. Legal pest control methods are explained and the public are requested not to interfere with these activities.

The campaign is promoted through literature produced by MAFF, SOAEFD and the DETR, videos, and exhibits used to target important areas where the message has the greatest impact. Talks and lectures are provided to organisations who may have an interest in the countryside and animals.

4.4.12 Problem pesticide groups

There are a number of pesticide types which regularly figure in incidents and the following is a summary of the main groups.

Insecticides are applied to crops in dilute formulations, but are extremely toxic when used on illegal baits as concentrates. The main types abused are usually organophosphorous or carbonate compounds.

Investigation Procedures

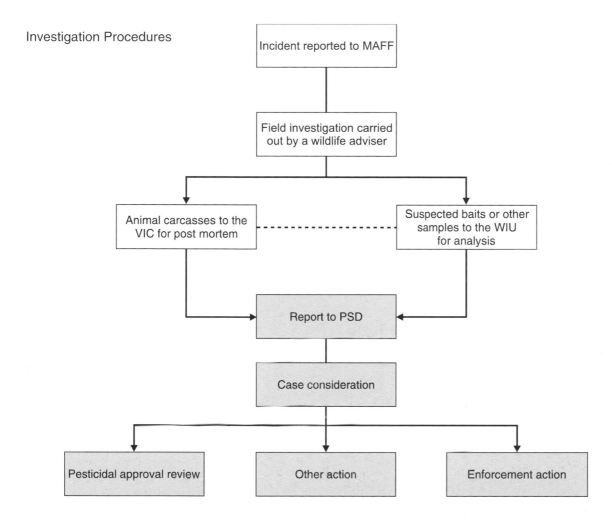

Other pesticides include:

- alpha-chloralose – a stupefying poison legally used for the control of mice and, under licence, certain pest species of birds.
- metaldehyde – a compound used in baits formulated for the control of slugs.
- rodenticides – virtually all cases involve anti-coagulant compounds which are widely used in the legal control of rats and mice.
- herbicides – most incidents in this category involve paraquat used in the control of weeds and other vegetation.
- Strychnine – this extremely toxic material can only be legally used on worm baits placed underground for the control of moles. The nature of the compound lends itself to abuse in baits.

- Fumigants – various formulations based on cyanide and phosphine are approved for the control of rabbits, rats and moles. Use against badgers and foxes is illegal.

4.4.13 Investigations

What to look for:

- carcasses which have been slit open and pegged down or tied to a tree or fence post (often rabbit, pigeon, other birds or casualty lambs), or pieces of chicken, other meat or fish dosed with powder, granules or liquid. They may have been injected with pesticides;
- dead birds of prey and/or corvids, either singly or a number beside a bait;

- hens' eggs are also injected and may be found in suspicious locations. Warning marks or coloration at the injection site can provide useful clues;

- pesticides may be mixed with proprietary animal foods such as cat or dog meat. Although close inspection may reveal the presence of granules or unusual discoloration, this is not always the case;

- other food which may attract target animals, including bread and grain, is also used;

- there is also the possibility that formulated pesticides might be deliberately or carelessly left in situations where animals can gain access. Treated grain, cereal-based pellets and rodenticide baits may be discovered.

Where there are suspicions that pesticides are being stored for illegal purposes, advisers may decide that searches of premises (excluding dwellings) should be made using their powers under the Food and Environment Protection Act.

Advisers will be looking for pesticides in containers such as flasks, bottles, bags or packages. These can be either in a properly labelled container or may have been decanted and stored unmarked. It is an offence to store a product other than in its original container or which no longer has approval under the COPR, and such a discovery could lead to enforcement action.

Suspicious materials may be seized by consultants and sent for pesticide analysis to the WIU.

4.4.14 Safety considerations

There are significant potential health risks to individuals who handle poisoned baits, contaminated carcasses and pesticides. These are increased by the fact that often the compound has not been identified and there may be a heavy concentration of pesticide involved.

Poisoning by pesticides can occur from ingestion or inhalation, through eye contamination or as a result of being absorbed through the skin. In addition to being toxic, chemicals may be irritant or corrosive.

Particular dangers are posed by gassing compounds. These react on contact with moisture and liberate toxic cyanide or phosphine gases. This has implications for the investigation of the suspected gassing of badger setts and fox earths. Such cases must only be dealt with by staff who are properly trained and equipped. Due to the hazards involved such materials are not removed or retained for analysis, but gas detection equipment may be used to obtain evidence.

Accordingly, it is important that adequate precautions are taken to minimise risks during the handling, transport and storage of toxic materials. The advice is that wherever possible this handling is left to advisers who are trained and equipped to deal with this aspect. Suitable protective clothing such as chemical-resistant gloves, coveralls and eye shields are used, and appropriate action taken with regard to packaging the evidence that is discovered. The matter of continuity of evidence is also a consideration.

Carcasses are placed in strong, liquid-proof bags, whilst suspected baits and containers of chemicals are usually initially bagged and all samples put into boxes to minimise the risks of spillage or leakage. Chemical-absorbent materials may be employed as a further precaution.

native plants

5.1 PLANTS SUBJECT TO PROTECTION

5.1.1 The general law

Schedule 8 of the Wildlife and Countryside Act 1981 (WCA) lists the wild plants that are protected, and Schedule 9 lists the plants that should not be planted or otherwise caused to grow in the wild.

These lists are the subject of quinquennial review by the Joint Nature Conservation Committee (JNCC). The results of the third review are expected in the spring of 1997. Details of the revisions may be obtained from English Nature (EN), Scottish Natural Heritage (SNH), the Countryside Council for Wales (CCW), or from the county ecologist.

For the European protected species of plants, see Schedule 4 of the Conservation (Natural Habitats, &c.) Regulations 1994. The species covered are also listed in Appendix A.

A growing plant is the legal property of someone, and thus is subject to the ordinary laws of property as well as to the special conservation laws. Some trees are subjects of Tree Preservation Orders.

The established law is that plants belong to the owner of the soil in which they stand. The legal consequence is that any unauthorised interference with a plant will amount to a civil wrong in common law. Therefore it may be that any deliberate or negligent harm caused to wild plants, if performed whilst being a trespasser, could give rise to a liability. It could follow that anyone picking wild flowers or even causing damage by walking on vegetation could face a civil action at the instance of the owner of the plants affected (Reid, C, *Nature Conservation Law*, 1994).

A major problem is that plants are not generally recognised as having any monetary value, and so a claimant may be unable to demonstrate that any loss has been suffered.

5.1.2 Powers of arrest

Cultivated plants, including shrubs and trees, that have been planted in a conservation habitat as part of the management plan are private property. They are protected by the general criminal law, and the execution of a power of arrest for theft or criminal damage may be appropriate. There is no power to detain or arrest for an offence of committing a Potentially Damaging Operation under Part II of the WCA, for which EN would initiate summary proceedings. In Scotland, SNH would report any apparent offences to the Procurator Fiscal, who would then decide whether a prosecution should take place. For all other offences discussed in this chapter, the general power of arrest under section 25 of the Police and Criminal Act 1984 is available in England and Wales. In Scotland, an individual suspected of committing an offence can be arrested under section 13 of the Criminal Procedure (Scotland) Act 1995.

5.1.3 Theft

A person who picks flowers, fruit or foliage from a plant growing wild, or who picks any fungus growing wild, does not steal them unless he does so for reward or for sale or for some other commercial purpose (section 4(3) of the Theft Act 1968). A theft charge is possible only if there is a commercial motive or if an entire plant is uprooted and taken, as opposed to merely parts of the plant being removed. In Scotland the common law crime of theft may apply.

A gypsy who cuts 'lucky' heather flowers for sale, could be liable to prosecution as follows:

- theft for commercial gain (section 4(3) of the Theft Act 1968); or

- not being an authorised person, intentionally uprooting a wild plant (section 13(1)(b) of the WCA).

5.1.4 Criminal damage

No offence is committed if the only property affected is any fungus growing wild or the flowers, fruit or foliage of a plant growing wild.

An offence of criminal damage may exist where a car has been dumped and set on fire, or where controlled waste has been dumped without authority, at a location where saplings or plant seeds have been planted as part of the management and habitat creation or maintenance of the site, and they have been destroyed by fire or poisoning. The management plan may give evidence of when the work was undertaken, and records from land agents or managers may provide the costs of the purchase of the seedlings, whips or seeds. Also there may be records of the length of time taken to sow the site. Therefore such a charge may be framed as there is a proper assessment of damage, and the plants were property as they had been purchased as seed or as immature plants.

The uprooting of a plant or its total destruction may give rise to prosecution, but lesser damage cannot (section 10(1) of the Criminal Damage Act 1971). In Scotland, damage to plants, flowers etc on someone's property could amount to the statutory offence of vandalism (Criminal Law (Consolidation)(Scotland) Act 1995, section 52) or the common law crime of malicious mischief. Each case would be judged on its merits by the Procurator Fiscal.

5.1.5   Wildlife and Countryside Act 1981 (WCA)

The statutory measures relating to wild plants mirror those for wild animals, with a general level of protection which is enhanced for certain species, whilst allowing for pest control and measures against the spread of disease. Under section 13(4) of the WCA 1981 the plant in question will be presumed to be wild unless the contrary is shown.

Two practical problems arise in an investigation of wild plant crime: those of species identification, and the fact that plants hybridise easily. Expert advice must be obtained. The current national reference book for the names of flora is the *New Flora of the British Isles* by Colin Stace, published by Cambridge University Press in 1991.

Section 27 (1) of the WCA provides the relevant definitions, as follows.

Authorised person – the owner or occupier, or any person authorised by the owner or occupier, of the land on which the action authorised is taken; or any person authorised in writing by the local authority for the area within which the action authorised is taken.

The authorisation of any person for the purposes of this definition shall not however, confer any right of entry upon any land.

Pick – in relation to a plant, means gather or pluck any part of the plant without uprooting it.

Sale – includes hire, barter and exchange, and cognate expressions shall be construed accordingly.

Uproot – in relation to a plant, means dig up or otherwise remove the plant from the land on which it is growing.

Vehicle – includes aircraft, hovercraft and boat.

Wild plant – any plant which is or (before it was picked, uprooted or destroyed) was growing wild and is of a kind which ordinarily grows in Great Britain in a wild state.

5.1.6   Protection of plants

> **Wildlife and Countryside Act 1981**
>
> **Section 13(1)(a)**
>
> It is an offence for any person to **intentionally pick, uproot or destroy** any wild plant on Schedule 8

Schedule 8 plants are those that are very rare or in danger of becoming extinct. Unfortunately there are collectors who will dig up these plants for their own gardens.

The 1994 Conservation Regulations make it an offence to cut or collect certain European species (see 5.1.1).

Wildlife and Countryside Act 1981

Section 13(1)(b)

It is an offence for any unauthorised person to
intentionally uproot any
wild plant

NOTE: Section 13(1)(b) of the WCA makes it illegal for an **unauthorised** person to uproot **any** plant whatsoever. (Compare this with offences of theft of or criminal damage to wild plants.)

EXAMPLES: A person picking a monkey orchid would commit an offence under section 13(1)(a) because the plant is on Schedule 8. A person who digs up bluebells to plant in their garden would commit an offence under section 13(1)(b), though they would **not** commit an offence if they were merely picking the bluebells as these plants are not on Schedule 8.

It is **not** an offence to pick, uproot or destroy a plant on Schedule 8 if this act was an incidental result of a lawful operation and could not **reasonably** have been avoided.

Wildlife and Countryside Act 1981

Section 13(2)(a)

It is an offence for any person to
sell, offer or expose for sale
or possess or transport for the purpose of sale
any live or dead wild plant
(or any part of or anything derived
from such a plant)
on Schedule 8

In any proceedings for an offence under subsection (2)(a) the plant in question shall be presumed to be a wild plant unless the contrary is shown.

Wildlife and Countryside Act 1981

Section 13(2)(b)

It is an offence for any person to publish or cause to be published any advertisement likely to be understood to convey that he
buy, sells or intends to buy or sell
any plant on Schedule 8
or any part of or anything derived from such a plant

NOTE: There is a trade in protected plants. The offences under section 13 have been introduced to try and prevent endangered plants from being wiped out by selfish collectors.

It is vitally important to obtain the assistance of an expert if ever you investigate possible offences relating to plants.

5.1.7 Introducing non-native species

When non-native species are introduced, whether accidentally or deliberately, they may threaten the native flora by competition for the same resources, and section 14(2) provides legislation concerning 'introductions'. Expert advice is required to investigate such an offence, and a person may commit an offence of intentionally obstructing a person who has been authorised by the Secretary of State to enter land to ascertain if an offence has been committed. Part II of Schedule 9 lists the plants concerned.

Wildlife and Countryside Act 1981

Section 14(2)

It is an offence for a person to
plant or otherwise cause to grow
in the **wild** any plant on Schedule 9 (Part 2)

NOTE: This offence is similar to the one relating to animals (section 14(1), though it applies only to plants on the list and not the non-native plants generally. The latter would be impossible as virtually every garden in the country is stocked with mainly non-native plants.

DEFENCE: It is a defence to a charge of committing offences under section 14 for a person to prove that he took all reasonable steps and exercised all due diligence to avoid committing the offence.

Wildlife and Countryside Act 1981

Section 18(1)

If any person
attempts to commit
an offence under sections 13 or 14, or for the purposes of committing such an offence,
has in his possession
anything capable of being used for committing the offence, he shall be guilty of an offence and may be punished as if he had committed the full offence

---

Section 19 contains powers for police officers to stop and search, seize and detain evidence, enter any land other than a dwelling house, and for a justice of the peace to grant a search warrant if satisfied by information on oath that there are reasonable grounds for suspecting that an offence under sections 13 or 14 has been committed.

Section 20 applies to any offence under section 13(1) involving the picking, uprooting or destruction of any wild plant, in that summary proceedings for an offence to which this section applies may be brought within a period of six months from the date on which evidence sufficient in the opinion of the prosecution to warrant the proceedings came to their knowledge.

Section 21(5) applies where an offence was committed in respect of more than one plant or other thing, in which case the maximum fine which may be imposed shall be determined as if the person convicted had been convicted of a separate offence in respect of each plant or thing.

The court by which any person is convicted of an offence shall order the forfeiture of any plant or other thing in respect of which the offence was committed; and may order the forfeiture of any vehicle, weapon or other thing which was used to commit the offence, and in the case of an offence under section 14, any animal or plant which is of the same kind as that in respect of which the offence was committed and was found in his possession.

habitat protection

6.1 INTRODUCTION

By itself, the criminal law protecting individual creatures can never secure their survival. Without suitable habitat offering food and shelter, no animal or plant can survive, and it is the loss of habitat which poses the greatest threat to most species today. If the law is going to seek the conservation of wildlife, it must ensure the continued existence of the range and expanse of habitat necessary for this (Reid 1994). Britain's 'natural' countryside is in fact the product of centuries of man's involvement with the land and its management.

As may be noted from the breadth of international conventions, governments are acknowledging that species in one country may depend on the resources in another, and that the viability of populations may depend on contacts with individuals on the other side of international frontiers, continents and hemispheres.

6.1.1 Definitions

Habitat – the natural home of an animal or plant. Examples of habitats include seashore, deciduous and coniferous woodland, chalk grassland, mountain, moorland, heathland, and wetlands such as lakes, rivers and water meadows.

Flora – the total vegetation assemblage that inhabits an area.

Fauna – the total animal population that inhabits an area.

6.1.2 The current levels of habitat protection

A wildlife officer should seek to know which habitats in his area have received any form of habitat designation.

There are over 80 types of statutory and non-statutory wildlife sites in the UK. Some, such as National Nature Reserves (NNRs) and Sites of Special Scientific Interest (SSSIs) are designated under Acts of Parliament. Then there are wildlife sites designated under international conventions or directives such as

Ramsar sites, special protection areas (SPAs) and special areas of conservation (SACs). These international sites are first notified by SSSI, as are NNRs. Other sites are selected by local authorities as either Local Nature Reserves (LNRs) or Sites of Importance for Nature Conservation (SINCs). Many other titles are given to non-statutory sites by local authorities, and their quality varies across the country.

6.2 STATUTORY DESIGNATIONS

National Nature Reserves (NNRs)

In NNRs the land is primarily dedicated to the interests of nature conservation, and much of the valuable habitat in Britain is provided by land which is used for other purposes, and can continue to be so used without damaging its value for wildlife.

NNRs are a suite of areas of high national or international importance for nature conservation, managed as nature reserves and formally declared as such by English Nature (EN), the Countryside Council for Wales (CCW) or Scottish Natural Heritage (SNH) under section 19 of the National Parks and Access to the Countryside Act 1949 and section 35 of the Wildlife and Countryside Act 1981 (WCA). Management is carried out in specific agreed ways by EN, the CCW and SNH as the owners or lessees of the land, or by agreement with EN, the CCW or SNH. Byelaws may be applied to NNRs. The criteria for selection of NNRs are primarily on biological/geological grounds.

Sites of Special Scientific Interest (SSSIs)

SSSIs were first introduced in 1949, with the objective of identifying sites of particular value to nature conservation, intended to represent the range of British ecosystems. Under section 28 of the 1981 Act, the Country Conservation Agencies have a duty to notify a site to be of special interest by reason of its flora, fauna, or geological or physiographical features.

Whilst the 1949 Act established SSSIs and required the then Nature Conservancy to notify local authorities, it was not until the WCA that owners and occupiers of such land were informed formally of the special nature of their property. Under this Act, the former Nature Conservancy Council (NCC) had to backtrack on all sites identified since 1949 and 'notify' them to owners and occupiers. The notification of SSSIs is also registered with the Land Registry as a local land charge. Thus when property changes hands, such notifications become known through legal searches.

A formal process of notifying SSSIs is prescribed in the 1981 Act and amended later under the Wildlife and Countryside (Amendment) Act 1985. A survey and assessment of biological sites of national and international importance was published on behalf of the former NCC and the Natural Environment Research Council in 1977. The review describes the main habitat types in Britain and sets out the criteria in selecting the 'key' sites listed. These sites are known as NCR sites. Since its publication, the former NCC and now the Joint Nature Conservation Committee (JNCC) have identified additional important sites and have added them to the list of NCR sites. NCR sites are identified as meeting certain criteria, and therefore of meeting the standard required of SSSIs.

Included in this process is the identification by the NCC/JNCC of any operation likely to damage the special interest. Such operations are listed as part of the package to owners and occupiers. Maps and details of the special interest are also included in the package.

Once a site is notified, owners and occupiers are required to give the NCC/JNCC written notice of their intention to carry out a listed operation. Failure to do so, or to obtain written consent, may lead to a prosecution. Once notified to local planning authorities, SSSIs and NNRs receive a degree of protection from development pressures, but national public interest may override that of wildlife. International sites, particularly SPAs and SACs which together form the Natura 2000 series, receive greater protection from development.

About 40 per cent are owned or managed by public bodies, such as Forestry Enterprise, Ministry of Defence and Crown Estate Commissioners, or by voluntary conservation bodies such as county wildlife

trusts and the RSPB. As at 31 March 1996, EN had designated in England 3,874 SSSIs covering a total of 920,696 hectares, and 913 sites in Wales covering a total of 216,647 hectares. In Scotland, 1,398 SSSIs covering an area of 892,840 hectares had been designated up to 31 March 1996.

Local Nature Reserves (LNRs)

LNRs are usually established, with the concurrence of EN, the CCW or SNH, on a suite of areas of local importance, in like manner to NNRs (although the approved body element is not applicable). Byelaws can be applied to LNRs. The criteria for the selection of LNRs are scientific in basis but are augmented to include wider issues such as education and public usage. They also contribute to the overall diversity of wildlife in Great Britain, providing stepping stones or wildlife corridors by linking with designated sites.

Ramsar wetland sites

In 1976 the UK Government ratified the Convention on Wetlands of International Importance, especially as Waterfowl Habitat – commonly referred to as the Ramsar Convention after its place of adoption at Ramsar, Iran, in 1971. The objectives are to stem the progressive encroachment on, and loss of, wetlands now and in the future, and to promote their wise use.

A wetland is defined as being an area of marsh, fen, peatland or water, whether natural or artificial, permanent or temporary, with water that is static or flowing, fresh, brackish or salt. This includes areas of marine water the depth of which at low tide does not exceed six metres.

The general criteria for using plants to identify wetlands of international importance are if:

- it supports an appreciable assemblage of rare, vulnerable or endangered species or subspecies of plant or an appreciable number of individuals of any one or more of these species;

- it is of special value for maintaining the genetic and ecological diversity of a region because of the quality and peculiarities of its flora;

- it is of special value as the habitat of plants at a critical stage of their biological cycles; or
- it is of special value for its endemic plant species or communities.

Special Areas of Conservation (SACs)

SACs were created under the Council Directive on the Conservation of Natural Habitats and Wild Fauna and Flora (92/43/EEC), adopted by member states of the European Union (EU) in May 1992. Like most EU legislation, the Directive is intended to provide a common standard across the EU, and gives a series of measures for nature conservation set out in 24 articles.

Under the Directive, the member states agree to establish a series of protected sites that are selected for their importance as natural habitat types and as habitats of the species listed in Annexes I and II, for habitats and species of 'Community interest', which, when designated, will be called Special Areas of Conservation.

Measures under the Directive include:

- protection of the designated sites;
- conservation of features in the landscape which are important for wildlife;
- the protection of listed species from damage, destruction or over-exploitation, and surveillance or monitoring of species and habitats.

The Directive is technically complex and, when designated, the SACs, along with the Special Protection Areas (SPAs) of the Birds Directive, will form a single pan-European 'Natura 2000' site series.

Implementation of the Directive in the UK was through the Conservation (Natural Habitats, &c.) Regulations 1994.

The Regulations are in part exercised through the existing provisions of Part I of the WCA, therefore any offences involving a European protected species of plant would be covered under current domestic legislation.

References in these Regulations to a 'European protected species' of plant are to any of those species of plants whose natural range includes any area in Great Britain and are listed in Schedule 4 to the Regulations.

Special Protection Areas (SPAs)

The UK is bound by the EU's Council Directive of 2 April 1979 (79/409/EEC) on the Conservation of Wild Birds. Under the Directive, EU member states are required to take special measures to protect the habitat of certain rare or vulnerable birds and also regularly-occurring migratory birds. These measures include the designation of Special Protection Areas. Member states are required to take appropriate steps to avoid pollution or deterioration of the habitat and disturbance to the birds.

Limestone Pavement Orders (LPOs)

LPOs are designated priority habitats under the Conservation (Natural Habitats, &c.) Regulations 1994. LPOs are the responsibility of local authorities working in conjunction with the Country Agencies.

Special provision is made for the protection of areas of limestone pavement, ie areas of limestone wholly or partly exposed on the surface of the ground and fissured by natural erosion (section 34(6) of the WCA). Such areas are of considerable botanical and geological value.

The Act refers to 'the removal of the limestone *or by its disturbance in any way*' where the character or appearance of any such designated land would be adversely affected, and if any person without reasonable excuse removes or disturbs limestone on or in any land designated by a Limestone Pavement Order he shall be liable:

- on summary conviction, to a fine not exceeding the statutory maximum; or
- on conviction on indictment, to a fine (section 34(4) of the WCA).

A reasonable excuse would be provided by the grant of planning permission to extract significant amounts of limestone, and the protection offered is in relation to operations which are incidental to other activities or which fall outside the scope of planning control. The limestone is much sought-after for use in gardens, and visitors may be tempted to remove pieces.

6.3   NON-STATUTORY DESIGNATIONS

6.3.1   County or regional Sites of Important Nature Conservation (SINCs)

These sites are identified on account of their flora and fauna which are of county or regional wildlife value, and are shown on local planning maps, to protect them from development which could destroy or adversely affect their nature conservation value. The selection is made by professional ecologists representing organisations such as county councils, wildlife trusts, farming and wildlife advisory groups.

6.3.2   Ancient woodland

Ancient woodland is that which has had a continuous woodland cover since at least 1600 AD and has only been cleared for underwood or timber production. They are important as many form surviving fragments of primeval forests, the climax vegetation of this country, and they have had a long time to acquire species and to form stable floral and faunal communities. Local planning departments retain maps of such sites.

6.3.3   Biogenetic Reserves

This is a Council of Europe project to list nature reserves containing typical, unique, rare or endangered ecosystems or species. Member states proposing areas for the network agree to protect them and to maintain their natural values. Predating the Bern Convention, the network does not have legal status.

6.4   NATIONAL LEGISLATION

National Parks and Access to the Countryside Act 1949

The Act established powers to declare NNRs; to notify SSSIs, and for local authorities to establish LNRs.

Wildlife and Countryside Act 1981 (WCA)

The Act consolidated and extended powers for protection of birds, animals and plants with functions in relation to licensing, scheduling of species, giving advice, enforcement, etc; notification of SSSIs; special protection of nationally important sites; establishment of Marine Nature Reserves; and powers for police to stop, search and obtain search warrants. In addition to describing the process of notifying SSSIs, the CCW and EN have the power to prosecute for habitat offences under sections 28 and 29 of the WCA. Section 29 also provides for the application to the Secretary of State for Nature Conservation Orders which provide additional protection for SSSIs of national importance.

Environmental Protection Act 1990

The Act abolished the NCC, and established the Nature Conservancy Council for England (English Nature), the CCW and the Nature Conservancy Council for Scotland (Scottish Natural Heritage), with the discharge of Great Britain's functions through the JNCC.

6.5   COMMUNITY DIRECTIVES AND INTERNATIONAL CONVENTIONS

Convention on the Conservation of European Wildlife and Natural Habitats (Bern Convention) – Seeks to conserve wild flora and fauna in their natural habitats, particularly endangered species, especially when conservation requires the co-operation of several states.

EC Council Directive on the Conservation of Natural Habitats and of Wild Fauna and Flora (the Habitats Directive) – Contributes to the conservation of biodiversity by requiring member states to take measures to maintain or restore natural habitats and wild species at a favourable conservation status, giving effect to both site and species protection objectives.

Convention on Wetlands of International Importance Especially as Waterfowl Habitat (Ramsar Convention) – Aims to stem the progressive encroachment on, and loss of, wetlands.

6.6 SECURING THE EVIDENCE

An officer investigating an apparent offence involving a habitat should emphasise, in statements from owners or wardens, the management aims for the site. Some land is of more value – by being of scientific, geological or aesthetic importance, rather than of agricultural value. Such important sites have over the years received protection from piecemeal Government legislation, and the sites are often referred to by the status that such protection grants, ie an SSSI or LNR.

Owners, land agents and managers of protected habitat may possess carefully researched and written management plans or site management statements, and these will often clearly state the aims of the site. These plans are frequently an excellent source of historical and scientific reference, and will include species lists that may aid the identification of remains, such as discarded stems, leaves, seed heads and flowers.

Other sources of evidence to substantiate that a habitat contained a protected plant that may have been picked, uprooted or damaged may be;

- site monitoring fixed-point photographs;

- video footage; and

- scientific reports from local field studies centres, ecology units and natural history societies.

Other evidence that could be of use in a prosecution would include:

- photographs of the site of the damage or theft, with a scale, and of the immediately surrounding habitat;

- historical evidence from past and current management plans that time and money are or were invested in the creation or maintenance of the habitat for the flora concerned, and the values involved;

- details/records when last observed in situ;

- explanation of level of protection to site – LNR, NNR, SSSI etc; and

- expert witness as to the probability and time-scales to repair or replace stolen or damaged species or habitat.

Note should be taken that a site may have different designations of protection, and the assumption should not be made that each designation shares the identical boundary as another designation on the same site. The site plan must be studied to ensure that the correct designation is applied to the location of the alleged offence (Ramsar, SPA, SAC and NNR sites follow SSSI boundaries).

6.6.1 Where may advice be obtained?

In the first place, advice should be sought from the on-site ranger, warden or owner, or any of their appointed staff. That person will provide most of the information that you require, including the level of protection designated for the site. A land agent or farm manager will also be in a position to assist. The problem is to assess the damage or impact of the event under investigation.

The Nature Conservancy Council for England operates under the name English Nature, and is responsible for providing advice to Government on wildlife conservation in England. Under section 24(4) of the WCA, EN has the power to advise and assist any constable in the enforcement of Part II of the Act. Its staff will provide advice on a wide range of topics including fly-tipping, travellers, and damage by burning dumped cars.

The national office of EN is at Northminster House, Peterborough PE1 1UA. Telephone 01733 340345. They operate 21 local offices across the country. Each local team is responsible for one or more counties in England. Each county has a conservation officer who can provide detailed information about special sites within that county. Most local offices have specialist information, especially on bats and badgers and other species protected under law. Local teams also have site managers who are responsible for the management of NNRs. EN produces a number of free quarterly publications, notably *English Nature, Sitelines* (a magazine for those involved with SSSIs). The booklet *What you should know about SSSIs* is also useful, and information on international sites is also available. The site safeguard officer is based in Peterborough and has overall responsibility for the protection of SSSIs in England.

Similar advice and assistance can be obtained from:
Scottish Natural Heritage (SNH)
Headquarters
12 Hope Terrace
Edinburgh EH9 2AS
Tel : 0131 447 4784

Countryside Council for Wales (CCW)
Headquarters
Plas Penrhos
Ffordd Penrhos
Bangor
Gwynedd LL57 2LQ
Tel: 01248 370444

Other reserves of protected habitat may be privately owned by organisations such as county wildlife trusts, which maybe contacted through the:
UK National Office of Wildlife Trusts
The Green
Witham Park
Waterside South
Lincoln LN5 7RJ
Tel: 01522 544400
Fax: 01522 511616

The Royal Society for the Protection of Birds (RSPB) is also a source of information.

An excellent source of information can be found in county council planning departments, as many counties now employ a county ecologist who maintains close links with all the statutory and voluntary bodies within the county. If one is not specifically employed, then often one or more of the planning officers will have an ecological responsibility to the county.

In 1994 the DoE issued *Planning Policy Guidance: Nature Conservation* (PPG9). This sets out the role of local planning authorities in protecting wildlife. All local plans should contain policies to safeguard rare or protected species and habitats, and the planning authorities play an important role in conservation.

At local authority level, assistance may be found from the parks and leisure department, where an officer with ecological or horticultural knowledge will be able to give advice on the status, management aims and initiatives in open public spaces, and the value of damaged trees and park furniture. Park staff can be sources of information regarding wildlife in the vicinity of the park, and are often competent at plant recognition. The Tree Preservation Order (TPO) officer may usually be contacted in the planning department (see TPOs in 6.8).

The Field Studies Council has regional field study centres, where botanists with experience of the area are available to provide assistance with plant identification. Further details may be obtained through:
The Field Studies Council
Preston Montford
Montford Bridge
Shrewsbury
Shropshire SY4 1HW
Tel: 01743 850674

6.6.2   Who should deal with offences?

EN and the CCW may initiate summary proceedings for offences under Part II of the WCA. In Scotland, SNH would report Part II offences to the Procurator Fiscal. The Country Conservation Agencies may seek the assistance of the police when an officer is called to or witness a breach in wildlife legislation, including a **Potentially Damaging Operation** – see list below (EN usually employs a Treasury Solicitor investigating officer to interview witnesses and obtain statements under caution for offences under Part II of the Act, in that he endeavours to seek the identity of the person involved, and obtain a statement under caution). The officer has no power to detain the person unless a criminal offence is established, or he fears a breach of the peace (also see 5.1.2). In Scotland, SNH would report offences to the Procurator Fiscal.

The following is a list of the more general Potentially Damaging Operations (PDOs).

- Cultivation, including ploughing, rotovating, harrowing and re-seeding.
- Grazing and changes in the grazing regime (including type of stock or intensity, or seasonal pattern of grazing and cessation of grazing).
- Stock feeding.
- Mowing or other methods of cutting vegetation.
- Application of manure, fertilisers and lime.
- Application of pesticides, including herbicides (weedkillers).
- Dumping, spreading or discharge of any materials.
- Burning.
- The release into the site of any wild, feral or domestic animal, plant or seed.
- The killing or removal of any wild animal, including pest control ('animal' includes ant, mammal, reptile, amphibian, bird, fish or invertebrate).
- The destruction, displacement, removal or cutting of any plant or plant remains (including tree, shrub, herb, hedge, dead or decaying wood, moss, lichen, fungus, leaf mould, turf).

- Tree and/or woodland management (including afforestation, planting, clear and selective felling, thinning, coppicing, modification of the stand or underwood, changes in species composition, cessation of management).
- Drainage (including the use of mole, tile, tunnel or other artificial drains).
- Modification of the structure of water courses (for example, rivers, streams, springs, ditches, drains), including their banks and beds, as by realignment, regrading and dredging.
- The changing of water levels and tables and water utilisation (including irrigation, storage and abstraction from existing water bodies and through boreholes).
- Infilling of ditches, drains, ponds, pools, marshes or pits.
- Freshwater fishery production and/or management, including sporting fishing and angling.
- Extraction of minerals, including peat, sand and gravel, and topsoil.
- Construction, removal or destruction of roads, tracks, walls, fences, hard-stands, banks, ditches or other earthworks, or the laying, maintenance or removal of pipelines and cables above and below ground.
- Storage of materials.
- Erection of permanent or temporary structures, or the undertaking of engineering works, including drilling.
- Use of vehicles or craft likely to damage or disturb features of interest.
- Recreational or other activities likely to damage or disturb features of interest.
- Game and waterfowl management and hunting practices.

EN is preparing a revised list to be referred to as 'Operations Likely to Damage' (OLDs).

6.7 LOCAL BYELAWS

County council and local authority byelaws may be of use if a criminal offence is not apparent. This legislation is very broad and is almost 'catch-all' in character, with phrases such as the following.

A person shall not:

- remove, cut or displace any soil, turf or plant;
- pluck any bud, blossom, flower or leaf or any tree, shrub or plant (Kingston upon Thames, Surrey); or
- light any fire likely to cause damage by fire to anything on the land, place or throw or let fall any lighted match, or any substances or thing in or among or near to grass, fern, heather, bushes or trees on the land (Surrey County Council).

A prosecution for criminal damage may be suitable if a sapling is vandalised in a local-authority-maintained open space, especially if the offence occurred during the annual National Tree Week (organised by the Tree Council), held usually in the last ten days of November, at the beginning of the tree-planting period. During this event, many council park departments plant several thousand pounds worth of saplings in streets and parks, and the thin and low-branched saplings are vulnerable to damage by vandals.

6.8 TREE PRESERVATION ORDERS (TPOs)

A TPO is an order made by a local planning authority, and sometimes a county council, which in general makes it an offence to cut down, top, lop, uproot, wilfully damage or wilfully destroy a tree without the planning authority's permission. The breach of such an order could carry a fine of up to £20,000 on summary conviction, or on indictment a liability to an unlimited fine. A replacement tree will normally have to be planted.

The purpose of the order is to protect trees for the public enjoyment. All types of tree are covered, including hedgerow trees, but not hedges, bushes or shrubs. The order can cover anything from a single tree to woodlands.

Any apparent infringement of a TPO should be fully reported to the local planning authority, which maintains a register of applications and decisions that the public may view.

wildlife law in Scotland

The Scottish legal system differs markedly from that of the rest of the United Kingdom. The prosecution of crime is a public function exercised by the Lord Advocate through local prosecutors known as Procurators Fiscal.

It is the Crown Office which decides whether cases will be prosecuted and which procedure (summary or solemn) they will be conducted under. The police act as investigators for the Procurator Fiscal. They are primarily public servants, however, operating under the direction of their chief constable, and are therefore independent of the prosecution system.

The development of the law in Scotland has resulted in there being virtually no private prosecutions. As a result the RSPB and SSPCA assist the police, who in turn report incidents to the Procurator Fiscal for an independent consideration for prosecution.

There are also other important differences in the way the law is applied in Scotland. For example, the Police and Criminal Evidence Act 1984 does not apply in Scotland, and a primary element of the law in Scotland, is the principle of corroboration. Although some statutory exemption now allows prosecution on the evidence of a single witness, the traditional application of Scots law requires evidence to be accounted for by two sources. While this may not necessarily mean two eye witnesses, interviews should for practical purposes be conducted by two people or forensic examination undertaken by two individuals (or one individual's work verified by another).

When cross-border enquiries are envisaged it is important that these differences are recognised and close liaison be made so that differences in evidential procedures are taken into account beforehand.

7.1 WILDLIFE LAW IN SCOTLAND

The majority of wildlife law applies throughout Great Britain and there are few particularly Scottish considerations, other than those presented by their different legal system.

Animal cruelty is dealt with under the **Protection of Animals (Scotland) Act 1912**, but this mirrors the 1911 statute used in England and Wales.

Scotland does, however, have its own statutes with regard to poaching. Essentially, the same type of behaviour or action will constitute an offence north or south of the border, only the legislation will differ. Poaching has traditionally been viewed as a serious offence in Scotland, given the substantial revenue raised through field sports. Recent years have, however, seen a reduction in the previously widespread commercial and 'gang' poaching activities. In the main this is due to the ready availability of farmed salmon and venison, which makes illegal taking of fish and deer less profitable. The right to take and kill 'game' in Scotland tends to be fiercely protected and lies with the landowner, or persons with his permission.

Scotland's traditional observance of the Sabbath also shines through in the prohibition, by statute or etiquette, of many field sports on Sundays.

The police are used to enforce legislation and there is little provision for gamekeepers to act on their own, as they might elsewhere than Scotland. Water bailiffs are employed by District Salmon Fishery Boards to patrol rivers and coastlines in the practical enforcement of salmon law, but the police are commonly involved in assisting with arrests and preparing reports to Procurators Fiscal.

The following is a brief overview of Scottish wildlife law.

7.2 GROUND GAME ACT 1880

This establishes the rights of occupiers of land to take and kill hares and rabbits, and provides for persons to show such right when required to do so.

No specific police powers are provided by this Act.

7.3 AGRICULTURE (SCOTLAND) ACT 1948

This is the primary legislation under which the style of spring traps and snares is approved. This statute also makes unlawful the use of firearms to kill rabbits or hares at night (one hour after sunset to one hour before sunrise), except by persons holding shooting rights for the land in question.

No specific police powers are provided by this Act.

7.4 GAME (SCOTLAND) ACT 1832

Section 1 of this Act established the offence of trespassing on land in search of 'game' (hares, pheasants, partridges, grouse, heath or moor game, black game and bustards, and also rabbits, woodcocks, snipes and wild ducks). Anyone failing to quit land on the request of the owner or his servant can be arrested by that person, but must then be brought before a sheriff (section 2).

No specific police powers are provided by this Act.

7.5 NIGHT POACHING ACT 1828

Section 1 of this Act creates the offence of unlawfully taking 'game' (as above), or going in search of game with a gun, net or engine between one hour after sunset and one hour before sunrise. Landowners and their servants or gamekeepers, or anyone assisting them (the police), may arrest an offender. Special penalties apply if three or more persons poach together with weapons under this law (section 9).

No specific police powers are provided by this Act.

7.6 POACHING PREVENTION ACT 1862

Section 2 of this Act allows any police officer in a public place who suspects a person to be coming from land where he has been unlawfully in search of game, to stop and search that person or his vehicle. He may then seize any game or other thing which may have been used to poach.

7.7 GAME LICENCES ACT 1860 AND GAME ACT 1831

These lay down the requirement for game licences and game dealer licences, but are regarded as somewhat archaic.

No specific police powers are provided.

7.8 DEER (SCOTLAND) ACT 1996

The Deer (Scotland) Act 1959 was amended by the Deer (Amendment) (Scotland) Act 1996. Subsequently, all existing Scottish deer legislation was consolidated into the Deer (Scotland) Act 1996.

The legal right to take or kill deer generally goes with the ownership of the land. However, there are various restrictions on the taking or killing of deer, for instance at night or during close seasons. Occupiers of agricultural land or forestry may also take action to prevent damage by deer, and the Deer Commission may authorise various actions to control deer under certain circumstances.

Section 5 – allows the setting of close seasons for the male and female of each species of deer and creates the offence of taking (alive) or wilfully killing or injuring deer during the close season.

Section 17 – creates the offence of taking or wilfully killing or injuring deer without lawful right or permission. The section also makes it an offence to kill or injure deer other than by shooting.

Section 18 – makes it an offence to take or wilfully kill or injure deer between one hour after sunset and one hour before sunrise.

Section 19 – makes it an offence to use a vehicle to drive deer with the intention of taking, killing or injuring them.

Section 20 – makes it an offence to shoot at deer from any moving vehicle.

Section 21 – allows the making of an order setting out the prescribed classes of firearms, ammunition and other equipment which may lawfully be used in connection with killing or taking deer, and creates the offence of failing to comply with such an order. This section also makes it an offence to wilfully injure deer by shooting.

Section 22 – creates a special penalty where two or more persons act together to commit a poaching offence.

Section 23 – creates the offence of the illegal possession of deer, firearms or ammunition in circumstances which make it reasonable to infer that a poaching offence had been committed. The evidence of one witness is sufficient to obtain a conviction for this offence.

Section 24 – makes it an offence to attempt to commit or do any act in preparation for the commission of an offence.

Section 27 – allows a police officer to seize any deer liable to be forfeited on conviction of an offence. The section also allows for the granting of a search warrant for premises or vehicles, and for the searching of any persons connected with such premises or vehicles, and for the seizure of evidence. The section also allows a constable to exercise the same powers of search and seizure without a warrant in cases of urgency.

Section 28 – allows a police officer to arrest any person for committing an offence under the Act.

Section 29 – deals with the circumstances where an offence under the Act has been committed by a body corporate, and allows proceedings against any official of that body who has consented to or connived in the offence or whose neglect has lead to the offence.

Section 30 – allows a court to convict an accused of an offence other than the offence charged if it is satisfied that he is guilty of this other offence.

Section 31 – sets out the penalties for the various offences under the Act and allows a court to cancel the firearm or shotgun certificate held by persons convicted under the Act.

7.9 DEER (CLOSE SEASONS) (SCOTLAND) ORDER 1984

The close season dates for red deer are set under the Deer (Amendment)(Scotland) Act 1996.

The following close season dates apply:		
Red deer	males	21 October to 30 June inclusive
	females	16 February to 20 October inclusive
Fallow deer	males	1 May to 31 July inclusive
	females	16 February to 20 October inclusive
Roe deer	males	21 October to 31 March inclusive
	females	1 April to 20 October inclusive
Sika deer	males	21 October to 30 June inclusive
	females	16 February to 20 October inclusive
Red/Sika deer hybrids share the close season of Sika deer.		

7.10 DEER (FIREARMS etc) (SCOTLAND) ORDER 1985

Minimum sizes of firearms and ammunition and muzzle velocities for killing deer were established by an order made under section 23A of the Deer (Scotland) Act 1959. The requirements vary from species to species, and also allow for the use of some types of shotguns under certain circumstances. Full details should be sought from the Deer Commission for Scotland.

7

7.11 SALMON AND FRESHWATER FISHERIES (PROTECTION) (SCOTLAND) ACT 1951

Section 1 – creates the offence of fishing for or taking salmon without legal right or permission.

Section 2 – prohibits salmon fishing methods other than rod and line or net and coble in inland waters.

Section 3 – creates special penalties for two or more persons poaching together.

Section 4 – prohibits the use of explosives, poisons or electrical devices to take salmon.

Section 6 – prohibits the taking of dead salmon or trout from rivers.

Section 7 – creates the offence of being in possession of salmon, instruments, explosives, poisons or noxious substances in circumstances which give grounds to suspect that the salmon were unlawfully obtained or the items are to be used to commit an offence **(evidence of one witness sufficient)**.

Section 7a – creates the offence of being in possession of salmon which has been illegally taken, killed or landed.

Section 8 – makes it an offence to attempt to commit any offence or do any act preparatory to committing an offence.

Section 10 – allows water bailiffs and police officers, with reasonable suspicion, to stop, search and seize in a similar manner to the powers granted under deer legislation.

Section 11 – provides for the grant of search warrants.

Section 12 – allows for the arrest of persons committing offences against the Act.

Section 13 – prohibits fishing for salmon by rod and line on Sundays.

Annual close seasons are established by order of the Secretary of State in consultation with District Salmon Fishery Boards, and vary throughout Scotland.

7.12 TROUT (SCOTLAND) ACT 1933

This Act prohibits the purchase or sale of trout less than eight inches in length.

7.13 FRESHWATER FISHERIES (SCOTLAND) ACT 1902

This Act establishes the annual close season for (brown) trout as being 7 October to 14 March inclusive. This does not apply to stocked waters, such as the popular trout fishing-farm ponds.

No specific police powers are provided by this Act.

It is important, however, to note that sea trout are regarded as salmon and enjoy the full protection of salmon legislation for the purposes of the law.

It should also be borne in mind that judicial decisions and case law have established some rod and line methods, such as sniggering, ripping and foul-hooking, to be unlawful. Some fishery boards also have orders prohibiting the use of certain baits, such as shrimps and prawns, and establishing when 'spinning' or 'fly' fishing must be employed. Liaison with local water bailiffs is vital for full details and expert advice.

7.14 SALMON ACT 1986

Section 20 – provides additional powers in respect of licensing and regulation of salmon dealing.

Section 21 – provides detailed of permitted methods of fishing for salmon.

Section 22 – amends section 7 of the Salmon and Freshwater Fisheries (Protection) (Scotland) Act 1951 for the offence of possessing salmon which has been illegally taken, killed or landed.

Section 23 – provides powers for the court in trying of one offence to convict of another.

Section 24 – prohibits the unauthorised introduction of salmon or salmon eggs into certain waters.

Section 25 – amends section 7 of the Salmon and Freshwater Fisheries (Protection)(Scotland) Act 1951, making it an offence to obstruct the free passage of salmon or use uncertificated fixed engines within the limits of the Solway Firth.

Section 26 – amends section 21 of the Salmon and Freshwater Fisheries (Protection) (Scotland) Act 1951 in respect of poaching in the Border Esk.

Section 27 – provides exemption from certain offences in respect of certain acts.

Section 28 – provides exemption from certain offences in respect of acts done for scientific purposes.

Section 30 – gives technical changes to prosecution offences under the Salmon Fisheries (Scotland) Act 1868, and provisions for persons to be convicted of these offences on the evidence of one witness.

The 1868 Act lists a number of offences: fishing during annual and weekly close times; fishing with illegal mesh size; fishing at falls; prevention of passage through passes; discharge of sawdust, chaff and shelling of corn; use of roe as bait; destroying young fish and disturbing spawning beds; taking unclean salmon; buying and selling in close time; provisions as to exportation of salmon, boats and gear removal during close time; and failure to observe weekly close time by netsmen.

7

wildlife law in Northern Ireland

8.1 INTRODUCTION

The statutory responsibility for nature conservation in Northern Ireland is carried solely by the Department of the Environment for Northern Ireland (DETR(NI)). The Environment and Heritage Service of the DETR(NI) carries out all the functions that are delegated to the statutory nature conservation organisations in mainland Great Britain, including all licensing under the wildlife legislation. This also includes licensing that is delegated to MAFF in England and Wales.

NOTE: The Wildlife and Countryside Act 1981 (WCA) does not apply in Northern Ireland

Wildlife in Northern Ireland is protected by the **Wildlife (NI) Order 1985** which, as in the WCA, classifies the species in various groups and affords varying levels of protection in Schedules to the Order.

Schedule 1 – Part I – Specially protected birds (all year).

Schedule 1 – Part II – Specially protected birds (during the close season).

Schedule 2 – Part I – Birds which may be taken or killed outside the close season (quarry list).

Schedule 2 – Part II – Birds which may be taken or killed at all times (pest list).

Schedule 3 – Birds which may be sold dead at all times.

Schedule 4 – Birds which may be shown for competitive purposes.

Schedule 5 – Animals other than birds which are protected at all times.

Schedule 6 – Animals other than birds which may not be killed or taken by certain methods.

Schedule 7 – Animals other than birds which may not be sold alive or dead at any time.

Schedule 8 – Protected plants.

Schedule 9 – Animals and plants established in the wild.

Schedule 10 – Close season for deer.

Schedule 11 – Prohibited firearms and ammunition.

The Schedules are reproduced in full at the end of this chapter.

Bird protection can be summarised as follows.
1. Birds cannot be killed, injured or taken.
2. Nests cannot be taken, damaged or destroyed.
3. Eggs cannot be taken or destroyed.
4. Live or dead wild birds (or anything derived thereof) cannot be possessed.
5. Eggs cannot be possessed.
6. Nesting birds cannot be disturbed.
7. Dependent young cannot be disturbed.
8. All birds are protected on a Sunday.
9. All birds are protected at night, ie the period between one hour after sunset to one hour before sunrise.

EXCEPTIONS: Pest species can be killed or taken and their nests and eggs/young destroyed by legal methods and authorised persons under the terms of general licences issued by Environment and Heritage Service DETR(NI). (NB. Items 8 and 9 above still apply.)

Quarry species (Part I of Schedule 2 and Part II of Schedule 1) of birds can be killed or taken in the open season (1 September – 31 January,) ie item 1 above does not apply in open season to authorised persons.

Other species receive protection under all nine items, with those mentioned in Part I of Schedule 1 receiving the protection of heavier fines for offences committed in respect of them.

Birds listed on Schedule 4 may be held in captivity, but only under licence from the DETR(NI). Such licences specify birds held all must be close-ringed to prove that they have been bred in captivity.

8

Common offences are similar to those occurring elsewhere in the United Kingdom. Principal amongst these are:

- illegal taking or killing birds by poisoning;
- trapping and possession of birds;
- taking non-pest species of birds;
- egg and chick stealing;
- digging out badgers;
- illegal hare-coursing;
- deer poaching; and
- lamping (hunting quarry by night with powerful lights).

8.2 ENFORCEMENT POWERS

These are contained in Article 25 of the Wildlife (NI) Order 1985.

Article 25(1)

If a police officer suspects with reasonable cause that any person is committing or has committed an offence under Parts II or III the police officer may without warrant:

a.   stop and search that person (if the police officer suspects with reasonable cause that the evidence of the commission of the offence is to be found on that person);

b.   search or examine any animal or thing which that person may then be using or have in his possession (if the police officer suspects with reasonable cause that evidence of the commission of the offence is to be found on that animal or thing);

e.   arrest as per Article 27 of the Police and Criminal Evidence Act 1984 (PACE) (general arrest powers); and

d.   seize and detain for the purposes of proceedings under this Order any thing which may be evidence of the commission of the offence or may be liable to be forfeited under Article 27.

A police officer can therefore stop and search any person for evidence of the commission of an offence under the Wildlife Order; search and examine any other thing which may be evidence of the commission of the offence; arrest the person if the general arrest conditions of PACE are satisfied; and seize and detain evidence of the commission of the offence or any other thing which may be forfeit to the court under Article 27.

Article 25(2): search without warrant

If a police officer suspects with reasonable cause that any person is committing an offence under Parts II or III he may, for the purpose of exercising the powers at paragraph (1), enter any land other than a dwelling house.

Article 25(3): warrants

If a justice of the peace is satisfied on a sworn complaint in writing that there are reasonable grounds for suspecting that:

a.   an offence under Article 4, 6, 9 or 16; or

b.   an offence under Article 7, 8, 10, 12(1) or (2), 13, 14, 15, 19 or 23

has been committed, and that evidence of the offence may be found on any premises, he may grant a warrant to any police officer, with or without other persons, to enter upon and search those premises for the purposes of obtaining that evidence.

Article 25(4): actions on seizure

Where under paragraph 1(d) a police officer seizes and detains any animal or any bird, egg or nest, he shall as soon as conveniently may be produce that animal or that bird, egg or nest to a magistrates court, and the court may order the animal or bird to be sold, liberated or destroyed, or the nest or egg to be sold or destroyed.

Article 27: penalties and forfeitures

Penalties

Where an offence is committed in respect of more than one bird, nest, egg or other animal, plant or other thing, the maximum fine which may be imposed shall be determined as if the person convicted had been convicted of a separate offence in respect of each bird, nest, egg, animal, plant or thing (Article 27(7)).

Birds	
Offences against all wild birds	fine of level 3 – £1,000
Offences against specially protected bird species	fine of level 5 – £5,000
Other animals	
Deer	fine of level 4 – £2,500 and/or three months' imprisonment
Badgers, bats etc	fine of level 5 – £5,000
Offences in relation to bird competitions	fine of level 4 – £2,500

Forfeitures

The court by which any person is convicted of an offence under this Order:

- shall order the forfeiture of any bird, nest, egg, other animal, plant or any thing in respect of which the offence was committed; and

- may order the forfeiture of any vehicle, animal, weapon or any thing which was used to commit the offence.

8.3   WELFARE OF ANIMALS ACT (NI) 1972

This supersedes the Protection of Animals Act 1911 and applies to all animals including wild animals. The Act is divided into four parts:

Part I Welfare of livestock and agricultural land	Part II Control of pet shops, animal boarding, riding and zoological establishments
Part III Protection of animals	Part IV Miscellaneous

NOTE:

- Pet shops and animal boarding, riding and zoological establishments have to be licensed.

- Zoological establishment includes any premises where animals are permanently kept primarily for the purpose of exhibition to the public.

- Part III covers a wide range of cruelty offences, including fighting, baiting and using non-approved traps or snares, and deals with the destruction of severely injured or diseased animals.

- A police officer may enter any premises at any reasonable time if he has reason to believe an offence is being committed under Part III.

- Northern Ireland has no dangerous wild animals legislation at present.

8.4   THE WILDLIFE (NI) ORDER

S1 1985/171 (NI 2) Schedule 1: Birds which are protected by special penalties
Articles 4, 5(6), 7(3) and 28

Part 1: at all times	
Bittern	Nightjar
Bunting, Corn	Osprey
Buzzard	Ousel, Ring
Chough	Owl, Barn
Corncrake	Owl, Long-eared
Crossbill	Petrel, Storm
Diver, Red-throated	Phalarope, Red-necked
Dotterel	Pipit, Tree
Dove, Turtle	Quail
Dunlin	Redstart
Eagle, Golden	Ruff
Eagle, White-tailed	Merlin

8

Falcon, Peregrine	Scoter, Common
Fieldfare	Swan, Bewick's
Firecrest	Swan, Whooper
Flycatcher, Pied	Tern, Arctic
Garganey	Tern, Common
Godwit, Black-tailed	Tern, Little
Goosander	Tern, Roseate
Goshawk	Tern, Sandwich
Grebe, Black-necked	Tit, Bearded
Greenshank	Twite
Harrier, Hen	Wagtail, Yellow (all races)
Harrier, Marsh	Warbler, Garden
Hawk, Sparrow	Warbler, Reed
Heron	Warbler, Wood
Kestrel	Whimbrel
Kingfisher	

Part II: during the close season

Gadwall	Pochard
Goldeneye	Scaup
Pintail	Shoveler
Plover, Golden	Wigeon

Schedule 2: Birds which may be killed or taken
Articles 4, 5, 6(4), 16(2) and 28

Part 1: outside the close season

Curlew	Pintail
Duck, Tufted	Plover, Golden
Gadwall	Pochard
Goldeneye	Scaup
Goose, Grey-lag	Shoveler
Goose, Pink-footed	Teal
Mallard	Wigeon

Part II: by authorised persons at all times

Crow, Hooded/Carrion	Pigeon, Feral
Gull, Great Black-backed	Pigeon, Wood

Gull, Herring	Rook
Gull, Lesser Black-backed	Sparrow, House
Jackdaw	Starling
Magpie	

Schedule 2, Part II has now been replaced by general licences which have the same effect.

Schedule 3: Birds which may be sold dead at all times
Articles 7(2) and 28

Woodpigeon

Schedule 4: Birds which may be shown for competitive purposes
Articles 8 and 28

Brambling	Linnet
Bullfinch	Magpie
Bunting, Reed	Redpoll
Chaffinch	Siskin
Goldfinch	Starling
Greenfinch	Twite
Jackdaw	Yellowhammer
Jay	

Schedule 5: Animals which are protected at all times
Articles 10, 11 and 28

Badger	Cetaceans (all species)
Bats (all species)	Lizard, Common or Viviparous
Butterfly, Brimstone	Marten, Pine
Butterfly, Dingy Skipper	Newt, Common
Butterfly, Holly Blue	Otter, Common
Butterfly, Large Heath	Seal, Common
Butterfly, Marsh Fritillary	Seal, Grey

Butterfly, Purple Hairstreak	Squirrel, Red
Butterfly, Small Blue	

Schedule 6: Animals which may not be killed or taken by certain methods
Articles 12 and 28

Badger	Lizard, Common or Viviparous
Bats (all species)	
Deer, Fallow	Marten, Pine
Deer, Red	Newt, Common
Deer, Sika	Otter, Common
Hare, Brown	Seal, Common
Hare, Irish	Seal, Grey
Hedgehog	Squirrel, Red

Schedule 7: Animals which may not be sold alive or dead at any time
Articles 13 and 28

Badger	Hedgehog
Bats (all species)	Lizard, Common or Viviparous
Butterfly, Brimstone	Marten, Pine
Butterfly, Dingy Skipper	Mussel, Freshwater
Butterfly, Holly Blue	Newt, Common
Butterfly, Large Heath	Otter, Common
Butterfly, Marsh Fritillary	Seal, Common
Butterfly, Purple Hairstreak	Seal, Grey
Butterfly, Small Blue	Sea-urchin, Common
Fox	Squirrel, Red
Frog, Common	

Schedule 8: Plants which are protected
Articles 14 and 28
Part I

Plants which are protected under article 14(1)(a) and (2)	
Avens, Mountain	Orchid, Bee
Barley, Wood	Orchid, Bird's Nest
Betony	Orchid, Bog
Broomrape, Ivy	Orchid, Green-winged
Buckthorn, Alder	Orchid, Irish Lady's Tresses
Bugle, Pyramidal	Orchid, Narrow-leaved Marsh
Campion, Moss	Orchid, Small white
Cat's-ear, Smooth	Oyster-plant
Centaury, Seaside	Pea, Marsh
Cloudberry	Pennyroyal
Clubmoss, Marsh	Pillwort
Cowslip	Rosemary, Bog
Cow-wheat, Wood	Saw-wort, Mountain
Cranesbill, Wood	Saxifrage, Purple
Cress, Shepherd's	Saxifrage, Yellow Marsh
Crowfoot, Water	Saxifrage, Yellow Mountain
Fern, Holly	Sea-lavender, Rock
Fern, Killarney	Sedge, Broad-leaved Mud
Fern, Oak	Sedge, Few-flowered
Fleabane, Blue	Small-reed, Northern
Globe-flower	Spike-rush
Grass, Blue-eyed	Thistle, Melancholy
Grass, Holy	Violet, Fen
Heath, Cornish	Violet, Water
Helleborine, Green-flowered	Waterwort, Eight-stamened
Helleborine, Marsh	Wintergreen, Serrated
Moschatel/Town Hall Clock	Yellow Bird's Nest
Mudwort	

8

Part II

Plants which are protected under article 14(1)(b) and (2)
Primrose

Schedule 9: Animals and plants to which Article 15 applies
Articles 15 and 28

Part I: Animals which are established in the wild	
Duck, Carolina Wood	Mink, American
Duck, Ruddy	Pheasant, Golden
Goose, Barnacle	Rat, Black
Goose, Canada	Squirrel, Grey
Goshawk	

Part II: Plants	
Hogweed, Giant	Pirri-pirri Bur
Kelp, Giant	Seaweed, Japanese
Knotweed	Spartina or Cord-grass
Knotwood, Japanese	

Schedule 10: Close seasons for deer
Articles 19(1) and (5), 23(3) and 28

Fallow deer	Buck:	1 May – 31 July inclusive
	Doe:	1 March – 31 October inclusive
Red deer	Stags:	1 May – 31 July inclusive
	Hinds:	1 March – 31 October inclusive
Sika deer	Stags:	1 May – 31 July inclusive
	Hinds:	1 March – 31 October inclusive

(In this Schedule, any reference to a species of deer includes a hybrid of that species.)

Schedule 11: Prohibited firearms and ammunition for deer – Articles 19(3) and 28

Firearms	Ammunition
• Any smooth-bore gun. • Any rifle having a calibre of less than .236 inches (6 millimetres). • Any pistol, revolver or other type of handgun other than a slaughtering instrument (within the meaning of Article 2(2) of the Firearms (Northern Ireland) Order 1981). • Any air-gun, air-rifle or air-pistol. • Any weapon which discharges a missile by means of a gas propellant.	• Any cartridge for use in a smooth-bore gun. • Any cartridge or load for use in a rifle other than a cartridge or load so designed that when fired in a rfle, the bullet discharged has a muzzle energy of not less than 1,700 foot pounds (2,305 joules). • Any bullet for use in a rifle other than: a bullet weighing not less than 100 grains (6.48 grammes); or an expanding bullet designed to deform in a predictable manner and thereby increase its effective diameter upon entering tissue.

the trade in non-native and endangered species

9.1 TACKLING THE TRADE IN ENDANGERED SPECIES AND THE WILDLIFE SMUGGLER

9.1.1 CITES

The **Convention on International Trade in Endangered Species of Wild Fauna and Flora**, commonly referred to as **CITES**, came into force in 1975. It sets down provisions for the regulation of international trade in specimens of animals and plants, and derivatives thereof, on the basis of a system of permits and certificates which are issued when certain conditions are met.

Over 140 countries are now party to the Convention, which is administered at an international level by a secretariat based in Switzerland. Conferences of the parties take place every two to three years. Major issues are discussed; ivory for example has been high on the agenda in recent years. The conferences also consider and adopt resolutions on issues such as the interpretation of the Convention, and recommendations for special measures to tackle problem species and countries, as well as reviewing the lists of species subject to protection under the Convention.

Each party to the Convention must designate a management authority to oversee the implementation and enforcement of the Convention as supplemented by conference resolutions, and for issuing permits and certificates where appropriate. The DETR is the management authority for Great Britain, while the Department of Agriculture (NI) carries out this function in Northern Ireland.

The two UK management authorities both take scientific advice from two separate scientific authorities. For plants this is the Royal Botanic Gardens, Kew, while the Joint Nature Conservation Committee (JNCC) advises on animals, including birds.

The plants and animals subject to CITES controls are listed in three appendices.

9.1.2 Appendix I

This includes those species which are threatened with extinction. The inclusion of any species in Appendix I means that all commercial trade in it is banned.

Individual exemptions may be permitted in exceptional circumstances, such as for scientific or zoological purposes, but these must be individually licensed by the CITES management authorities of both the importing and exporting countries. In such cases the trader must obtain an import certificate before he can apply for an export certificate. There are also exemptions for captive-bred and artificially-propagated specimens.

Some of the species included in Appendix I are:
* tigers
* rhinoceros
* elephants
* sea turtles
* most bears
* the great whales
* the great apes
* many parrots, macaws and cockatoos
* some orchids and cacti.

9.1.3 Appendix II

This lists species which, whilst not immediately threatened with extinction, may become so if trade in them is not controlled. Commercial trade in these species is permitted under CITES only when the country of origin has issued an export permit.

Appendix II includes, amongst others, all species of:
* bears
* parrots
* spotted cats
* crocodilians
* orchids
* many birds of prey
* carnivorous plants

which are not already included in Appendix I.

9

The appendices also include 'look-alike' species which may not be threatened themselves, but closely resemble species which are. This has been done specifically to assist law enforcement.

9.1.4   Appendix III

This allows signatory countries to list any of their own protected species about which they seek international co-operation to control trade. Broadly, this allows the provisions of Appendix II to be applied to these species. For example, India has listed several species of civets which are protected within its own borders but which are used in some countries in the manufacture of cosmetics.

9.2   THE EC WILDLIFE TRADE REGULATION

CITES is implemented within the European Union by EC Regulations 338 and 939 of 1997. The Regulation has four annexes. Annex A is broadly equivalent to Appendix I of the Convention. It includes all Appendix I species, together with almost 200 Appendix II and III species, and some non-CITES species. All of those CITES species which are strictly protected under the Birds and Habitats Directives are included in this most protected category.

Annex B is broadly equivalent to Appendix II, including all the remaining Appendix II species not on Annex A, but subject to individual species/country bans as previously provided for under Annex C2 of EC Regulation 3626/82, together with over 50 Appendix III and non-CITES species. Annex C includes approximately 200 Appendix III species, while Annex D contains non-CITES specimens imported into the Community in such numbers as to warrant monitoring by a simple notification procedure.

The Regulation introduces changes to internal controls on sales, purchase, possession and movement. There are now provisions for antiques, and a new definition of 'offering for sale' which will specifically include invitation to treat.

In the UK, the penalties for import and export offences are set out in the Customs and Excise Management Act 1979. The penalties for 'domestic' offences are provided for in the Control of Trade in Endangered Species (Enforcement) Regulations 1997 (COTES).

HM Customs and Excise are primarily responsible for enforcing import and export controls. The police have responsibility for enforcing sales and other 'domestic' controls.

It is not an offence merely to be in possession of a CITES item (an ivory antique, for example), but it is an offence to attempt to purchase, sell or display for commercial purposes any Annex A specimen without an exemption or evidence of legal acquisition – including an import permit (for Annex B specimens) issued by the UK CITES management authority, the DETR or DANI in Northern Ireland.

The provisions of CITES apply to living and dead animals and plants, their body parts or any derivatives obtained from them. This means that a tiger, for instance, enjoys the same level of protection from trade whether it is sold as a living creature, a carcass, a skin, bones which are used as raw materials in oriental medicines, or a manufactured medicinal product claiming to contain tiger derivatives.

9.3   INTER-AGENCY LIAISON

CITES recognises that, next to habitat destruction, illegal trade in endangered species offers the greatest threat to the world's rarest animals and plants. It is also thought that, after narcotics, such illegal trade is now the second largest criminal activity in the world. It is estimated to generate profits equivalent to about five billion US dollars annually.

Wildlife smuggling is only gradually receiving the attention it deserves amongst law enforcement agencies, and nowhere is this more true than in the United Kingdom. Yet evidence already exists to demonstrate that many persons active in this field have links with Britain. Illegal trade in species is completely global, and the UK's relatively few enquiries in this field have already necessitated liaison with agencies in the

USA, Canada, Thailand, Hong Kong, Australia and New Zealand, apart from the obvious links to our counterparts on the European continent.

Police officers may traditionally suffer from a trend to concentrate on their own patch or beat. Where wildlife is concerned, it is vital to think big. Early contact with colleagues in **HM Customs and Excise** opens a new horizon of intelligence-gathering possibilities. Their international network, the **World Customs Organisation,** allows for the global picture to be considered too. Seek out, and feed in, information via **Interpol.** Its **Wildlife Crime Sub-Group,** established in 1993, has led to a much greater emphasis on this type of crime, and Interpol's records and contacts can produce extremely useful information and assistance.

Liaison between the police and Customs, as demonstrated by successes against drug trafficking, can be extremely effective. Customs officers have built up a vast knowledge of smuggling trends and methods of moving both people and goods around the world. Their links with airlines and shipping companies can be very helpful. In foreign countries, they often also have useful intelligence on immigration records that can aid in tracking smugglers. The police, meanwhile, are more used to gathering data on individuals and collating the evidence required to bring cases to court. Put together, these elements can be a very effective combination against the international criminal.

Never forget, too, the CITES Secretariat in Switzerland. Together with the experience and technical knowledge of its staff, particularly the enforcement officers, CITES plays a vital role in supporting the work of national agencies.

CITES management authorities in nations around the world can also provide details of persons engaged in species trade. Experience has shown that a considerable amount of criminal activity makes fraudulent use of otherwise apparently legitimate CITES documents.

The United Kingdom features principally in CITES offences in one of three ways; import, export and in-transit. UK citizens or businesses are just as likely to be end-users or customers for species or derivatives as

anywhere else in the world. Many of our native birds of prey feature in CITES appendices, as do some of our animals and plants.

It is important, therefore, for police officers to be aware that they are empowered to use legislation normally enforced by Customs staff, and some knowledge of it is essential in dealing with CITES and COTES offences. It should also be noted that those engaged in wildlife crime often know their subject very well indeed.

It can be all too easy to overlook the fact that Britain is a target nation for wildlife criminals, and that these may not always be live birds or eggs; carcasses are also sought out for the black market in taxidermy and substantial profits can be obtained in such trade. The UK, and particularly Scotland, attracts large numbers of foreign field sportsmen each year. For example, in the first nine months of 1995, three Scottish police forces alone issued over 4,000 firearm and/or shotgun visitor permits.

Whilst the majority of such sportsmen will clearly be legitimate and law-abiding persons, experience has shown a strong 'trophy-collecting' element within this fraternity.

In dealing with any export offence, one must bear in mind the question of how the species has firstly been obtained; this is where police and Customs legislation and officials must work together.

The Wildlife and Countryside Act 1981 (WCA) creates a range of offences that can be committed involving wildlife, and provides powers of search and seizure to the police. However, it must be noted that the Act's power of arrest is conditional and limited.

9

Typical offences that might be encountered in an export scenario would include the following.

The Wildlife and Countryside Act 1981

Section 1(2)

It is an offence for any person to
have in his possession or control
any live or dead wild bird or any part of, or
anything derived from, such a bird
or
an egg of a wild bird or any part of such an
egg

No offence would be committed if a licence has been issued under section 16 of the WCA.

The Wildlife and Countryside Act 1981

Section 9(2)

It is an offence for any person to
have in his possession or control
any live or dead wild animal in Schedule 5 or
any part of, or anything derived from, such an
animal

However, no offence will be committed if a licence has been issued under section 16 of the WCA.

Sections 5 and 11 – list illegal methods of taking and killing birds and animals, and possession of items (described later) that might fall within these categories could render persons liable to prosecution depending on circumstances. Shooting parties have been known to use such methods.

The Wildlife and Countryside Act 1981

Section 13

It is an offence to
possess or transport for sale
any live or dead wild plant in Schedule 8

However, no offence will be committed if a licence has been issued under section 16 of the WCA.

The Conservation (Natural Habitats, &c.) Regulations 1994 also create offences that the police can deal with. Identical powers, and limitations, exist as per the WCA.

The Conservation (Natural Habitats, &c.) Regulations 1994

Regulations 39(2) and (4)

It is an offence to
keep, transport, sell or exchange
any live or dead animal of a European
protected species or part of,
or anything derived from,
such an animal

This includes such as wildcats and otters. Offences can be committed if other species, such as mountain hares, pine martens and seals, are taken using illegal methods.

The Conservation (Natural Habitats, &c.) Regulations 1994

Regulations 41 and 43(5)

Lists prohibited methods of
taking or killing animals
and can include tape recorders, stunning
devices, sighting devices for
night shooting, nets, crossbows
and poisons

Regulation 43

It is an offence to
possess plants
of European protected species

9.4 IMPORT AND EXPORT CONTROLS

9.4.1 Customs and Excise Management Act 1979

The Customs and Excise Management Act 1979 creates the offence of exporting, shipping as stores, or bringing to any place in the UK for the purpose of being exported or shipped as stores, goods prohibited or restricted by other enactments (section 68(1)(a) and (b)). It is this section that would be invoked if persons attempted to take protected species out of the UK unlawfully to another country. Sections 170(1) and (2) provide for similar offences in relation to import.

Although normally enforced by Customs and Excise officers, police officers may be authorised by a Commissioner of Customs and Excise to use specified powers provided by the 1979 Act. Under Section 11 of the Act it is the duty of every constable to assist in the enforcement of the law relating to the Commissioner's responsibilities.

Specific sections of the statute are worthy of note.

Section 139 – allows for seizure and detention of goods liable to forfeiture under the Customs and Excise Acts by the police where proceedings may be taken under other legislation (ie domestic wildlife law)

Section 161 – allows Customs officers using their 'writ of assistance' to search any premises when the presence of goods liable to forfeiture under the Customs and Excise Acts is suspected, but they must be accompanied by a police officer at night (between 11pm and 5am).

Section 163 – allows for search of vehicles and vessels by Customs officers if they are suspected to be carrying goods liable to forfeiture under the Customs and Excise Acts.

9.4.2 The EC Wildlife Trade Regulation

EC Regulations 338 and 939 of 1997 set out the rules for the import, export and re-export of the species to which they apply. The regulation of trade is based on a system of permits and certificates which may only be issued when certain conditions are met.

Applications for permits and certificates are considered by the DETR (DANI in Northern Ireland). Permits must be obtained before:

- any Annex A, B or C specimen can be exported or re-exported;
- any Annex A or B specimen can be imported.

People importing Annex C or D specimens must complete a standard notification form.

Slightly different rules apply if the specimen is a personal or household effect.

The DETR, through the enforcement co-ordinator, can confirm whether or not the necessary permits have been issued.

9.4.3 The Control of Trade in Endangered Species (Enforcement) Regulations 1997

The Control of Trade in Endangered Species (Enforcement) Regulations 1997 No 1372 may also be employed when dealing with CITES goods suspected of being illegally exported or imported.

Regulation 5 – allows for any specimen brought to any place for the purpose of export to be forfeited if proof of lawful exportation is not furnished. Similarly, specimens that have been imported can be forfeited if proof of lawful importation is not furnished.

Regulation 7 – deals with the movement of live specimens.

Regulation 6 – deals with breach of conditions of permits issued by the management authority.

9

119

Traditional East Asian medicines

For more detailed advice when dealing with such offences, you are recommended to liaise with CITES-trained police wildlife liaison officers, HM Customs and Excise CITES liaison and intelligence officers (a specialised CITES enforcement team is based at Heathrow Airport) and the UK management authority.

It is important to agree at an early stage which agency is best able to carry enquiries forward (unless the circumstances warrant a joint investigation).

For details see Appendix E – Useful Contacts.

9.5 SPECIFIC OFFENCES IN THE TRADE IN ENDANGERED SPECIES

9.5.1 Traditional East Asian medicines

Many species of animals and plants have been used in traditional East Asian medicines (TEAMs) for hundreds, perhaps thousands, of years. For example, it is known that bear bile has been valued as a medicine for at least 1,300 years, and the first published reference in China to the use of tiger bone in medicine appeared in 500 AD.

The Chinese have an ancient culture in which traditions are strong and many of the old remedies remain in use today. The growth in prosperity in the Far East and the increasing interest in alternative and natural remedies in the West has increased the demand for the animals and plants used in their preparation at a time when their wild populations are, in many cases, declining. The vast majority of TEAMs do not contain ingredients of species covered by the CITES Convention, but others do, and these are traded in Oriental communities throughout the world.

Manufactured medicines are made in a number of countries in South-East Asia, principally the People's Republic of China, from where they are exported to both the East and also the West via the west coast of the USA. 'Raw materials' such as bones, antelope and rhinoceros horn, snake skins and orchids also enter the UK illegally to be made into remedies and treatments by TEAM pharmacists and practitioners here in Britain.

9.5.2 Species involved

Tiger

Most tiger body parts have a use in traditional East Asian medicines. For example, the whiskers are prescribed to cure toothache, the brain to cure laziness and the tail to cure skin diseases. However, the most highly prized of all body parts are the bones, which are used as a treatment for rheumatism, stiffness of the joints and muscles, and other aches and strains.

There is a huge demand for tiger bone around the world, and this poses the greatest threat to the continued survival of the species in the wild. Tiger bone products come in many forms, from pills to tablets to wine which is drunk as a general tonic, but perhaps the best known are tiger-bone plasters, sold in small packets which often portray a tiger design on the packaging. Tiger-bone plasters are produced in huge quantities under many different brand names, and have been found in Chinese communities within Britain on a number of occasions.

Rhinoceros

The rhinoceros has been pushed to the brink of extinction in recent years by the huge demand for rhinoceros horn. In Oriental medicine, rhinoceros horn is believed to reduce fever; it is not normally used as an aphrodisiac. As with the tiger, rhinoceros horn is used as an ingredient in a range of products, most often in the form of tablets and herbal teas, although raw horn has also been found in Britain.

Bear

With the exception of the giant panda, all of the world's bear species are hunted for their gall bladders and the bile salts they produce, which are often used in Oriental medicines. Many bear species are listed in CITES Appendix I and so should not be in international trade or bought or sold in the UK.

Bear bile is believed to reduce swelling and is also used in the treatment of some serious conditions such as cancer, heart disease and cirrhosis of the liver. Tests have shown that bears are unique in producing a chemical called ursodeoxycholic acid (UDCA) which appears to have some medicinal value in humans, but this can be manufactured synthetically.

Bear products are marketed under a number of different brand names and typically come in the form of pills, tablets and herbal teas.

NOTE: Not all bears are listed in Appendix I, so some trade may be legal.

A wide range of other species covered by the CITES Convention is also known to be used in TEAMs.

9.5.3   Organising a search operation

In 1995 the Metropolitan Police launched 'Operation Charm', the first police operation of its kind to investigate the illegal use of endangered species in TEAMs in Britain. The experience which the forces involved gained from this has been invaluable, and will also be of value to any police officers planning such an enquiry in future. The publicity given to 'Operation Charm' has had the effect of increasing public awareness of this issue and this, in turn, has led to more information on the sale of endangered species products being passed to police. As our role in the enforcement of CITES becomes better known, it is likely that more operations like 'Charm' will take place in future.

Three other successful cases are described at the end of this chapter.

9.5.4   Obtaining a warrant

Regulation 9 of the COTES Regulations includes the provision for a constable to apply for a warrant to search premises for unlawfully imported specimens. A warrant can be applied for if any of the following conditions apply:

• that admission to the premises has been refused;

• that refusal is apprehended;

• that the case is one of urgency;

• that an application for admission to the premises would defeat the object of the entry.

Justices of the peace may not always be familiar with the COTES Regulations, so it is advisable to take a copy of EC Regulation 338/97, listing the species you have evidence of, to show to them. The status of the species listed in the Regulations is reviewed from time to time, so make sure that you have the latest version. The DETR enforcement co-ordinator can check this for you, as well as confirming that no sales licences have been issued.

9.5.5   Knowing what to look for

Chinese medicine products can be marketed in English, Chinese or in Chinese characters. You will need some expert assistance to help in identification. TRAFFIC International, the wildlife trade monitoring arm of the WWF and IUCN have an enforcement assistance officer who can provide expert help both in the preparations and during the search itself.

Some Chinese medicine products, for example brands of tiger-bone plasters, will have a bold tiger design on the packaging, but almost invariably product packaging will list the ingredients, either on the box or on a sheet of paper inside. This also applies to orchids for example, Herba dendrobi (Dendrobium species).

9

Remember that under COTES it is not necessary to prove that a product which claims to contain a particular ingredient actually does contain that ingredient, so police officers should seize any product which claims to contain, for example:

- tiger bone
- rhinoceros horn
- bear bile.

9.5.6 Sales offences

Regulation 8(1) of the COTES Regulations 1997 makes it an offence to purchase, offer to purchase, acquire for commercial purposes, display to the public for commercial purposes, use for commercial gain, sell, keep for sale, offer for sale or transport for sale any specimen of a species listed in Annex A of the EC Wildlife Trade Regulation.

Regulation 8(2) makes it an offence to sell any Annex B specimen if it has been illegally imported.

Within the EC Wildlife Trade Regulation there is provision to permit the purchase, sale, display etc of certain specimens. The CITES management authority can issue a certificate for the purposes listed in Article 8.3 of the EC Regulation.

If a certificate has been issued for a sale, a separate certificate is not required for the purchase of the specimen. However, certificates are holder-specific and valid for just one transaction. The new owner must apply for a further certificate if he or she wishes to sell it.

Certificates can be issued by the CITES management authority if for example the specimen is captive-bred or artificially propagated; for breeding or propagation purposes; for research or education aimed at the conservation of the species; is a worked specimen acquired more than 50 years previously; or meets one of the other purposes set down in Article 8 of the EC Wildlife Trade Regulation.

It is worth checking with the DETR whether any certificates have been issued.

Annex A species include tigers, rhinos, leopards, most bears and some orchids.

All other bears are included in Annex B; Regulation 8(2) of COTES extends to these animals (but only if the item has been imported unlawfully). In a recent prosecution, the Crown Prosecution Service were satisfied that since these plants and animals can only be obtained outside the UK, they must have been unlawfully imported.

Defences relevant to the above offences are set out in Regulations 8(4) and (5) of COTES. They include that if the accused:

- proves to the court that he did not believe it was a specimen listed in Annex A or B; or
- enquired whether the goods were unlawfully imported and had no reason to believe they were imported unlawfully,

an offence will not have been committed.

In 'Operation Charm' the Crown Prosecution Service have been satisfied that if goods are anywhere in the shop premises, they are there for sale. It is important to ask for any appropriate documentation and ask questions about each of those supplied, as some documentation could be a defence.

If there is any evidence or suspicion of unlicensed importation from a third country, then more serious offences may have been committed and Customs and Excise should be involved (see 9.4.2).

9.5.7 Checklist of questions to ask

1. Are the products displayed or kept for sale?
2. Are they readily identifiable or marked with their ingredient?
3. Do they contain or claim to contain species listed in Annex A?
4. Do they contain or claim to contain species listed in Annex B and, if so, have they been unlawfully imported?
5. Who is responsible for the shop, ie manager/owner?
6. Do the proprietors know they should not sell a listed item?

7. Is there any documentation covering the original supply of the products to the shop?
8. Does the proprietor know what the products contain?

9.5.8 On the day of the search

Even fairly small shops often carry large stocks, so make sure that you have sufficient officers available to carry out a thorough search.

You will also need some expert assistance to help with identification. TRAFFIC International may be able to help with this and can be contacted through their Cambridge office, details of which are included in the list of useful addresses in Appendix E.

An interpreter will be essential to assist with interviewing staff. There are different dialects of Chinese and so, ideally, your interpreter should speak Cantonese and Mandarin.

There is no power of arrest under COTES, so you will need to report for prosecution any individuals appearing to commit such an offence. In 'Operation Charm' policy has been to report the manager or proprietor of the premises rather than taking action against shop assistants.

In Scotland, because COTES allows for imprisonment as a sentencing option, section 14 detentions under the Criminal Procedure (Scotland) Act 1995 may be employed. This is an important consideration for Scottish officers and COTES should always be contemplated, where relevant, when dealing with wildlife crime. At the conclusion of the six-hour detention period, common law powers of arrest could then be used if destruction of evidence, interference with witnesses, likelihood of absconding and so forth was thought to be a risk.

9.5.9 Identification and analysis of seized items

It is not necessary to prove that products which claim to contain a particular species do, in fact, do so. However, in the case of any body parts or other raw materials seized it may be necessary to have these identified.

Items such as bones or other reasonably complete body parts can probably be identified by expert staff at the National History Museum in London (see list of useful addresses in Appendix E). However, any items in ground or powdered form will need to be identified by scientific analysis. In these cases the Forensic Science Laboratory should be able to help. The Royal Botanic Gardens, Kew, will assist in plant identification.

Many of the more recently imported medicinal products containing endangered species no longer list the species included in the ingredients, although in all other respects the packaging is identical. This is probably a deliberate attempt to get around the provision in British law that a product's claims are taken as read, and in such cases forensic analysis of these products will be necessary to secure convictions in future. At the time of writing work is still being done on the development of a test to identify tiger bone in manufactured products, but a test to identify bear bile is available.

Some products may also contravene the legislation controlling the sale of medicines. The Department of Health's Medicines Control Agency can advise you on this. See list of useful addresses in Appendix E.

9.6 LEGISLATION

9.6.1 The Control of Trade in Endangered Species (Enforcement) Regulations 1997 (COTES)

The COTES Regulations allow for offences in relation to breaches of the EC Regulation implementing CITES, and contain powers of search and entry for enforcement officers. The Regulations apply throughout the United Kingdom. Regulation 3 of

COTES includes the provision for any person who, for the purpose of obtaining a permit or certificate, provides false information or documentation to be guilty of an offence.

COTES also includes provision for offences by corporate bodies.

Penalties under the COTES Regulations include fines of up to £5,000 per offence, imprisonment for up to two years, or both.

9.6.2 The Endangered Species (Import & Export) Act 1976

This Act was the United Kingdom's first legislation to give effect to the CITES Convention, but it has been largely superseded by EC Regulations 3626/82 and 3418/83, and more recently by EC Regulations 338 and 939 of 1997.

The Act was substantially amended by Statutory Instruments 2677 and 2684 of 1996. SI 2677 removes import and export controls on non-CITES species. SI 2684 removes from the Act import and export controls on CITES species which are now implemented through the EC Wildlife Trade Regulation. This SI also removes the duplication between the Act and the Regulation on the sale of certain species.

As a result of these changes, the Act could no longer be used to implement the EC Seals Directive. The Import of Seal Skins Regulations 1996 (SI 1996 No 2686) now effects this by banning the import of harp and hooded seal pup skins.

9.7 CITES: SOME COMMON QUESTIONS ANSWERED

Q. *I am returning from holiday in the Far East. I bought souvenirs which were openly on display and which Customs there made no attempt to take from me. These include ivory carvings, a jaguar-skin handbag and some beautiful coral. Am I breaking the law?*

A. Depending on the country you visited and the products bought, it may or may not have been illegal for persons to sell you those items. However, even though it may have been against that nation's legislation, many countries do not enforce such laws. To import such items without an export permit from the exporting country would be contrary to the provisions of the Customs and Excise Management Act 1979 (CEMA). Such exports are only permitted for personal effects, not commercial consignments.

NB. It may be legal to import ivory carvings/ elephant hide articles from *Zimbabwe only* providing these are for personal use (ie not commercial) only.

Q. *What does captive-bred mean?*

A. CITES provisions relating to this are very strict. To be considered as captive-bred, a bird or animal must be what is termed 'second generation' (F2). This is not as simple as it may sound. If a person mates a male and female taken from the wild, their offspring are not captive-bred. However, if males and females from such offspring subsequently mate, their offspring are captive-bred because they are considered second generation. Where Appendix 1 species are concerned, and someone is considering a commercial operation, then it must be registered with the CITES Secretariat and the specimens must be marked.

False declarations of species having been captive-bred or artificially propagated is the second most common type of CITES fraud.

It is recommended that advice is sought from the management and scientific authorities when trying to establish whether a specimen meets captive-bred definitions.

Q. *I inherited a tiger skin from a relative. I now wish to sell this as I'm told it could be valuable.*

A. You must apply to the DETR for a licence or risk contravening COTES.

Q. *My local taxidermist's shop has a stuffed grizzly bear in its window. It attracts a lot of attention but has a 'Not For Sale' sticker on it. Is this legal?*

A. Possibly not. Unless the taxidermist is covered by a DETR licence, this is likely to contravene the 'commercial display' element of Regulation 8 of COTES.

Q. *I am a police officer. I have received information that a person from an embassy in London has obtained a peregrine falcon which was taken from the wild in Scotland. He intends returning to his country and will transport the bird in the 'diplomatic bag'. Can I take any action?*

A. If this person can claim diplomatic immunity, then he may well escape prosecution from offences under the WCA. However, there is no diplomatic immunity from CITES provisions and all specimens must be accompanied by valid CITES permits. In their absence, CITES specimens are liable to forfeiture, but legal proceedings are unlikely under CEMA because of his diplomatic immunity.

Q. *I am a police officer. I have received information that someone is selling items which are subject to CITES provisions in a local shop. Can I obtain a warrant under COTES to search the premises?*

A. Yes.

Q. *I was at a flower show and saw rare species of orchids and cacti on display, and some were for sale. Can this be legal?*

A. It probably is. Many of the world's rare plant species are artificially propagated and traded legally on a widespread basis.

Q. *If it is relatively easy to artificially propagate such plants, why do people smuggle species such as orchids and cacti from abroad?*

A. Plant collectors will sometimes want to acquire plants from the wild, even though these, to the layman, may appear to be in much poorer condition than those reared in a glasshouse. A

botanist may well be able to tell the difference between the two, as can most people when shown the tell-tale signs.

Q. *If I am simply in possession of an imported CITES specimen from outside the EU within mainland UK, does the law apply to me?*

A. Yes. Regulation 5 of COTES means you may have to furnish proof of its lawful importation to a Customs officer or someone authorised by them. The specimen is liable to forfeiture if you can not.

NOTE: Publicity material, produced by the DETR and HM Customs, has been directed at holiday and business travellers who may inadvertently be breaking the law by bringing souvenirs made from endangered species back from trips abroad. The DETR has produced a leaflet and bookmark which, together with posters suitable for display in police stations or Customs-controlled areas in ports and airports, are available from:

The Department of the Environment, Transport and the Regions
Publications Despatch Centre
Blackhorse Road
London SE99 6TT

The DETR also produces newsletters and guidance notes. If you want to be put on the mailing list, contact the DETR on 0117 987 8366, or write to:
Global Wildlife Division
Department of the Environment,
Transport and the Regions
Room 806
Tollgate House
Houlton Street
Bristol BS2 9DJ

The DETR can also supply other leaflets for educational activities and Customs can loan seized items – for example, ivory tusks and reptile-skin bags – for use in school visits and similar public awareness exercises.

9

Some non-governmental organisations (for example, the World Wide Fund for Nature (WWF), the Royal Society for the Protection of Birds (RSPB) and TRAFFIC International) will also supply materials for educational use.

9.8 MAJOR CITES OPERATIONS

Operation Dorian

A man was arrested on 12 October 1994 while trying to leave Australia carrying 29 parrot eggs valued at £105,000. A search of the premises he had been staying at revealed a further six eggs with a total value of £750,000. He was sentenced to six months' imprisonment and a fine of AUS$1,000.

HM Customs and Excise officers, assisted by a wildlife inspector, TRAFFIC investigator and a local police wildlife liaison officer, searched the premises of his known associates and family in December 1994.

Twenty-two birds were seized and three people were arrested. A further six birds were seized the following day.

Associates of the arrested man were successfully prosecuted. Three people received prison sentences of eight months, two months and six weeks. Two others were each given 200 hours community service. The judge further ordered payment of £2,500 towards the cost of the case and £29,500 worth of assets were seized.

Operation Monty

On 20 July 1994 two people were intercepted by a Customs officer after arriving at Heathrow from Karachi, Pakistan. One of them was carrying a large polystyrene box and a rucksack which he claimed contained 60 lizards and legless lizards which were not CITES controlled and for which he had a licence.

The reptiles and documents were detained for examination and identification. In all, 109 reptiles were identified, some of which had died. The legless lizards were confirmed to be CITES-controlled snakes. The lizards comprised a mixture of non-CITES and CITES species. The reptiles were valued at £5,500.

A subsequent search of the person's property led to the discovery of many more reptiles and the acquisition of a Caiman crocodile.

The judge sentenced the person to four months' imprisonment, and commented that this was being imposed to let others know of the seriousness of the offence and to stand as a warning.

Operation Indiana

In August 1995 officers from Customs, the police, the RSPB and TRAFFIC executed a warrant acting on information that the skull of a Philippine eagle was at a certain premises. The search of the premises revealed a home and outbuildings crammed full of dead endangered species in various degrees of preparation and finished mounts.

Amongst the 500 specimens removed from the house was a red panda, a number of chimpanzees and the skull of a Philippine eagle. The person was found to be carrying out a global business, and premises in Belgium were quickly identified as also being used by him. Belgian Customs officers raided them and recovered a further 1,000 specimens. He was successfully prosecuted and was sentenced to two years' imprisonment.

Operation Morello

In September 1996, South East Regional Crime Squad officers seized rhino horn to the estimated value of almost £3m. The raid took place in London, and the haul was the largest ever known there.

This case exemplifies the value of the partnership approach to combatting wildlife crime. The police worked closely with the RSPCA, and the DETR was also involved.

The police are currently questioning several people and are pursuing their inquiries.

miscellaneous legislation

10.1 ABANDONMENT OF ANIMALS ACT 1960

The Abandonment of Animals Act 1960 was introduced to cope with the growing problem resulting from what is often looked upon as the 'puppy for Christmas' scenario, where a family tires of a pet or it outgrows the home environment. The law takes effect when an animal is abandoned, whether permanently or not, in circumstances likely to cause unnecessary suffering.

Although perhaps not immediately apparent, this can be an extremely useful piece of legislation for the wildlife officer. The 1960 Act shares the same definition of 'animal' as the Protection of Animals Acts. Consequently any non-domestic species, including birds, reptiles and fish, that have been taken into captivity fall within its terms. This allows the police to deal with the individual who may abandon exotic species and even the wildlife rehabilitator who may choose to engage in 'releases' in an inappropriate fashion. Such powers might, for instance, be brought to bear if previously injured and hand-reared badgers were returned to the countryside without sufficient pre-planning and supervision.

One must also presume, since legislators chose to include the phrase 'whether permanently or not', that enforcement officials could use this statute against persons leaving species unattended for lengthy periods, as well as the more obvious situation of the young dog being cast out to wander the streets as a stray.

10.2 DANGEROUS WILD ANIMALS ACT 1976

The Dangerous Wild Animals Act 1976 was introduced to tackle the increasing fashion in the late 1960s and early 1970s for people to keep exotic pets which were all too often from the more dangerous species. It became unacceptable, simply from a public safety point of view, for the average citizen to be free to purchase an animal from the 'big cat' families, a crocodile or venomous snake without some form of control.

The Act's schedule designates the species covered, such as many primates, carnivores, bears, larger reptiles, dangerous spiders and scorpions. Keeping such animals without a local authority licence is unlawful, and the authority is also entitled to specify where and how the animal is to be kept. This law also requires keepers to have their animals covered by a satisfactory liability insurance policy.

It is thought the enactment of this law led to a number of releases into the UK countryside, including some that may have subsequently produced the 'big cat' sightings that are often reported. Indeed, in 1978 a puma was captured in Inverness-shire and, despite extensive enquiries, its origin was never established. However, it would have made a perfect prosecution under the abandonment legislation had its keeper been traced. It would also, of course, have been an offence under **section 14 of the Wildlife and Countryside Act 1981** – releasing or allowing to escape into the wild any animal not ordinarily resident in Great Britain.

The Dangerous Wild Animals Act 1976, although targeted at a specific problem, again offers wider scope to enforcement officers, since its schedule includes many CITES species, and its potential should never be ignored.

One normally finds that it is environmental health departments within local authorities which are given the task of administering this legislation. No specific powers are granted to the police under this Act. However, local authorities are entitled to authorise veterinary surgeons and such other competent persons to inspect premises where animals are to be kept. Animals kept contrary to the Act are also subject to seizure by the authority.

10.3 PET ANIMALS ACT 1951

Properly licensed zoos and pet shops are exempt from the provisions of the Dangerous Wild Animals Act 1976, as are circuses. Whilst the Pet Animals Act 1951 provides for the licensing of pet shops by local authorities, and prohibits the selling of animals for pets in any road or public place or to a person under 12 years of age, the police have no power of entry for inspection into pet shops.

10.4   ZOO LICENSING ACT 1981

This Act requires that all zoos in Great Britain are licensed and regularly inspected. The aim of the Act is to ensure that where animals are kept in caged surroundings they are kept in adequate space and properly provided for.

Licensing is carried out by district councils (usually the environmental health department) with the DETR having responsibility for maintaining a list of zoo inspectors and setting detailed standards for zoo management.

Zoo inspections are carried out by local authorities, using inspectors who are appointed as necessary by the DETR. Inspectors are veterinary practitioners or persons competent to advise on animal-keeping and zoo management.

Smaller zoos, for example butterfly houses and seaside aquaria, can obtain dispensation from the full inspection procedures but must still comply with the set standards of modern zoo practice.

No specific police powers are provided by the Act.

10.5   PERFORMING ANIMALS (REGULATION) ACT 1925

The Performing Animals (Regulation) Act 1925 controls the exhibition and training of animals for any entertainment to which the public have access, whether on payment or not. No person can exhibit or train an animal unless they are registered with the local authority. The expression 'animal' is not specifically defined by the Act but does exclude invertebrates.

Any police officer may enter and inspect, at all reasonable times, any premises in which any performing animals are being exhibited or trained, or kept for either purpose, and any animal found there. He may also require any trainer or exhibitor to produce his certificate of registration from the local authority.

10.6   PROTECTION OF ANIMALS ACT 1934

The Protection of Animals Act 1934 prohibits any public performance where unbroken or untrained horses or bulls are thrown, casted with ropes or appliances, wrestled, fought, struggled or ridden. The offence under this statute is committed by any person who promotes, causes or permits any such performance, or takes part in such a performance.

This Act would appear to outlaw in Great Britain the rodeos or bullfights popular elsewhere in the world. No specific powers are granted to the police under this legislation.

10.7   CINEMATOGRAPH FILMS (ANIMALS) ACT 1937

The Cinematograph Films (Animals) Act 1937 prohibits the showing or supply of any film in which a scene represents the cruel infliction of pain or terror on any animal. 'Animal' has the same meaning as in the Protection of Animals Act 1911 (1912 in Scotland).

10.8   THE PROTECTION OF ANIMALS (AMENDMENT) ACT 1988

The Protection of Animals (Amendment) Act 1988 inserted into the Protection of Animals Acts 1911 (1912 in Scotland) the offences of being present at animal fights or advertising such fights. This legislation is employed where unlawful dog fights or badger baiting take place.

10.9   OPERATIONS ETC INVOLVING ANIMALS AND THE SLAUGHTER OF ANIMALS

Various statutes have been enacted to protect animals from unnecessary pain during otherwise lawful operations. Whilst wildlife law enforcers are unlikely to be called upon to deal with these situations, it is worth knowing that such legislation exists. The **Protection of Animals (Anaesthetics) Acts 1954 and 1964** specify procedures where anaesthetics must be employed, including such as docking of tails, de-horning, castration, etc. However, this field of law is complicated and advice should be sought from the Royal College of Veterinary Surgeons or MAFF. Similarly, the **Animals (Scientific Procedures) Act 1986** provides for a system of licensing control of experimental and other scientific work carried out on living animals. The Home Office is responsible for the regulation of this Act, and the involvement of the police or courts is likely to be very rare.

Even the simple act of shoeing horses is controlled, so that persons wishing to do so must be registered under the **Farriers (Registration) Act 1975**.

Similarly, considerable legislation provides for the control of the slaughtering of animals, slaughterhouses, keeping of animals prior to slaughter, knackeries, and Jewish and Muslim methods of slaughter. These statutes are primarily enforced by local authorities and MAFF. Acts governing these fields commonly provide power of entry for inspection purpose to constables, but the police would be well advised to seek expert advice before attempting to enforce this area of the law.

10.10 ANIMAL HEALTH ACT 1981

This is the primary legislation under which Secretaries of State are entitled to introduce Orders governing a wide range of animal health matters, including transport, quarantine, rabies and notifiable diseases. Liaison with such as MAFF, local authority diseases of animals inspectors or RSPCA/SSPCA inspectors is recommended, as they have considerable experience of the intricacies of the legislation and can provide the essential evidential expert knowledge required.

However, the police should be aware of their own powers under section 60 of the Act.

- Any person seen committing an offence or suspected of being engaged in committing an offence can be stopped and detained by a police officer.

- That person can then be arrested, without warrant, if he fails to give his name and address to the police officer's satisfaction.

- The police officer may also stop, detain and examine any animal, vehicle, boat or thing to which the offence or suspected offence relates.

Further powers relating specifically to rabies are granted, and these refer to situations where persons land or attempt to land animals in contravention of Orders made to prevent the introduction of rabies to Great Britain; to the failure of persons in charge of any vessel or boat to comply with those Orders; or where movement is being made of animals from or into a place declared to be infected with rabies.

- A police officer may arrest, without warrant, any person committing or suspected of committing such an offence (section 61).

- He may also enter (if need be, by force) and search any vessel, boat, aircraft or vehicle in which that person is or in which the police officer reasonably suspects him to be. Similar power is granted to enter, search for and seize any animal (section 62).

10.11 DUMPED WASTE – ENVIRONMENTAL PROTECTION ACT 1990

On 1 April 1996 a new national agency, the Environment Agency, was created from the regional Waste Control Areas, and will provide a 24-hour national emergency advice service when telephoned on 0800 807060.

The Agency will provide expert evidence and initiate proceedings in cases where waste has been abandoned. Such waste would include oil and oil filters, oil solvent, petrol and its derivatives, paint, chairs and fridges; in other words, the purposeful disposal of waste in an anti-social manner. Two types of waste exist, special and controlled. Special waste includes prescription – only medicine, toxic substances, and inflammable and tissue – damaging substances. Controlled waste is any household, commercial or industrial waste.

10

Section 33 of the Act prohibits the unauthorised or harmful depositing, treatment or disposal of waste in or on any land in a manner likely to cause pollution to the environment or harm to human health.

On summary conviction of disposing of controlled waste, there may be a fine of up to £20,000 and/or six months' imprisonment may be imposed. On indictment, the imprisonment may be up to two years for controlled waste and five years' imprisonment for special waste.

The difficulty in investigating these type of offences is often one of the continuity of evidence, but the officer does have recourse to the general arrest provisions of section 25 of the Police and Criminal Evidence Act 1984 in England and Wales. In Scotland, an individual suspected of committing an offence can be arrested under section 13 of the Criminal Procedure (Scotland) Act 1995. The powers granted under the environmental protection legislation apply to police officers too. Indeed, the presence of a police officer may often be required in order to stop vehicles for inspection purposes.

In Scotland the relevant body is the Scottish Environment Protection Agency (SEPA).

appendix a

the Schedules to the Wildlife and Countryside Act 1981

THE SCHEDULES

Schedule 1

Part 1 – Birds protected by special penalties at all times

Any species of bird not mentioned in Schedule 1 or Schedule 2 is fully protected throughout the year. See also checklist of legal status of selected British birds in Appendix B.

Common names are given here for guidance only. In cases of dispute or proceedings, scientific names should be used. See Appendix D.

Avocet	Fieldfare	Owl, Barn Snowy	Shrike, Red-backed
Bee-eater	Firecrest		Spoonbill
Bittern	Garganey	Peregrine	Stilt, Black-winged
Bittern, Little	Godwit, Black-tailed	Petrel, Leach's	
Bluethroat	Goshawk	Phalarope, Red-necked	Stint, Temminck's
Brambling	Grebe, Black-necked Slavonian	Plover, Kentish Little Ringed	Stone-curlew
Bunting, Cirl Lapland Snow	Greenshank	Quail, Common	Swan, Bewick's Whooper
Buzzard, Honey	Gull, Little Mediterranean	Redstart, Black	Tern, Black Little Roseate
Chough		Redwing	
Corncrake	Harriers (all species)	Rosefinch, Scarlet	Tit, Bearded Crested
Crake, Spotted	Heron, Purple	Ruff	
Crossbill (all species)	Hobby	Sandpiper, Green Purple Wood	Treecreeper, Short-toed
Divers (all species)	Hoopoe		Warbler, Cetti's Dartford Marsh Savi's
Dotterel	Kingfisher	Scaup	
Duck, Long-tailed	Kite, Red	Scoter, Common Velvet	
Eagle, Golden White-tailed	Merlin	Serin	Whimbrel
	Oriole, Golden		Woodlark
Falcon, Gyr	Osprey	Shorelark	Wryneck

Part II – Birds and their eggs protected by special penalties during the close season, 1 February to 31 August (21 February to 31 August below high-water mark), but which may be killed or taken at other times

Goldeneye	Greylag Goose (*in Outer Hebrides, Caithness, Sutherland and Wester Ross only*)	Pintail

Schedule 2

Birds which may be killed or taken outside the close season, 1 February to 31 August, except where indicated otherwise

Part I

Note: The close season for ducks and geese when below high-water mark is 21 February to 31 August.

Capercaillie *(close season 1 Feb–30 Sep)*	Mallard	Woodcock *(close season 1 Feb–30 Sep, except in Scotland where 1 Feb–31 Aug)*
	Moorhen	
Coot	Pintail	
Duck, Tufted	Plover, Golden	
Gadwall	Pochard	
Goldeneye	Shoveler	
Goose, Canada Greylag Pink-footed White-fronted *(fully protected in Scotland)*	Snipe, Common *(close season 1 Feb–11 Aug)*	
	Teal	
	Wigeon	

Part II

Birds which may be killed or taken by authorised persons:

This section has been replaced by general licences with the same effect.

Crow, Carrion	Jackdaw	Starling
Dove, Collared	Jay	Wood Pigeon
Gull, Great Black-backed Herring Lesser Black-backed	Magpie	
	Pigeon, Feral	
	Rook	
	Sparrow, House	

Schedule 3

Birds which may be sold alive at all times if ringed and bred in captivity

Part I

Blackbird	Greenfinch	Siskin
Brambling	Jackdaw	Starling
Bullfinch	Jay	Thrush, Song
Bunting, Reed	Linnet	Twite
Chaffinch	Magpie	Yellowhammer
Dunnock	Owl, Barn	
Goldfinch	Redpoll	

Note: Certain birds on Schedule 4 may also be sold under licence provided they are registered with the DETR; for details see legal status checklist – Appendix B.

Part II

Birds which may be sold dead at all times

Woodpigeon

Part III

Birds which may be sold dead from 1 September to 28 February

Capercaillie	Pintail	Snipe, Common
Coot	Plover, Golden	Teal
Duck, Tufted	Pochard	Wigeon
Mallard	Shoveler	Woodcock

Note: It is illegal to offer for sale at any time of the year any wild goose, moorhen, gadwall or goldeneye, although they are legitimate quarry species outside the close season.

Schedule 4

Birds which must be registered and ringed if kept in captivity

Bunting,
Cirl
Lapland
Snow

Buzzard, Honey

Eagle,
Adalbert's
Golden
Great Phillipine
Imperial
New Guinea
White-tailed

Chough

**Crossbills
(all species)**

Falcon,
Barbary
Gyr
Peregrine

Fieldfare

Firecrest

**Fish-eagle,
Madagascar**

**Forest-falcon,
Plumbeous**

Goshawk

Harrier,
Hen
Marsh
Montagu's
Galapagos
Grey-backed
Hawaiian
Ridgway's
White-necked

**Hawk-eagle,
Wallace's**

Hobby

**Honey Buzzard,
Black**

Kestrel,
Lesser
Mauritius

Kite, Red

Merlin

Oriole, Golden

Osprey

Redstart, Black

Redwing

Sea-eagle,
Pallas'
Steller's

Serin

Serpent-eagle,
Andaman
Madagascar
Mountain

Shorelark

**Shrike,
Red-backed**

Sparrowhawk,
New Britain
Gundlach's
Imitator
Small

Tit,
Bearded
Crested

Warbler,
Cetti's
Dartford
Marsh
Savi's

Woodlark

Wryneck

Any bird, one of whose parents or other lineal ancestor was a bird of a kind specified in the above list.

Schedule 5

Protected animals

Adder
(*section 9(1)* *'killing and injuring' and 9(5) 'sale' only*)

Anemone,
Ivell's Sea
Pink Sea Fan
Starlet Sea

Apus Tadpole Shrimp

Bats, Horseshoe (all species)

Bats, Typical (all species)

Beetle
Bembridge
Lesser
Silver Water
Long-horned
Mire Pill
Mocass
Rainbow Leaf
Spangled Water
Violet Click

Burbot

Butterfly
Adonis Blue*
Black Hairstreak*
Chalkhill Blue*
Chequered Skipper*

Duke of Burgundy Fritillary*
Glanville Fritillary*
Heath Fritillary*
High Brown Fritillary*
Large Blue*
Large Copper*
Large Heath*
Large Tortoiseshell*
Lulworth Skipper*
Marsh Fritillary*
Mountain Ringlet*
Northern Brown Argus*
Pearl-Bordered Fritillary*
Purple Emperor*
Silver-spotted Skipper*
Silver-studded Blue*
Small Blue*
Swallowtail*
White Letter* Hairstreak
Wood White*
* denotes Section 9(5) 'sale' only)

Cat, Wild

Cicada, New Forest

Crayfish, Atlantic Stream
(*section 9(1)* *'taking' and 9(5) 'sale' only*)

Cricket,
Field
Mole

Dolphins

Dormouse

Dragonfly
Norfolk Aeshna
Orange-spotted Emerald

Frog, Common
(*Section 9(5) 'sale' only*)

Grasshopper, Wart-biter

Hatchet Shell, Northern

Lagoon Snail

Lagoon Snail, De Folin's

Lagoon Worm, Tentacled

Leech, Medicinal

Lizard,
Sand
Viviparous
(*Section 9(1)* *'killing & injuring' and 9(5) 'sale' only*)

Marten, Pine

Moth,
Barberry Carpet
Curzon's sphinx
Black-veined
Essex Emerald
New Forest Burnet
Reddish Buff
Sussex Emerald
Viper's Bugloss

Mussel, Freshwater Pearl
(*section 9(1)* *'killing & injuring' only*)

Newt,
Great Crested (or Warty)
Palmate [+]
Smooth [+]
[+] (*Section 9(5) 'sale' only*)

Otter, Common

Porpoises

Sandworm, Lagoon

Sea Fan, Pink
(*section 9(1)* *'killing, injuring & taking', 9(2) 'possession' and 9(5) 'sale' only*)

Sea Mat, Trembling

Sea Slug, Lagoon

Shad, Allis
(*Section 9(1)* *'killing & injuring' and 9(5) 'sale' only*)

Shrimp,
Fairy
Lagoon Sand
Tadpole

Slow Worm
(*section 9(1)* *'killing & injuring' and 9(5) 'sale' only*)

Snail,
Glutinous
Lagoon
Sandbowl

Snake
Grass
(*section 9(1)* *'killing & injuring' and 9(5) 'sale' only*)
Smooth

Spider,
Fen Raft
Ladybird

Squirrel, Red

Sturgeon

Toad,
Common
(*section 9(5) 'sale' only*)
Natterjack

Turtles, Marine

Vendace

Walrus

Whales

Whitefish

Worm, Tentacled Lagoon

Note: Where a species is annotated with an asterisk, protection is only afforded against the actions referred to.

Schedule 6

Animals which may not be killed or taken by certain methods

Badger	Bats, Typical (all species)	Dolphin, Bottle-nosed	Hedgehog	Porpoise, Harbour (otherwise known as Common Porpoise)	Shrews (all species)
Bats, Horseshoe (all species)	Cat, Wild	Dormice (all species)	Marten, Pine		Squirrel, Red
			Otter, Common		
			Polecat		

Schedule 8

Protected plants

Adder's Tongue, Least

Alison, Small

Blackwort

Broomrape,
Bedstraw
Oxtongue
Thistle

Cabbage, Lundy

Calamint, Wood

Caloplaca, Snow

Catapyrenium, Tree

Catchfly, Alpine

Catillaria, Laurer's

Centaury, Slender

Cinquefoil, Rock

Cladonia, Upright Mountain

Clary, Meadow

Club-rush, Triangular

Colt's-foot, Purple

Cotoneaster, Wild

Cottongrass, Slender

Cow-wheat, Field

Crocus, Sand

Crystalwort, Lizard

Cudweed,
Broad-leaved
Jersey
Red-tipped

Diapensia

Dock, Shore

Earwort, Marsh

Eryngo, Field

Fern,
Dickie's Bladder
Killarney

Flapwort, Norfolk

Fleabane,
Alpine
Small

Frostwort, Pointed

Galingale, Brown

Gentian,
Alpine
Dune
Early
Fringed
Spring

Germander,
Cut-leaved
Water

Gladiolus, Wild

Goosefoot, Stinking

Grass-poly

Crimmia, Blunt-leaved

Gyalecta, Elm

Hare's-ear,
Sickle-leaved
Small

Hawk's-beard, Stinking

Hawkweed,
Northroe
Shetland
Weak-leaved

Heath, Blue

Helleborine,
Red
Young's

Horsetail, Branched

Hound's-tongue, Green

Knawel, Perennial

Knotgrass, Sea

Lady's-slipper, Sea

Lady's-slipper

Lecanactis, Churchyard

Lecanora, Tarn

Lecidea, Copper

Leek, Round-headed

Lettuce, Least

Lichen,
Artic Kidney
Ciliate Strap
Coralloid Rosette
Ear-lobed Dog

Forked Hair
Golden Hair
Orange-fruited Elm
River Jelly
Scaly Breck
Stary Breck

Lily, Snowdon

Liverwort,
Lindenberg's Leafy

Marsh-mallow, Rough

Marshwort, Creeping

Milk-parsley, Cambridge

Moss
Alpine Copper
Baltic Bog
Blue Dew
Blunt-leaved Bristle
Bright Green
Cave
Cordate Beard
Cornish Path
Derbyshire Feather
Dune Thread
Glaucous Beard
Green Shield
Hair Silk
Knothole
Large Yellow Feather
Millimetre
Multifruited River
Nowell's lime-stone
Rigid Apple
Round-leaved feather
Scleicher's Thread
Triangular Pygmy

Vaucher's Feather

Mudworth, Welsh

Naiad
Holly-leaved
Slender

Orache, Stalked

Orchid,
Early Spider
Fen
Ghost
Lapland Marsh
Late Spider
Lizard
Military
Monkey

Panneria, Caledonia

Parmelia, New Forest

Parmentaria, Oil Stain

Pear, Plymouth

Penny-cress, Perfoliate

Pennyroyal

Pertusaria, Alpine Moss

Physcia, Southern Grey

Pigmyweed

Pine, Ground

Pink,
Cheddar
Childing

Plantain, Floating Water

Pseudo-cyphell-aria, Ragged

Psora, Rusty Alpine

Ragwort, Fen

Ramping-fumitory, Martin's

Rampion, Spiked

Restharrow, Small

Rock-cress,
Alpine
Bristol

Rustwort, Western

Sandwort
Norwegian
Teesdale

Saxifrage,
Drooping
Marsh
Tufted

Solenopsora, Serpentine

Soloman's Seal, Whorled

Sow-thistle, Alpine

Spearwort, Adder's-tongue

Speedwell,
Fingered
Spiked

Star-of-Bethlem, Early

Starfruit

Schedule 8 – Continued...

Stonewort,
Foxtail
Bearded

Strapwort

Turpswort

Violet, Fen

Viper's-grass

Water-plantain, Ribbon-leaved

Wood-sedge, Starved

Woodsia,
Alpine
Oblong

Wormwood, Field

Woundwort,
Downy
Limestone

Yellow-rattle, Greater Ragged

Schedule 9

Animals and plants to which Section 14 applies (ie may not be released into or grown in the wild)

Part 1: Birds and other animals

Bass,
Large-mouthed
Black
Rock

Bitterling

Budgerigar

Capercaillie

Coypu

Crayfish,
Noble
Signal
Turkish

Deer,
Sika
Muntjak

Dormouse, Fat

Duck,
Carolina Wood
Mandarin
Ruddy

Eagle,
White-tailed

Flatworm, New Zealand

Frog,
Edible
European Tree
(otherwise known as Common Tree Frog)
Marsh

Gerbil,
Mongolian

Goose,
Canada
Egyptian

Heron, Night

Lizard, Common Wall

Marmot, Prairie
(otherwise known as Prairie Dog)

Mink, American

Newt,
Alpine
Italian Crested

Owl, Barn

Parakeet,
Ring-necked

Partridge,
Chukar
Rock

Pheasant,
Golden
Lady Amherst's
Reeves'
Silver

Porcupine,
Crested
Himalayan

Pumpkinseed
(otherwise known as Sun-fish or Pond-perch)

Quail, Bobwhite

Rat, Black

Snake,
Aescupapian

Squirrel, Grey

Terrapin,
European Pond

Toad,
African Clawed
Midwife

Wallaby,
Red-necked

Wels (otherwise known as European Catfish)

Part II: Plants

Hogweed, Giant

Kelp, Giant

Kelp, Japanese

Knotweed, Japanese

Seafingers, Green

Seaweed,
Californian Red
Hooked Asparagus
Japanese
Laver (except native species)

Wakame

Schedule 2: European protected species of animals

Bats, Horseshoe (all species)	Dolphins, Porpoises and Whales (all species)	Otter, Common
Bats, Typical (all species)		Snake, Smooth
		Sturgeon
Butterfly, Large Blue	Dormouse	Toad, Natterjack
	Lizard, Sand	
Cat, Wild	Newt, Great Crested (or Warty)	Turtles, Marine

Schedule 4: European protected species of plants

Dock, Shore	Marshwort, Creeping	Plantain, Floating-leaved Water
Fern, Killarney		
Gentian, Early	Naiad, Slender	
	Orchid, Fen	Saxifrage, Yellow Marsh
Lady's-slipper		

appendix b

checklist of legal status of selected British birds

CHECKLIST OF LEGAL STATUS OF SELECTED BRITISH BIRDS

Reprinted by kind permission of the RSPB

This list indicates the legal status of all birds in the Schedules and many other common species of British birds.

Any species not listed **below** is protected at all times.

Auk, Little	Protected at all times.
Avocet	Specially protected at all times.
Bee-eater	Specially protected at all times.
Bittern	Specially protected at all times.
Bittern, Little	Specially protected at all times.
Blackbird	Protected at all times.
Blackcap	Protected at all times.
Bluethroat	Specially protected at all times.
Brambling	Specially protected at all times. May be competitively exhibited or sold if captive-bred and fitted with an approved close ring.
Bullfinch	Protected at all times but may also be killed under general licence in certain fruit-growing areas. May be competitively exhibited or sold if captive-bred and fitted with an approved close ring.
Bunting, Cirl	Specially protected at all times; must be ringed and registered if kept in captivity.
Bunting, Corn	Protected at all times.
Bunting, Lapland	Specially protected at all times; must be ringed and registered if kept in captivity.
Bunting, Reed	Protected at all times. May be competitively exhibited or sold if captive-bred and fitted with an approved close ring.

Bunting, Snow	Specially protected at all times; must be ringed and registered if kept in captivity.
Buzzard	Protected at all times. Subject to new sales controls under COTES 1997.
Buzzard, Honey	Specially protected at all times; must be ringed and registered if kept in captivity. Subject to new sales controls under COTES 1997.
Buzzard, Rough-legged	Protected at all times. Subject to new sales controls under COTES 1997.
Capercaillie	Protected in close season; may be shot from 1 October – 31 January; may be sold (dead) from 1 September – 28 February.
Chaffinch	Protected at all times. May be competitively exhibited or sold if captive-bred and fitted with an approved close ring.
Chiffchaff	Protected at all times.
Chough	Specially protected at all times; must be ringed and registered if kept in captivity.
Coot	Protected in close season; may be shot from 1 September – 31 January; may be sold (dead) from 1 September – 28 February.
Cormorant	Protected at all times.
Corncrake	Specially protected at all times
Crake, Spotted	Specially protected at all times.
Crane	Protected at all times.
Crossbill (all species)	Specially protected at all times; must be ringed and registered if kept in captivity.
Crow, Carrion and Hooded	May be killed or taken (including destruction of nests/eggs) under the terms of a general licence.

Cuckoo	Protected at all times.
Curlew	Protected at all times.
Dipper	Protected at all times.
Diver (all species)	Specially protected at all times.
Dotterel	Specially protected at all times
Dove, Collared	May be killed or taken (including destruction of nests/eggs) under the terms of a general licence.
Dove, Rock	Protected at all times.
Dove, Stock	Protected at all times.
Dove, Turtle	Protected at all times.
Duck, Long-tailed	Specially protected at all times.
Duck, Tufted	Protected in close season; may be shot from 1 September – 31 January (to 20 February in areas below high-water mark); may be sold (dead) from 1 September– 28 February. General licence permits sale of captive-bred birds and their eggs.
Dunlin	Protected at all times.
Dunnock	Protected at all times. May be competitively exhibited or sold if captive-bred and fitted with an approved close ring.
Eagle, Golden	Specially protected at all times; must be ringed and registered if kept in captivity. General licence permits registered birds to be sold.
Eagle, White-tailed	Specially protected at all times; must be ringed and registered if kept in captivity. Subject to new sales controls under COTES 1997.
Eider	Protected at all times. General licence permits sale of captive-bred birds and their eggs.
Falcon, Gyr	Specially protected at all times; must be ringed and registered if kept in captivity. Subject to new sales controls under COTES 1997.
Falcon, Peregrine	Specially protected at all times; must be ringed and registered if kept in captivity. Subject to new sales controls under COTES 1997.
Fieldfare	Specially protected at all times; must be ringed and registered if kept in captivity.
Firecrest	Specially protected at all times; must be ringed and registered if kept in captivity.
Flycatcher (all species)	Protected at all times.
Fulmar	Protected at all times.
Gadwall	Protected in close season; may be shot from 1 September – 31 January (to 20 February in areas below high-water mark). General licence permits sale of captive-bred birds and their eggs.
Gannet	Protected at all times. Provision exists for licence to be granted permitting taking for food for human consumption on Sula Sgeir only.
Garganey	Specially protected at all times. Subject to new sales controls under COTES 1997.
Godwit, Bar-tailed	Protected at all times.
Godwit, Black-tailed	Specially protected at all times.
Goldcrest	Protected at all times.

Goldeneye	Specially protected during close season; may be shot from 1 September – 31 January (to 20 February in areas below high-water mark).
Goldfinch	Protected at all times. May be competitively exhibited or sold if captive-bred and fitted with an approved close ring.
Goosander	Protected at all times.
Goose, Barnacle	Protected at all times. General licence permits sale of captive-bred birds and their eggs.
Goose, Bean	Protected at all times. General licence permits sale of captive-bred birds and their eggs.
Goose, Brent	Protected at all times.
Goose, Canada	Protected in close season; may be shot from 1 September – 31 January (to 20 February in areas below high-water mark). General licence permits sale of captive-bred birds and their eggs.
Goose, Greylag	Protected in close season; may be shot from 1 September – 31 January (to 20 February in areas below high-water mark). General licence permits sale of captive-bred birds and their eggs. NB. In Outer Hebrides, Caithness, Sutherland and Wester Ross, specially protected in close season.
Goose, Lesser White-fronted	Protected at all times. General licence permits sale of captive-bred birds and their eggs.
Goose, Pink-footed	Protected in close season; may be shot from 1 September – 31 January (to 20 February in areas below high-water mark). General licence permits sale of captive-bred birds and their eggs.
Goose, Snow	Protected at all times.
Goose, White-fronted	Scotland: Protected at all times. England and Wales: Protected in close season; may be shot from 1 September – 31 January (to 20 February in areas below high-water mark). General licence permits sale of captive-bred birds and their eggs.
Goshawk	Specially protected at all times; must be ringed and registered if kept in captivity. Subject to new sales controls under COTES 1997.
Grebe, Black-necked	Specially protected at all times.
Grebe, Slavonian	Specially protected at all times.
Grebe (all other species)	Protected at all times.
Greenfinch	Protected at all times. May be competitively exhibited or sold if captive-bred and fitted with an approved close ring.
Greenshank	Specially protected at all times.
Grouse, Black	Covered by Game Acts which protect it in close season and allow it to be shot from 20 August – 10 December.
Grouse, Red	Covered by Game Acts which protect it in close season and allow it to be shot from 12 August – 10 December.
Guillemot (all species)	Protected at all times.
Gull, Black-headed	Protected at all times. General licence permits authorised persons to kill and take birds and to destroy their nests and eggs at certain aerodromes.

Gull, Common	Protected at all times. General licence permits authorised persons to kill and take birds and to destroy their nests and eggs at certain aerodromes.
Gull, Great Black-backed	May be killed or taken under the terms of a general licence. General Licence permits sale of eggs for human consumption.
Gull, Herring	May be killed or taken under the terms of a general licence. General licence permits sale of eggs for human consumption.
Gull, Lesser Black-backed	May be killed or taken under the terms of a general licence. General licence permits sale of eggs for human consumption.
Gull, Little	Specially protected at all times.
Gull, Mediterranean	Specially protected at all times.
Harrier (all species)	Specially protected at all times; must be ringed and registered if kept in captivity. Subject to new sales controls under COTES 1997.
Hawfinch	Protected at all times.
Heron, Grey	Protected at all times.
Heron, Purple	Specially protected at all times.
Hobby	Specially protected at all times; must be ringed and registered if kept in captivity. Subject to new sales controls under COTES 1997.
Hoopoe	Specially protected at all times.
Jackdaw	May be killed or taken under the terms of a general licence. May be competitively exhibited or sold if captive-bred and fitted with an approved close ring.
Jay	May be killed or taken under the terms of a general licence. May be competitively exhibited or sold if captive-bred and fitted with an approved close ring.
Kestrel	Protected at all times. Subject to new sales controls under COTES 1997.
Kingfisher	Specially protected at all times.
Kite, Red	Specially protected at all times; must be ringed and registered if kept in captivity. Subject to new sales controls under COTES 1997.
Kittiwake	Protected at all times.
Knot	Protected at all times.
Lapwing	Protected at all times. General licence permits authorised persons to take birds and destroy their nests and eggs at certain aerodromes. Provision exists for licence to permit taking of eggs before 15 April for food for human consumption.
Linnet	Protected at all times.
Magpie	May be killed or taken under the terms of a general licence. May be competitively exhibited or sold if ringed and bred in captivity.
Mallard	Protected in close season; may be shot from 1 September – 31 January (to 20 February in areas below high-water mark); may be sold (dead) 1 September – 28 February. General licence permits (1) authorised persons to take eggs for incubation; (2) selling of captive-bred birds and their eggs.
Martin (all species)	Protected at all times.

Merganser, Red-breasted	Protected at all times.
Merlin	Specially protected at all times; must be ringed and registered if kept in captivity. Subject to new sales controls under COTES 1997.
Moorhen	Protected in close season; may be shot from 1 September – 31 January.
Nightingale	Protected at all times.
Nightjar	Protected at all times.
Nuthatch	Protected at all times.
Oriole, Golden	Specially protected at all times; must be ringed and registered if kept in captivity.
Osprey	Specially protected at all times; must be ringed and registered if kept in captivity. Subject to new sales controls under COTES 1997.
Ouzel, Ring	Protected at all times.
Owl, Barn	Specially protected at all times; may be competitively exhibited or sold if ringed and bred in captivity. Also included on Schedule 9 of the Act. Subject to new sales controls under COTES 1997.
Owl, Little	Protected at all times. Subject to new sales controls under COTES 1997.
Owl, Long-eared	Protected at all times. Subject to new sales controls under COTES 1997.
Owl, Short-eared	Protected at all times. Subject to new sales controls under COTES 1997.
Owl, Snowy	Specially protected at all times. Subject to new sales controls under COTES 1997.
Owl, Tawny	Protected at all times. Subject to new sales controls under COTES 1997.
Oystercatcher	Protected at all times. General licence permits authorised persons to kill or take birds and destroy their nests and eggs at certain aerodromes.
Partridge (all species)	Covered by Game Acts which give protection in close season and allow shooting from 1 September – 1 February.
Petrel, Leach's	Specially protected at all times.
Petrel, Storm	Protected at all times.
Phalarope, Grey	Protected at all times.
Phalarope, Red-necked	Specially protected at all times.
Pheasant	Covered by Game Acts which protect it in the close season and allow it to be shot from 1 October – 1 February.
Pigeon, Feral	May be killed or taken (including destruction of nests/eggs) under the terms of a general licence.
Pintail	Specially protected in close season; may be shot from 1 September – 31 January (to 20 February in areas below high-water mark); may be sold (dead) from 1 September – 28 February. General licence permits the sale of captive-bred birds and their eggs.
Pipit (all species)	Protected at all times.
Plover, Golden	Protected in close season; may be shot from 1 September – 28 February.
Plover, Grey	Protected at all times.
Plover, Kentish	Specially protected at all times.

Plover, Little Ringed	Specially protected at all times.
Plover, Ringed	Protected at all times.
Pochard	Protected in close season; may be shot from 1 September – 31 January (to 20 February in areas below high water mark); may be sold (dead) from 1 September – 28 February. General Licence permits sale of captive-bred birds and their eggs.
Ptarmigan	Covered by Game Acts which protect it at all times in England and Wales; protected in Scotland in close season but may be shot from 12 August – 10 December.
Puffin	Protected at all times.
Quail, Common	Specially protected at all times.
Rail, Water	Protected at all times.
Raven	Protected at all times.
Razorbill	Protected at all times.
Redpoll	Protected at all times. May be competitively exhibited or sold if captive bred and fitted with an approved close-ring.
Redshank	Protected at all times.
Redshank, Spotted	Protected at all times.
Redstart	Protected at all times.
Redstart, Black	Specially protected at all times; must be ringed and registered if kept in captivity.
Redwing	Specially protected at all times; must be ringed and registered if kept in captivity.
Robin	Protected at all times.

Rook	May be killed or taken under the terms of a General Licence.
Rosefinch, Scarlet	Specially protected at all times.
Ruff	Specially protected at all times.
Sanderling	Protected at all times.
Sandpiper, Common	Protected at all times.
Sandpiper, Curlew	Protected at all times.
Sandpiper, Green	Specially protected at all times.
Sandpiper, Purple	Specially protected at all times.
Sandpiper, Wood	Specially protected at all times.
Scaup	Specially protected at all times. General Licence permits sale of captive-bred birds and their eggs.
Scoter, Common	Specially protected at all times.
Scoter , Velvet	Specially protected at all times.
Serin	Specially protected at all times; must be ringed and registered if kept in captivity.
Shag	Protected at all times.
Shearwater, Manx	Protected at all times.
Shelduck	Protected at all times. General Licence permits sale of captive-bred birds and their eggs.
Shorelark	Specially protected at all times; must be ringed and registered if kept in captivity.

Shoveler	Protected in close season; may be shot from 1 September – 31 January (to 20 February in areas below high-water mark); may be sold (dead) from 1 September –28 February. General licence permits sale of captive-bred birds and their eggs.
Shrike, Great Grey	Protected at all times.
Shrike, Red-backed	Specially protected at all times; must be ringed and registered if kept in captivity.
Siskin	Protected at all times; may be competitively exhibited or sold if ringed and bred in captivity.
Skua (all species)	Protected at all times.
Skylark	Protected at all times.
Smew	Protected at all times. General licence permits sales of captive-bred birds and their eggs.
Snipe, Common	Protected in close season; may be shot from 12 August – 31 January; may be sold (dead) from 1 September – 28 February.
Snipe, Jack	Protected at all times.
Sparrow, House	May be killed or taken (including destruction of nests/eggs) under the terms of a general licence.
Sparrow, Tree	Protected at all times.
Sparrowhawk	Protected at all times. Subject to new sales controls under COTES 1997.
Spoonbill	Specially protected at all times.
Starling	May be killed or taken under the terms of a general licence.
Stilt, Black-winged	Specially protected at all times.

Stint, Little	Protected at all times.
Stint, Temminck's	Specially protected at all times.
Stonechat	Protected at all times.
Stone-curlew	Specially protected at all times.
Swallow	Protected at all times.
Swan, Bewick's	Specially protected at all times.
Swan, Mute	Protected at all times.
Swan, Whooper	Specially protected at all times. General licence permits sale of captive-bred birds and their eggs.
Swift	Protected at all times.
Teal	Protected in close season; may be shot from 1 September – 31 January (to 20 February in areas below high-water mark); may be sold (dead) from 1 September – 28 February. General licence permits sale of captive-bred birds and their eggs.
Tern, Arctic	Protected at all times.
Tern, Black	Specially protected at all times.
Tern, Common	Protected at all times.
Tern, Little	Specially protected at all times.
Tern, Roseate	Specially protected at all times.
Tern, Sandwich	Protected at all times.
Thrush, Mistle	Protected at all times.
Thrush, Song	Protected at all times. May be competitively exhibited or sold if captive-bred and fitted with an approved close ring.
Tit, Bearded	Specially protected at all times; must be ringed and registered if kept in captivity.
Tit, Crested	Specially protected at all times; must be ringed and registered if kept in captivity.

Tit (all other species)	Protected at all times.
Treecreeper	Protected at all times.
Treecreeper, Short-toed	Specially protected at all times.
Turnstone	Protected at all times.
Twite	Protected at all times. May be competitively exhibited or sold if captive bred and fitted with an approved close-ring.
Wagtail (all species)	Protected at all times.
Warbler, Cetti's	Specially protected at all times; must be ringed and registered if kept in captivity.
Warbler, Dartford	Specially protected at all times; must be ringed and registered if kept in captivity.
Warbler, Marsh	Specially protected at all times; must be ringed and registered if kept in captivity.
Warbler, Savi's	Specially protected at all times; must be ringed and registered if kept in captivity.
Warbler (all other species)	Protected at all times.
Waxwing	Protected at all times.
Wheatear	Protected at all times.
Whimbrel	Specially protected at all times.
Whinchat	Protected at all times.
Whitethroat (all species)	Protected at all times.
Wigeon	Protected in close season; may be shot from 1 September – 31 January (to 20 February in areas below high-water mark); may be sold (dead) from 1 September – 28 February. General licence permits sale of captive-bred birds and their eggs.
Woodcock	England and Wales: Protected in close season; may be shot from 1 October – 31 January. Scotland: Protected in close season; may be shot from 1 September – 31 January.
Woodlark	Specially protected at all times; must be ringed and registered if kept in captivity.
Woodpecker (all species)	Protected at all times.
Woodpigeon	May be killed or taken (including destruction of nests/eggs) under the terms of a general licence.
Wren	Protected at all times.
Wryneck	Specially protected at all times; must be ringed and registered if kept in captivity.
Yellowhammer	Protected at all times. May be competitively exhibited or sold if captive-bred and fitted with an approved close ring.

appendix c
guide to general licences

Only brief details are given, but copies of the actual licences under the Wildlife and Countryisde Act 1981 (WCA) can be obtained from the Government department responsible for their issue, ie:

- the Department of the Environment, Transport and the Regions (DETR)

- the Ministry of Agriculture, Fisheries and Food (MAFF)

- the Scottish Office Agriculture, Environment and Fisheries Department (SOAEFD).

Unless otherwise stated, the licence permits authorised persons (in some cases anyone) to carry out the licensable act in England, Wales and Scotland. **General licences need not be applied for.**

The numbering sequence is purely for convenience; it does not refer to the actual number on the licence, as this can vary with their revocation and the issuing of new licences. The abbreviation in brackets is the Government Department responsible for their issue.

1. **Bullfinches** – permits the killing or taking in cage traps of bullfinches by an authorised person for the purpose of preventing serious damage to the buds of fruit trees in the areas listed below. As from 28 September 1985 live-trapped bullfinches may be given to an aviculturalist provided the DETR receives details of the birds supplied.

   - Cambridgeshire – *Districts of East Cambridgeshire, Fenland, Huntingdon and South Cambridgeshire.*

   - Essex – *Whole county.*

   - Kent – *Whole county.*

   - Suffolk – *Whole county.*

   - Warwickshire – *District of Stratford-on-Avon, and the parishes of Brandon and Bretford, Monks Kirby and Sherbourne.*

2. **Killing of birds to prevent serious damage to agriculture** – permits the killing or taking of certain birds, including the taking, damaging or destruction of their eggs, by an authorised person for the purpose of preventing serious damage to livestock, crops, vegetables, fruit, growing timber, fisheries or inland waters. Control is

either by shooting, a cage trap or net. This applies to the following species (MAFF, SOAEFD, WOAD).

   - Carrion crow
   - Collared dove
   - Great black-backed gull
   - Lesser black-backed gull
   - Herring gull
   - Jackdaw
   - Jay
   - Magpie
   - Feral pigeon
   - Rook
   - House sparrow
   - Starling
   - Woodpigeon

3. **Killing of birds to preserve public health/air safety** – permits the killing or taking of certain birds, including the taking, damaging or destruction of their nests or the taking or destruction of their eggs, by an authorised person for the purpose of preserving public health or air safety. This applies to species as at 2 above. (DETR, SOAEFD, WOAD)

4. **Killing of birds to conserve wild birds** – permits the killing or taking of certain birds, including the taking, damaging or destruction of their nests, by an authorised person for the purpose of conserving wild birds. This applies to the following species. (DETR, SOAEFD, WOAD)

   - Carrion crow
   - Great black-backed gull
   - Lesser black-backed gull
   - Herring gull
   - Jackdaw
   - Jay
   - Magpie
   - Feral pigeon
   - Rook

5. **Sale of gulls' eggs** – permits the sale and advertising for sale of eggs of great black-backed, lesser black-backed and herring gulls for food for human consumption (DETR, SOAEFD, WOAD).

6. **Eggs in nestboxes** – permits the removal of eggs from nestboxes from 1 August to 31 January (DETR, SOAEFD, WOAD).

7. **Taking of mallard eggs** – permits the taking of mallard eggs before 31 March (in England and Wales) and 10 April (Scotland). Any bird hatched from an egg so taken must be released before 31 July in the same year (DETR, SOAEFD and WOAD).

8. **Sale of dead birds** – permits the sale of dead wild birds providing that such birds were bred in captivity, or had not been illegally taken from the wild, and that each sale is accompanied by documentary evidence that the bird was captive-bred or legally removed from the wild. The seller should submit a report of such sales to the DETR by 31 December each year (DETR, SOAEFD, WOAD).

9. **Sale of wildfowl** – permits the sale of certain wildfowl (which regularly breed in captivity) or their eggs. Birds must have been bred in captivity, from parents lawfully held; documentary evidence must accompany sale (DETR, SOAEFD, WOAD).

10. **Sale of feathers and parts** – Permits the sale of feathers and parts of dead wild birds of species as mentioned in 2 above and Schedule 3, part III (DETR, SOAEFD, WOAD).

    NOTE: This is essentially to cover sales in the fly fishing and feather picture trade.

11. **Exhibition of captive birds** – two licences exist. One permits the competitive exhibition of certain captive birds of species which have occurred as vagrants in Britain providing that they have been bred in captivity from parents lawfully held in captivity. A second licence permits the competitive showing of other wild birds (not listed in Schedule 3, Part 1) providing that they have been bred in captivity and are ringed with an individually-numbered metal close ring (DETR).

12. **Veterinary surgeons** – permits vets to keep Schedule 4 species which are receiving treatment for up to six weeks without the need to register them (DETR, SOAEFD, WOAD).

13. **Keeping illegally-taken birds** – permits the police, Customs, RSPB, RSPCA and SSPCA to keep any bird, pending legal proceedings (DETR, SOAEFD, WOAD).

14. **Keeping disabled birds** – permits RSPB wardens, RSPB teacher naturalists, regional and area officers, and RSPCA and SSPCA inspectors to keep disabled Schedule 4 species for up to 15 days (DETR, SOAEFD, WOAD).

15. **Semi-automatic weapons** – permits the use of semi-automatic weapons to kill certain species, as mentioned in 2 above, by an authorised person for the purpose of preserving public health, air safety and preventing serious damage to agriculture (DETR, SOAEFD, WOAD).

16. **Artificial light** – permits the use of artificial light, sighting devices, mirrors, dazzling devices for the killing of:
    - feral pigeon
    - house sparrow
    - starling

    by an authorised person for the purpose of preserving public health, air safety and preventing serious damage to agriculture (DETR, SOAEFD, WOAD).

17. **Killing of birds on airfields** – permits the killing and destruction of nests and eggs of black-headed gull, common gull and lapwing on Civil Aviation Authority and certain other named aerodromes for the purpose of preserving air safety where there is no other satisfactory course of action. Also permits the killing or destruction of nests and eggs of oystercatcher on named aerodromes (DETR, SOAEFD, WOAD).

18. **Keeping captive-bred birds in show cages** – permits birds listed on Schedule 3, Part I to be kept in small cages for training purposes. No bird shall be confined in such a cage for more than one hour in 24 hours and the minimum dimensions permissible are: 10" x 9½" x 40½" (height x breadth x depth) (DETR).

19. **Keeping birds in Larsen traps** – permits the keeping or confining of a carrion crow, jackdaw, jay, magpie or rook by an authorised person in a Larsen cage trap for the purpose of conserving wild birds, protecting any collection of wild birds and preventing serious damage to livestock, foodstuffs for livestock, crops, vegetables, fruit, growing timber or fisheries. This allows this particular type of cage trap to be used with a live

decoy bird providing the trap is inspected at least once during any 24-hour period (DETR).

PROHIBITION OF SHOOTING ON SUNDAYS

The following Orders made under the Protection of Birds Acts remain in force under the WCA. They prohibit the Sunday shooting of Schedule 2, Part I birds (quarry species) in the following administrative counties:

- Anglesey
- Brecknock
- Caernarvon
- Cardigan
- Carmarthen
- Cornwall
- Denbigh
- Devon
- Glamorgan
- Isle of Ely
- Merioneth
- Montgomery
- Norfolk
- Pembroke
- Somerset
- Yorkshire North Riding
- Yorkshire West Riding

and in the county boroughs of

- Doncaster
- Great Yarmouth
- Leeds

Shooting of quarry species (Schedule 2, Part I) on Sundays and Christmas Day is illegal in Scotland.

appendix d
species list with scientific names

ANIMALS AND BIRDS

Adder	*Vipera berus*
Avocet	*Recurvirostra avosetta*
Badger	*Meles meles*
Bass, Large-mouthed Black	*Micropterus salmoides*
Bass, Rock	*Ambioplites rupestris*
Bat, Horseshoe	*Rhinolophidae*
Bat, Typical	*Vespertilionidae*
Bee-eater	*Merops apiaster*
Beetle, Rainbow Leaf	*Chrysolina cerealis*
Bitterling	*Rhodeus sericeus*
Bittern	*Botaurus stellaris*
Bittern, Little	*Ixobrychus minutus*
Blackbird	*Turdus merula*
Bluethroat	*Luscinia svecica*
Brambling	*Fringilia montifringilla*
Budgerigar	*Melopsittacus undulatus*
Bullfinch	*Pyrrhula pyrrhula*
Bunting, Reed	*Emberiza schoeniclus*
Bunting, Cirl	*Emberiza cirlus*
Bunting, Lapland	*Calcarius lapponicus*
Bunting, Snow	*Plectrophenax nivalis*
Burbot	*Lota lota*
Butterfly, Chequered Skipper	*Carterocephalus palaemon*
Butterfly, Heath Fritillary	*Meilicta athalia (otherwise known as Melitaea athalia)*
Butterfly, Large Blue	*Maculinea arion*
Butterfly, Swallowtail	*Papilio machaon*
Buzzard, Ferruginous	*Buteo regalis*
Buzzard, Honey	*Pernis apivorus*
Buzzard, Red-tailed	*Buteo jamaicensus*
Capercaillie	*Tetrao urogallus*
Cat, Wild	*Felis silvestris*
Chaffinch	*Fringilla coelebs*
Chough	*Pyrrhocorax pyrrhocorax*
Coot	*Fulica atra*
Corncrake	*Crex crex*
Coypu	*Myocastor coypus*
Crake, Spotted	*Porzana porzana*
Cricket, Field	*Cryllus campestris*
Cricket, Mole	*Gryllotalpa gyllotalpa*
Crossbills (all species)	*Loxia*
Crow, Carrion	*Corvus corone*
Divers (all species)	*Gavia*
Dolphin, Bottle-nosed	*Tursiops truncatus (otherwise known as Tursiops tursio)*
Dolphin, Common	*Delphinus delphis*
Dormice (all species)	*Gliridae*
Dormouse, Fat	*Glis glis*
Dotterel	*Charadrius morinellus*
Dove, Collared	*Streptopelia decaocto*
Dragonfly, Norfolk Aeshna	*Aeshna isosceles*
Duck, Carolina Wood	*Aix sponsa*
Duck, Mandarin	*Aid galericulata*
Duck, Ruddy	*Oxyura jamaicensis*
Duck, Tufted	*Aythya fuligula*
Duck, Long-tailed	*Clangula hyemalis*
Dunnock	*Prunela modularis*
Eagle, Adalbert's	*Aquila adalberti*
Eagle, Golden	*Aquila chrysaetos*

Eagle, Great Phillipine	*Pithecophaga jefferyi*
Eagle, Imperial	*Aquila helica*
Eagle, New Guinea	*Harpyopsis novaeguineae*
Eagle, White-tailed	*Haliaetus albicilla*
Falcon, Barbary	*Falco pelegrinoides*
Falcon, Gyr	*Falco rusticolus*
Falcon, Lanner	*Falco biarmicus*
Falcon, Peregrine	*Falco peregrinus*
Falcon, Saker	*Falco cherrug*
Fieldfare	*Turdus pilaris*
Firecrest	*Regulus ignicapillus*
Fish Eagle, Madagascar	*Haliaeetus vociferoides*
Forest Falcon, Plumbeous	*Micrastur plumbeus*
Frog, Common	*Rana temporaria*
Frog, Edible	*Rana esculenta*
Frog, European Tree (otherwise known as Common Tree Frog)	*Hyla arborea*
Frog, Marsh	*Rana ridibunda*
Gadwall	*Anas strepera*
Garganey	*Anas querquedula*
Gerbil, Mongolian	*Meriones unguiculatus*
Godwit, Black-tailed	*Limosa limosa*
Goldeneye	*Bucephala clangula*
Goldfinch	*Carduelis carduelis*
Goose, Canada	*Branta canadensis*
Goose, Egyptian	*Alopochen aegyptiacus*
Goose, Greylag	*Anser anser*
Goose, White-fronted	*Anser albifrons*
Goose, Pink-footed	*Anser brachyrhynchus*
Goshawk	*Accipiter gentilis*
Grasshopper, Wart-biter	*Decticus verrucivorus*
Grebe, Black-necked	*Podiceps nigricollis*
Grebe, Slavonian	*Podiceps auritus*
Greenfinch	*Carduelis chloris*
Greenshank	*Tringa nebularia*
Gull, Herring	*Larus argentatus*
Gull, Little	*Larus minutus*
Gull, Great Black-backed	*Larus marinus*
Gull, Lesser Black-backed	*Larus fuscus*
Gull, Mediterranean	*Larus melanocephalus*
Harrier, Hen	*Circus cyaneus*
Harrier, Marsh	*Circus aeruginosus*
Harrier, Montagu's	*Circus pygargus*
Hawk, Galapagos	*Buteo galapagoensis*
Hawk, Grey-backed	*Leucopternis occidentalis*
Hawk, Harris	*Parabuteo unicinctus*
Hawk, Hawaiian	*Buteo solitarius*
Hawk, Ridgway's	*Buteo ridgwayi*
Hawk, White-necked	*Leucopternis lacernulata*
Hawk-Eagle, Wallace's	*Spizaetus nanus*
Hedgehog	*Erinaceus europaeus*
Heron, Night	*Nycticorax nycticorax*
Heron, Purple	*Ardea purpurea*
Hobby	*Falco subbuteo*
Honey Buzzard, Black	*Henicopernis infuscata*
Hoopoe	*Upupa epops*
Jackdaw	*Corvus monedula*
Jay	*Garrulus glandarius*
Kestrel	*Falco tinnunculus*
Kestrel, Lesser	*Falco naumanni*
Kestrel, Mauritius	*Falco punctatus*

Kingfisher	*Alcedo atthis*
Kite, Red	*Milvus milvus*
Linnet	*Carduelis cannabina*
Lizzard, Common Wall	*Podarcis muralis*
Lizzard, Sand	*Lacerta agilis*
Lizard, Viviparous	*Lacerta vivipara*
Magpie	*Pica pica*
Mallard	*Anas platyrhynchos*
Marmot, Prairie (otherwise known as Prairie Dog)	*Cynomys*
Marten, Pine	*Martes martes*
Merlin	*Falco columbarius*
Mink, American	*Mustela vison*
Moorhen	*Gallinula chloropus*
Moth, Barberry Carpet	*Pareulype berberata*
Moth, Black-veined	*Siona lineata (otherwise known as Idaea lineata)*
Moth, Essex Emerald	*Thetidia smaragdaria*
Moth, New Forest Burnet	*Zygaena viciae*
Moth, Reddish Buff	*Acosmetia caliginosa*
Newt, Alpine	*Triturus alpestris*
Newt, Great Crested (otherwise known as Warty Newt)	*Triturus cristatus*
Newt, Palmate	*Triturus helveticus*
Newt, Smooth	*Triturus vulgaris*
Oriole, Golden	*Oriolus oriolus*
Osprey	*Pandion haliaetus*
Otter, Common	*Lutra lutra*
Owl, Barn	*Tyto alba*
Owl, Bengal Eagle	*Bubo bubo bengalenisis*
Owl, Eagle	*Bubo bubo*
Owl, Scops	*Otus scops*
Owl, Tengmalms'	*Aegolius funereus*
Owl, Snowy	*Nyctea scandiaca*
Parakeet, Ring-necked	*Psittacula krameri*
Partridge, Chukar	*Alectoris chukar*
Partridge, Rock	*Alectoris graeca*
Petrel, Leach's	*Oceanodroma leucorhoa*
Phalarope, Red-necked	*Phalaropus lobatus*
Pheasant, Golden	*Chrysolophus pictus*
Pheasant, Lady Amherst's	*Chrysolophus amherstiae*
Pheasant, Reeves'	*Syrmaticus revesii*
Pheasant, Silver	*Lophura nycthemera*
Pigeon, Feral	*Columba livia*
Pintail	*Anas acuta*
Plover, Kentish	*Charadrius alexandrinus*
Plover, Little Ringed	*Charadrius dubius*
Plover, Golden	*Aythya ferina*
Porcupine, Crested	*Hystrix cristata*
Porcupine, Himalayan	*Hystrix hodgsonii*
Polecat	*Mustela putorius*
Porpoise, Harbour (otherwise known as Common Porpoise)	*Phocaena phocaena*
Pumpkinseed (otherwise known as Sun-fish or Pond-perch)	*Lepomis gibbosus*
Quail, Bobwhite	*Colinus virginianus*
Quail, Common	*Coturnix coturnix*
Rat, Black	*Rattus rattus*
Redpoll	*Carduelis flammea*
Redstart, Black	*Phoenicurus ochruros*

Redwing	*Turdis iliacus*	Sparrow, House	*Passer domesticus*
Rook	*Corvus frugilegus*	Sparrowhawk	*Accipiter nisus*
Rosefinch, Scarlet	*Carpodacus erythrinus*	Sparrowhawk, New Britain	*Accipiter brachyurus*
Ruff	*Philomachus pugnax*	Sparrowhawk, Gundlach's	*Accipiter gundlachii*
Sandpiper, Wood	*Tringa ochropus*		
Sandpiper, Purple	*Calidris maritima*	Sparrowhawk, Imitator	*Accipiter imitator*
Sandpiper, Green	*Tringa ochropus*	Sparrowhawk, Small	*Accipiter nanus*
Scaup	*Aythya marila*	Spoonbill	*Platalea leucorodia*
Scoter, Common	*Melanitta nigra*	Starling	*Sturnus vulgaris*
Scoter, Velvet	*Melanitta fusca*	Stone Curlew	*Burhinus oedicnemus*
Sea-Eagle, Pallas'	*Haliaeetus leucoryphus*	Stilt, Black-winged	*Himantopus himantopus*
Sea-Eagle, Steller's	*Haliaeetus pelagicu*	Stint, Temminck's	*Calidris temminckii*
Serin	*Serinus serinus*	Swan, Whooper	*Cygnus cygnus*
Serpent Eagle, Andaman	*Spilornis eigini*	Swan, Bewick's	*Cygnus bewickii*
Serpent-Eagle, Madagascar	*Eurtiorchis astur*	Teal	*Anas Crecca*
		Tern, Black	*Chlidonias niger*
Serpent-Eagle, Mountain	*Spilornis kinabaluensis*	Tern, Little	*Sterna albifrons*
Shrews (all species)	*Soricidae*	Tern, Roseate	*Sterna dougallii*
Shorelark	*Eremophila alpestris*	Terrapin, European Pond	*Emys orbicularis*
Shoveler	*Anas clypeata*	Thrush, Song	*Turdus philomelos*
Shrike, Red-backed	*Lanius collurio*	Tit, Bearded	*Panurus biarmicus*
Siskin	*Carduelis spinus*	Tit, Crested	*Parus cristatus*
Slow-worm	*Anguis fragilis*	Treecreeper, Short-toed	*Certhia brachydactyla*
Snail, Carthusian	*Monacha cartusiana*	Toad, African Clawed	*Xenopus laevis*
Snail, Glutinous	*Myxas glutinosa*	Toad, Common	*Bufo bufo*
Snail, Sandbowl	*Catinella arenaria*	Toad, Midwife	*Alytes obstetricans*
Snake, Grass	*Natrix helvetica*	Toad, Natterjack	*Bufo calamita*
Snake, Smooth	*Coronella austriaca*	Toad, Yellow-bellied	*Bombina variegata*
Spider, Fen Raft	*Dolomedes plantarius*	Twite	*Carduelis flavirostris*
Spider, Ladybird	*Eresus niger*	Wallaby, Red-necked	*Macropus rufogriseus*
Squirrel, Red	*Sciurus vulgaris*	Warbler, Cetti's	*Cettia cetti*
Snipe, Common	*Gallinago gallinago*		

Warbler, Dartford	*Sylvia undata*
Warbler, Marsh	*Acrocephalus palustris*
Warbler, Savi's	*Locustella luscinioides*
Wels (otherwise known as European Catfish)	*Silurus glanis*
Whimbrel	*Numenius phaeopus*
Wigeon	*Anas penelope*
Woodcock	*Scolopax rusticola*
Woodlark	*Lullula arborea*
Woodpigeon	*Columba palumbus*
Wryneck	*Jynx torquillia*
Yellowhammer	*Emberiza citrinella*
Zander	*Stizostedion lucioperca*

PLANTS

Alison, Small	*Alyssum alyssoides*
Broomrape, Bedstraw	*Orobanche caryophyllacea*
Broomrape, Oxtongue	*Orobanche loricata*
Broomrape, Thistle	*Orobanche reticulata*
Calamint, Wood	*Calmintha sylvatica*
Catchfly, Alpine	*Lychnis alpina*
Cinquefoil, Rock	*Potentilla rupestris*
Club-rush, Triangular	*Scirpus triquetrus*
Cotoneaster, Wild	*Cotoneaster integerrimus*
Cow-wheat, Field	*Melampyrum arvense*
Cudweed, Jersey	*Gnaphalium luteoalum*
Diapensia	*Diapensia lapponica*
Eryngo, Field	*Eryngium campestre*
Fern, Dickie's Bladder	*Cystopteris dickieana*
Fern, Killarney	*Trichomanes speciosum*
Galingale, Brown	*Cyperus fuscus*
Gentian, Alpine	*Gentiana nivalis*

Gentian, Spring	*Gentiana verna*
Germander, Water	*Teucrium scordium*
Gladiolus, Wild	*Gladiols illyricus*
Hare's-ear, Sickle-leaved	*Bupleurum falcatum*
Hare's-ear, Small	*Bupleurum baldense*
Heath, Blue	*Phyllodoce caerulea*
Helleborine, Red	*Cephalanthera rubra*
Hogweed, Giant	*Heracleum mantegazzianum*
Kelp, Giant	*Macrocystis pyrifera*
Knawel, Perennial	*Scleranthus perennis*
Knotgrass, Sea	*Polygonum maritimum*
Knotweed, Japanese	*Polygonum cuspidatum*
Lady's-slipper	*Cypripedium calceolus*
Lavender, Sea	*Limonium paradoxum/Limonium recurvum*
Leek, Round-headed	*Allium sphaerocephalon*
Lettuce, Least	*Lactuca saligna*
Lily, Snowdon	*Lloydia serotina*
Marsh-mallow, Rough	*Althaea hirsuta*
Orchid, Early Spider	*Ophrys sphegodes*
Orchid, Fen	*Liparis loeselii*
Orchid, Ghost	*Epipoglum aphyllum*
Orchid, Late Spider	*Ophrys fuciflora*
Orchid, Lizard	*Himantoglossum hircinum*
Orchid, Military	*Orchis militaris*
Orchid, Monkey	*Orchis simia*
Pear, Plymouth	*Pyrus cordata*
Pink, Cheddar	*Dianthus gratianopolitanus*
Pink, Childling	*Petroraghia nanteuilii*
Sandwort, Norwegian	*Atenaria norvegica*

Sandwort, Teesdale	*Minuartia stricta*
Saxifrage, Drooping	*Saxifraga cernua*
Saxifrage, Tufted	*Saxifraga cespitosa*
Seaweed, Japanese	*Sargassum muticum*
Solomon's Seal, Whorled	*Polygonatum verticillatum*
Sow-thistle, Alpine	*Cicerbita, alpina*
Spearwort, Adder's-tongue	*Ranunculus ophioglossifolius*
Speedwell, Spiked	*Veronica spicata*
Spurge, Purple	*Euphorbia peplis*
Starfruit	*Damasonium alisma*
Violet, Fen	*Viola persicifolia*
Water-plantain, Ribbon-leaved	*Alisma gramineum*
Wood-sedge, Starved	*Carex depauperata*
Woodsia, Alpine	*Woodsia alpina*
Woodsia, Oblong	*Woodsia ilvensis*
Wormwood, Field	*Artemisia campestris*
Woundwort, Downy	*Stachys germanica*
Woundwort, Limestone	*Stachys alpina*
Yellow-rattle, Greater	*Rhinanthus serotinus*

appendix e
useful addresses

Person/organisation	Area of authority/specialist knowledge
Department of the Environment, Transport and the Regions Global Wildlife Division Tollgate House Houlton Street Bristol BS2 9DJ Tel: 0117 987 8000 Tel: 0117 987 8132 Fax: 0117 987 8393 (Lynn Garvey – Enforcement Co-ordinator) Tel: 0117 987 8154 Fax: 0117 987 8393 (Nick P Williams – Chief Wildlife Inspector)	*Principal UK authority for WCA licensing and registration; UK Management Authority for CITES. Will advise on all aspects of WCA and CITES enforcement, legislation, licensing and exemptions.*
Home Office Constitutional and Community Policy Directorate Queen Anne's Gate London SW1H 9AT Tel: 0171 273 2316 Fax: 0171 273 2029	*Animal welfare issues including the Wild Mammals (Protection) Act 1996, the Deer Acts, the Game Acts, the Conservation of Seals Acts, field sports and hunting issues.*
Ministry of Agriculture, Fisheries and Food (MAFF) Hook Rise South Tolworth Surbiton Surrey KT6 7NF Tel: 0181 330 8169 Fax: 0181 330 6678	*Import licences in respect of health regulations.*
Department of the Environment, Transport and the Regions Chemicals and Biotechnology Unit Rm B357 Romney House 43 Marsham St London SW1P 3PY Tel: 0171 276 8336 Fax: 0171 276 8333	*Licences for releasing non-native species (Dr W E G Parish).*

MAFF Regional Service Centres

(See page 163)

Licensing for killing or taking birds causing agricultural damage.
Licensing for interfering with badgers or their setts for the purpose of preventing damage to property or agriculture.

Scottish Office Agriculture, Environment & Fisheries
Department (SOAEFD)
Pentland House
47 Robbs Loan
Edinburgh EH14 1TY
Tel: 0131 556 8400

Licensing.
Licences to remove dogs from setts.

Welsh Office Agriculture Department (WOAD)
Cathays Park
Cardiff CF1 3NQ
Tel: 01222 825111
        01222 823553
        01222 825203

Licences in Wales for killing birds causing agricultural damage.
Licences for badger sett disturbance.
Licences for some wildlife activities.

English Nature (EN)
Northminster House
Peterborough PE1 1UA
Tel: 01733 340345

Licences for Schedule 1 bird nest examination and photography.
Licences for badger sett disturbance.
Expert advice on badgers.

Countryside Council for Wales (CCW)
Plas Penrhos
Fford Penrhos
Bangor
Gwynedd LL57 2LQ
Tel: 01248 385500

Licences for badgers and setts – section 10(1) of the Protection of Badgers Act 1992.

Bat licences, Schedule 8 plant licences, Schedules 5 and 6 animal licences – section 16(3) of the WCA 1981 and in some cases, Regulation 44(2) a–e of the Conservation (Natural Habitats, &c.) Regulation 1994.

Removal of deer licences – section 11 of the Deer Act 1991.

Bird licences – section 16(1) a–c and n of the WCA 1981.

Scottish Natural Heritage (SNH)
Research and Advisory Service
Bonnington Bond
2–5 Anderson Place
Edinburgh EH6 5NP
Tel: 0131 554 9797

Licensing badger setts.
Licences for Schedule 1 bird nest examination and photography.

Deer Commission for Scotland
Knowlsey
82 Fairfield Road
Inverness IV3 5LH
Tel: 01463 231751

(formerly Red Deer Commission)
Authorised to enter land for deer counts.
Authorised to cull deer out of season in cases of excessive damage by deer and to set up control schemes (Scotland only).

Countryside Commission
John Dower House
Crescent Place
Cheltenham
Gloucestershire GL50 3RA
Tel: 01242 521381
Fax: 01242 584270

Advice on public access to the countryside.

Forestry Authority
231 Corstophine Road
Edinburgh EH12 7AT
Tel: 0131 334 0303
There are regional offices throughout Britain

(formerly Forestry Commission)
Advice on planting/cutting.
Issues felling licences.

DNA TESTING

Professor David Parkin
Department of Genetics
Queens Medical Centre
Nottingham NG7 2UH
Tel: 0115 9709399
Fax: 0115 9709906

Nottingham University has pioneered avian DNA research and will undertake DNA analysis in wildlife investigations.
Other laboratories are also becoming available.

ORGANISATIONS WITH CITES EXPERTISE

Department of the Environment, Transport
and the Regions
Global Wildlife Division
Tollgate House
Houlton Street
Bristol BS2 9DJ
Tel: 0117 987 8000

Tel: 0117 987 8132
Fax: 0117 987 8393
(Lynn Garvey – Enforcement Co-ordinator)

Tel: 0117 987 8154
Fax: 0117 987 8282
(Nick P Williams – Chief Wildlife Inspector)

*Principal UK authority for WCA licensing and
registration; UK management authority for CITES. Will
advise on all aspects of WCA and CITES enforcement,
legislation, licensing and exemptions.*

Animal Health Division
Department of Agriculture for Northern Ireland
Dundonald House
Upper Newtownards Road
Belfast BT4 3SB

CITES management authority for Northern Ireland.

CITES Secretariat
15 Chemin des Anemones
Case Postale 456
CH 1219 Chatelaine – Geneve
Switzerland
Tel: 0041 22 979 9129/9140
Fax: 0041 22 797 3417

*International CITES headquarters.
Enforcement/infraction officers will provide advice and
guidance.*

National Criminal Intelligence Service (NCIS)
Interpol UK
PO Box 8000
Spring Gardens
Tinworth Street
London SE11 5EN
Tel: 0171 238 8000/8431

TRAFFIC International
219C Huntingdon Road
Cambridge CB3 0DL
Tel: 01223 277427
Fax: 01223 277237
Email: traffic@wcmc.org.uk

TRAFFIC monitors the international wildlife trade. Their enforcement assistance officer can provide specialist expertise in identification of items, products, etc.

US Department of the Interior
Fish and Wildlife Service
Forensics Laboratory
1490 East Main Street
Ashland
Oregon 97520
USA
Tel: 001 503 482 4191

The world's only wildlife forensic science laboratory, designed to meet the needs of wildlife law enforcement agencies in all CITES signatory countries.

The Natural History Museum
Cromwell Road
London SW7
Tel: 0171 938 9123

Can provide expert identification of body parts, bones, etc.

Royal Museum of Scotland
Natural History Department
Chambers Street
Edinburgh EH1 1JF
Tel: 0131 225 7534
Fax: 0131 220 4819

Can provide expert identification of body parts, bones etc.

Department of Health
Medicines Control Agency
Enforcement Unit
Market Towers
1 Nine Elms Lane
London SW8 5NQ

Specialist agency of Department of Health responsible for the enforcement of laws controlling the sale of medicines and similar products. Can provide assistance in cases involving the sale of TEAMs.

World Wide Fund for Nature
Panda House
Weyside Park
Godalming
Surrey
Tel: 01483 426444

CITES Enforcement Team
HM Customs & Excise
Building 353
Cargo Village
Shoreham Road East
Hounslow
Middlesex TW6 3RD
Tel: 0181 910 3830
Fax: 0181 910 3833

Specialist Customs team with a great deal of experience of CITES enforcement.

LIST OF OTHER CITES LIAISON AND INTELLIGENCE OFFICERS

Executive unit	Name – in post 1/98	Location	Telephone number
Anglia	Claire Kalinowska	CCU, Haven House, Ipswich	01473 235732
Central England	Jill Cox	Birmingham Airport	0121 782 6655 ext 153
Eastern England	Phil Weaver	ICU, Bowman House, Nottingham	0115 971 2295 Fax: 0115 971 2291
London Central	Rob Farrow	CCU Thomas Paine House London	0171 865 3544
Northern England	Jim May	Newcastle Airport	0191 286 0966 ext 4448
Northern Ireland	Michael Patterson	CCU, Carne House, Belfast	01232 358371
North West England	Geoff Conner	FIT, Manchester Airport	0161 912 6943
North West England	Andy Chesters	Queen Dock Buildings, Liverpool	0151 703 1115
Scotland	Mike Wallace	EPU, Glasgow Airport	0141 887 7557
South East England	Dick Bunting	Priory Court, Dover	01304 206789
Southern England	Denis McAlister	Portcullis House, No 4 Gate, Southampton	01202 685157 ext. 311
South London & Thames	Kathy Thornton	The Boathouse, Custom House, Gravesend	01375 853070
Thames Valley	Glen Packham	Intelligence Team, Eldon Court, Reading	01734 644200
Wales, the West & Borders	Ritchie Thomas	Intelligence Unit, Pembroke Dock	01646 622777/8

Wales, the West & Borders	Debbie Walker	CIU, Custom House, Avonmouth	0117 982 2962
National Investigation Service	Dave Wendholt	Customs 'E', Custom House, London	0171 665 7192
Isle of Man	Mark Shuttleworth	North Quay, Douglas	01624 648110

MAFF REGIONAL SERVICE CENTRES

Region	Counties covered	Address	Telephone number
Northern	Cumbria, Lancashire, Northumberland, Tyne and Wear	Eden Bridge House, Lowther Street, Carlisle CA3 8DX	01228 23400
North East	Cleveland, Durham, Humberside, North Yorkshire, South Yorkshire, West Yorkshire	Government Buildings, Crosby Road, Northallerton DL6 1AD	01609 773751
North Mercia	Cheshire, Greater Manchester, Merseyside, Shropshire, Staffordshire	Berkeley Towers, Nantwich Road, Crewe CW2 6PT	01270 69211
South Mercia	West Midlands, Gloucestershire, Hereford and Worcester, Warwickshire	Government Buildings, Block C, Whittington Road, Worcester WR5 2LQ	01905 763355
East Midlands	Derbyshire, Leicestershire, Lincolnshire, Northamptonshire, Nottinghamshire	Block 7, Chalfont Drive, Nottingham NG8 3SN	01159 291191
Anglia	Bedfordshire, Cambridgeshire, Essex, Hertfordshire, Norfolk, Suffolk	Block B, Government Buildings, Brooklands Avenue, Cambridge CB2 2DR	01223 462727
South East	Berkshire, Buckinghamshire, Greater London, Hampshire, Isle of Wight, Kent, Oxfordshire, Surrey, East Sussex, West Sussex	Block A, Government Offices, Coley Park, Reading RG1 6DT	01734 581222

Wessex	Avon, Dorset, Somerset, Wiltshire	Block III, Government Buildings, Burghill Road, Westbury-on-Trym, Bristol BS10 6NJ	0117 959100
South West	Cornwall, Devon, Isles of Scilly	Government Buildings, Alphington Road, Exeter EX2 8NQ	01392 77951

RSPB OFFICES

RSPB Investigation Section staff will provide advice and expert witnesses to assist in operations and prosecutions.

UK Headquarters
RSPB
The Lodge
Sandy
Bedfordshire SG19 2DL
Tel: 01767 680551

Scottish Headquarters
17 Regent Terrace
Edinburgh EH7 5BN
Tel: 0131 557 3136

Wales Office
Bryn Aderyn
The Bank
Newtown
Powys SY16 2AB
Tel: 01686 626678

Northern Ireland Office
Belvoir Park Forest
Belfast BT8 4QT
Tel: 01232 491547

CRUELTY CASES

England & Wales
RSPCA (Head Office and Prosecution)
Causeway
Horsham
West Sussex RH12 1HG
Tel: 01403 264181
Fax: 01403 241048
DX No: 57628
Helpline: 0990 555 999
RSPCA inspectors are located throughout England and Wales

Scotland
SSPCA
Braehead Manor
603 Queensferry Road
Edinburgh EH14 6EA
Tel: 0131 339 0222
Fax: 0131 339 4777
SSPCA inspectors are located throughout Scotland

Northern Ireland
USPCA
11 Drumview Road
Lisburn
Northern Ireland BT27 6YF
Tel: 01232 813178/813126
Fax: 01232 812260

POISONING

In cases of suspected poisoning the following are contact addresses.
Remember there is a freephone number: 0800 321600.

England

Wildlife Incident Unit
Central Science Laboratory
London Road
Slough SL3 7HJ
Tel: 01753 734626

Scotland

Scottish Agricultural Science Agency
East Craigs
Edinburgh EH12 8NJ
Tel: 0131 244 8864

Wales

ADAS Wales
Yr Hen Ysgol
Fford Alexandra
Aberystwyth SY23 1LF
Tel: 01970 627762

Northern Ireland

Department of Agriculture for Northern Ireland
Dundonald House
Upper Newtownards Road
Belfast BT4 3SB
Tel: 01232 650111

FALCONRY

Jemima Parry-Jones
National Bird of Prey Centre
Newent
Gloucestershire
Tel: 01531 820286

Jim Chick (Chairman of the Hawk Board)
Moonrakers
Allington
Salisbury
Wiltshire
Tel: 01980 610594

Mick Cunningham (Chairman of Raptor Rescue)
8 Harvey Road
Handacre
Rugeley
Staffordshire
Tel: 01543 491712

Neil Forbes Bvet Med MRCVS
(Avian Veterinary Surgeon)
Lansdown Veterinary Surgeons
Clockhouse Veterinary Hospital
Wallbridge
Stroud
Gloucestershire
Tel: 01453 752555

Carol Scott (The Hawk Board)
Lynn Drive
Eaglesham
Glasgow G76 0JJ
Tel: 01355 302671

Adrian Williams (Welsh Hawking Club)
Church Village
Pontypridd
South Wales CF38 1SY
Tel: 01443 206333

Philip and Jenny Wray
Independent Bird Register (IBR)
184 Warwick Road
Kenilworth
Warwickshire CV8 1HU
Tel: 01926 850000

Peter Mulholland
Raptor Registration (RR)
Beckside Cottage
Moortown
Lincolnshire LN7 6JA
Tel: 01652 678492

NOTE: See also specialist police contacts.

SUPPLIERS OF MICROCHIPS

R S Biotech
R S Biotech
Brook Street
Alva
Clackmannanshire FK12 5JJ
Tel: 01259 760335
Fax: 01259 762824
Mobile: 0831 416249

Pettrac
AVID plc
Holroyd Suite
Oak Hall
Sheffield Park
Uckfield
East Sussex TN22 3QY
Tel: 01825 791069
Fax: 01825 791006

Identichip
Animalcare Ltd
Common Road
Dunnington
York YO1 5RU
Tel: 01904 488661
Fax: 01904 488184

Trovan
UK ID Systems Ltd
Riverside Industrial Park
Catterall
Preston
Lancashire PR3 0HP

AVICULTURE

National Council for Aviculture
PO Box 234
Woking
Surrey GU21 1WR
Tel/Fax: 01483 776801

Maintains national register of bird thefts. Will advise on identification and avian crime intelligence.
(Graham Wellstead)

BIRD RINGING

British Trust for Ornithology
National Centre for Ornithology
The Nunnery
Thetford
Norfolk IP24 2PU
Tel: 01842 750050

Issue licences to bird ringers, for production on demand.

FIELD SPORTS ORGANISATIONS

British Field Sports Society
59 Kennington Road
London SE1 7PZ
Tel: 0171 928 4742
Fax: 0171 620 1401

All aspects of field sports.

British Deer Society
Fordingbridge
Hampshire SP6 1EF
Tel/Fax: 01425 655 433

All matters relating to deer.

British Association for Shooting and Conservation
(BASC)
Marford Mill
Rossett
Wrexham LL12 0HL
Tel: 01244 573000
Fax: 01244 573001

Produce useful leaflet advice, eg code of practice for fox snaring and night shooting.
(Stewart Scull)

Scottish Association of Country Sports
Riverside Lodge
Tochry
By Dunkeld
Tayside PH8 0DY
Tel: 01532 723259
Fax: 01532 723259

All aspects of country sports in Scotland.
(David Cant)

Game Conservancy Ltd
Fordingbridge
Hampshire SP6 1EF
Tel: 01425 652381
Fax: 01425 655848

All aspects of practical game management.

BADGERS

National Federation of Badger Groups
15 Cloisters House
Cloisters Business Centre
8 Battersea Park Road
London SW8 4BG
Tel: 0171 498 3220
Fax: 0171 498 4459

Conservation officer will liaise with police and provide
details of local badger groups.
(Elaine King)

Chris Cheeseman
Central Science Laboratory
Brownshill
Stroud
Gloucestershire GL6 8AP
Tel/Fax: 01453 855105

Adviser on all aspects of badger law and conservation.

BATS

Bat Conservation Trust
15 Cloisters House
8 Battersea Park Road
London SW8 4BG
Tel: 0171 627 2629
Fax: 0171 627 2628

Provides details of local bat groups and produces
information pack.
(Jill Bradley)

MARINE MAMMALS – SEALS, DOLPHINS, PORPOISES AND WHALES

Sea Mammal Research Unit
School of Biological and Medicinal Sciences
Bute Buildings
University of St Andrews
KY16 8LB
Tel: 01334 476161

Provides expert advice and assistance on marine mammals.

Sea Birds and Cetacean Branch
Joint Nature Conservation Committee
Thistle House
7 Thistle Place
Aberdeen AB10 1UZ
(Mark Tasker)
Tel: 01224 655701
Fax: 01224 621488

Institute of Zoology
Regents Parks
London NW1 4RY
Tel: 0171 722 3333/
0171 449 6691 (Direct)
Fax: 0171 586 1457

Advice regarding stranded dolphins, porpoises and whales in England and Wales.
(Paul Jepson)

Scottish Stranding Co-ordinator
SAC Veterinary Services
Drummondhill
Stratherrick Road
Inverness IV2 4JZ
Tel: 01463 243030
Fax: 01463 711103

Advice on all strandings in Scotland.
(Robert Reid)

The Ulster Museum
Botanic Gardens
Belfast BT5 AB
Tel: 01232 383000

Advice on all strandings in Northern Ireland (Terry Bruton or Lynn Rendell).

HABITAT

UK National Office of Wildlife Trusts
The Green
Witham Park
Waterside South
Lincoln LN5 7RJ
Tel: 01522 544400
Fax: 01522 511616

Protection of species and their habitat through 47 wildlife trusts.

Field Studies Council
Preston Montford
Montford Bridge
Shrewsbury
Shropshire SY4 1HW
Tel: 01743 850674

Provide details of botanists to identify plants and give advice.

Farming and Wildlife Advisory Group
National Agricultural Centre
Stoneleigh
Kenilworth
Warwickshire CV8 2RX
Tel: 01203 696699

Regional officers will advise on best practice to benefit both farming and wildlife. Useful booklets produced.

SPECIALIST POLICE CONTACTS

Deputy Chief Constable Mick Brewer
Warwickshire Police Headquarters
PO Box 4
Leek Wootton
Warwick CV35 7QB
Tel: 01926 415000
Fax: 01926 415022

Wildlife Adviser to the Association of Chief Police Officers (ACPO).
Co-Chairman, Wildlife Law Enforcement Steering Group.

PC Paul Beecroft
Thames Valley Police
Henley Police Station
2 Kings Road
Henley on Thames
Oxon RG9 2AJ
Mobile: 0589 167488

Maintains national list of stolen birds of prey.
Maintains lost-and-found service for Raptor Rescue.
Maintains a list of persons willing to take in seized birds of prey.

Inspector Phil Cannings
Bedfordshire Police
Ampthill Police Station
Woburn Street
Ampthill
Bedfordshire MK43 2HX
Tel: 01234 842666
Fax: 01234 842605
Pager: 0941 100200 (ref: 177775)

Advice on birds of prey, wild birds, bird ringing, DNA cases.

Andy Fisher
Wildlife Liaison Officer
Room 913
New Scotland Yard
Broadway
London SW1H 0BG
Tel: 0171 230 3641
Fax: 0171 230 2152

WLO liaison for all Metropolitan Police enquiries. Operation Charm liaison.

Inspector Steve Kourik
Hertfordshire Police WLO
County Police Station
Ware Road
Hertford SG13 7HD
Tel: 01992 533099
Fax: 01992 5330009

Specialist on mammals, particularly bats and badgers.

Inspector Charlie Parkes
Derbyshire Police WLO
Chesterfield Police Station
Beetwell Street
Chesterfield S40 1QP
Tel: 01246 220100 ext 2307

Game laws, poaching and field sports.

Chief Inspector Robert Philpott
Wiltshire Police Headquarters
Devizes
Wiltshire
Tel: 01380 729715
Wildlife Ansaphone: 01380 734070

Major egg-collecting and taxidermy case experience.

Inspector John Sellar
Grampian Police
Banchory Station
High Street
Banchory
Aberdeenshire AB31 5RP
Tel: 01330 822252
Fax: 01330 825518

Sergeant Peter Slimon
Metropolitan Police
113 High Street
Esher
Surrey KT10 9QQ
Tel: 0181 247 5391
Fax: 0181 247 5391

*Wildlife adviser to ACPO (Scotland).
Experience of wildlife smuggling cases and joint operations
with HM Customs and Excise. Useful contacts with
wildlife law enforcement agencies on the European
continent, USA, Canada, Australia and New Zealand.*

Specialist WLO for plants and habitat conservation.

appendix f
further reading

There are many books currently available which deal with the various aspects of wildlife law enforcement covered in this Guide.

The following list gives details of some publications which readers may find useful in providing further general or specialist information.

GENERAL

Species Conservation Handbook	Compiled by Dr A Gent (EN) and obtainable from English Nature (ISBN 1-85716-149-1)

Fair Game *A comprehensive and useful guide to the law on field sports and many other aspects of wildlife law enforcement.*	Authors: Publishers:	Charlie Parkes and John Thornley (Wildlife Liaison Officers, Derbyshire Police) Pelham (ISBN 0-7207-2030-3)

Nature Conservation Law	Author: Publishers:	Colin Reid Sweet and Maxwell 1994 (ISBN 0-414-00998-3)

SPECIES IDENTIFICATION

There are a number of excellent pocket reference guides to the identification of birds and other wildlife. Available at most bookshops, useful publications include the following:

The Complete Guide to British Wildlife *Contains details of birds, animals and plant life.*	Authors: Publishers:	N Arlott, R Fitter and A Fitter Collins (ISBN 0-00-219212-8)

The Birds of Britain and Europe, North Africa and the Middle East	Authors: Publishers:	Herman Heinzel, Richard Fitter and John Parslow Collins (ISBN 0-00-219894-0)

Field Guide to the Birds of Britain and Europe	Authors:	Roger Tory Peterson, Guy Mountfort, PAD Hollom
	Publishers:	Collins
		(ISBN 0-00-219900-9)

Butterflies and Moths of Britain and Europe	Authors:	H Hofmann and T Marktanner
	Publishers:	Collins
		(ISBN 0-00-220029-5)

Trees of Britain and Northern Europe	Authors:	Alan Mitchell and John Wilkinson
	Publishers:	Collins
		(ISBN 0-00-219857-6)

Wild Flowers of Britain and Europe	Authors:	M Blamey, R Fitter and A Fitter
	Publishers:	Collins
		(ISBN 0-00-219715-4)

Whales, Dolphins and Porpoises	Author:	Mark Carwardine
	Publishers:	Dorling & Kindersley
		(ISBN 0-7513-1030-1)

FALCONRY

Falconry, Art and Practice	Author:	Emma Ford
	Publishers:	Blandford
		(ISBN 0-7137-2248-7)

Falconry (Care, Captive Breeding and Conservation)	Author:	Jemima Parry-Jones
	Publishers:	David & Charles
		(ISBN 0-7153-8914-9)

AVICULTURE

Keeping British Birds	Author:	Frank Meaden
A full guide to British aviculture	Publishers:	Blandford
		(ISBN 0-7137-2388-2)

BADGERS

Badgers	Authors:	Ernest Neal and Chris Cheeseman
	Publisher:	TAD Poyser, Natural History Series

Problems with Badgers	Booklet produced by RSPCA
	(ISBN 0-85661-082-8)

Badgers and Developers	Booklet produced by English Nature

Badger Protection	Fact-sheets are produced by the National Federation of Badger Groups

FOX AND PEST CONTROL

Pest Control
Fox Snaring   Leaflets produced by BASC
Lamping

The Evolution of CITES *A reference guide to the Convention on International Trade in Endangered Species of Wild Flora and Fauna.*	Authors: Publishers:	Willem Wijnstekers CITES Secretariat
International Wildlife Trade A CITES Sourcebook	Author: Publishers:	Ginette Hemley Long Island Press, Washington DC 1994 (ISBN 1-55963-348-4)
Prescription for Extinction. Endangered Species and Patented Oriental Medicine in Trade	Authors: Publishers:	Andrea Goski and Kurt Johson TRAFFIC International 1994 (ISBN 1-85850-031-1)
Killed for a Cure: A Review of the Worldwide Trade in Tiger Bone	Authors: Publishers:	Judy Mills and Peter Jackson TRAFFIC International 1994 (ISBN 1-85850-049-4)

appendix g
abbreviations

BASC	–	British Association for Shooting and Conservation
CCW	–	Countryside Council for Wales
CITES	–	Convention on International Trade in Endangered Species of Wild Flora and Fauna
COPR	–	Control of Pesticides Regulations 1986
COTES	–	Control of Trade in Endangered Species (Enforcement) Regulations 1997
CPS	–	Crown Prosecution Service
DANI	–	Department of Agriculture for Northern Ireland
DETR	–	Department of the Environment, Transport and the Regions
DNA	–	Deoxyribonucleic acid
EN	–	English Nature
FEPA	–	Food and Environment Protection Act 1985
ITE	–	Institute of Terrestrial Ecology
IUCN	–	International Union for the Conservation of Nature and Natural Resources
JNCC	–	Joint Nature Conservation Committee
LNR	–	Local Nature Reserve
MAFF	–	Ministry of Agriculture, Fisheries and Food
NCA	–	National Council for Aviculture
NCC	–	Nature Conservancy Council
NNR	–	National Nature Reserve
PACE	–	Police and Criminal Evidence Act 1984
PSD		Pesticides Safety Directorate
PWLO	–	Police Wildlife Liaison Officer
RSPB	–	Royal Society for the Protection of Birds
RSPCA	–	Royal Society for Prevention of Cruelty to Animals
SINC	–	Site of Important Nature Conservation
SNH	–	Scottish Natural Heritage
SOAEFD	–	Scottish Office, Agriculture, Environment and Fisheries Department
SSPCA	–	Scottish Society for Prevention of Cruelty to Animals
SSSI	–	Site of Special Scientific Interest
TRAFFIC		Trade Records and Analysis of Flora and Fauna in Commerce
WCA	–	Wildlife and Countryside Act 1981
WIIS	–	Wildlife Incident Investigation Scheme
WOAD	–	Welsh Office Agriculture Department
WWF	–	World Wide Fund for Nature

PERSONAL CONTACT INFORMATION

NAME:

ADDRESS:

TEL:

NAME:

ADDRESS:

TEL:

NAME:

ADDRESS:

TEL:

NAME:

ADDRESS:

TEL:

NAME:

ADDRESS:

TEL:

NAME:

ADDRESS:

TEL:

NAME:

ADDRESS:

TEL:

NAME:

ADDRESS:

TEL:

NAME:

ADDRESS:

TEL:

d

e

f

Printed in the United Kingdom for the Stationery Office
J40406   C10   6/98   065536   21/42773